AF362463

# WEEKLY BUDDHIST DISCOURSE CHANTING

# Vol. 1

Composed
by
**Bhikṣuṇī TN Giới Hương**

Hong Duc Publishing

**HUONG SEN BUDDHIST TEMPLE**

19865 Seaton Avenue

Perris, CA 92570, USA

Tel: 951-657-7272, Cell: 951-616-8620

Email: huongsentemple@gmail.com

thichnugioihuong@yahoo.com

https://www.facebook.com/Huong.Sen.Riverside

Web: www.huongsentemple.com

First edition © 2023 Huong Sen Buddhist Temple

# CONTENT


The First Words     9

**Chapter 1: INTRODUCTION**     **12**

1. Introduction     12
2. The incense offering     12
3. Salutation     13

    Gratitude the Buddhas and Bodhisattvas     13

    Gratitude the Buddhas in the past     14

    Gratitude the Arahats     15

    Gratitude the Ancestors     16

1. The Repentance Gatha     17
2. Opening verse     17

**Chapter 2: THE BUDDHIST DISCOURSES**     **18**

1. The Heirs in Dhamma     18
2. The Discourse on Effacement     20
3. The Discourse on Right View     26
4. The Greater Discourse on Ways of Undertaking Things     34
5. The Ways of the Forest     43
6. Two Sorts of Thinking     45
7. The Simile of the Snake     52
8. The Ignoble and Noble Searchs     55
9. The Shorter Simile of the Elephant's Footprint     58

10. The Shorter Discourse on the Simile
of the Heartwood   65

11. The Greater Cowherd Discourse   74

12. The Shorter Discourse on the Cowherd   82

13. The Longer Discourse on the Ending
of Craving   86

14. The Great Classification   95

15. The Shorter Set of Questions-and-Answers   109

16. The Diamond That Cuts through Illusion   118

17. Discourse on Love (Metta Sutta)   128

18. Flower Garland: The Ten Great Aspirations
of Samantabhadra Bodhisattva   130

19. The Five Ways of Putting an End to Anger   135

20. Discourse on the Full Awareness of Breathing   141

21. Discourse the Universal Door
(The Lotus of the Wonderful Dharma)   154

22. Discourse on the Eight Realizations
of the Great Beings   160

23. Five Practices for Nourishing Happiness   164

24. The Four Establishments of Mindfulness   183

25. The Protecting and Transforming   200

26. The Middle Way   203

27. The Measuring and Reflecting   206

28. Knowing the Better Way To Live Alone   212

29. Taking Refuge in the Amitbha Buddha   217

30. Store of Precious Virtues: Practice
of the Highest Understanding   220

31. The Dharma Seal   235

32. Venerable Anuradha   239

33. Awakening the Source of Love   243

34. The Three Earth-Touchings   247

35. Knowing the Better Way to Catch a Snake   254

36. The Land of Great Happiness   266

37. The Teachings to Be Given to the Sick   275

38. The Happiness in the Present Moment   284

39. We Are Truly Present   287

40. The Happiness   289

41. The Youth and Happiness   292

42. The Deep Kindness of Parent   299

43. The Kalama Sutra
    - The Instruction to the Kalamas   329

44. Mastering of Anger   343

45. The Ten Wholesome Ways of Actions   346

46. Turning to the Tathagata   357

47. The Forty-two Section Discourse   362

48. The Karma Discourse   389

49. The Innumerable Meanings   399

50. Meditating Four Immeasure
    of Loving-Kindness   408

51. The Larger Sukhavativyuha Discourse   420

52. Bring Anew   427

53. Taking refuge in Oneself   432

54. Joyfully Sharing the Merit   435

## CONCLUSION 439


1.  The Insight that brings us to the other shore 439
2.  Invoking the bodhisattvas' names 441
3.  Read the Names of Buddhas & Bodhisattvas 445
4.  Taking refuge in Amitabha Buddha 447
5.  May the day & night be well 449
6.  Gatha on Impermanence 451
7.  Prayer 451
8.  Salutation thousands Buddha in three Times 452
9.  Taking refuge at three jewels 453
10. Sharing the merit & verse for closing 455
11. The Divine Gatha 456

**BẢO ANH LẠC Bookshelf** 458

# THE FIRST WORDS

Every day Nuns and Buddhists at Hương Sen Buddhist Temple, California, USA, have practiced and recited following the Vietnamese scripture, "Nghi Lễ Hàng Ngày – 50 Kinh Tụng và các Lễ Vía trong Năm" (Daily Chanting – Fifty Discourses and Annual Festivals) of the Pureland Sect, which was composed in 2021 by Bhikkhunī Thích Nữ Giới Hương. It is based on the original ritual of her late Master, the Venerable Elder Hải Triều Âm at Liên Hoa Temple and Dược Sư Temple.[1]

Since many Vietnamese-Americans, Hispanic, native Americans, and English speakers have come to Huong Sen Temple in search of practice and ritual, Bhikkhunī Giới Hương composed 3 volumes of the English version of **WEEKLY BUDDHIST DISCOURSE CHANTING.**

The first volume includes 54 popular Buddhist discourses from the sources of "The Middle Length Discourses of The Buddha" (Majjhima Nikāya), "The Connected Discourses of the Buddha" (Samyukta Agama), "Increased by One Discourses" (Anguttara Nikaya), "Chanting from the Heart" (Buddhist Ceremonies and Daily Practices) of Thích Nhất Hạnh, "Daily Chanting – 50 Discourses and Annual Festivals" of Huong Sen Temple and others.

We should chant at least once a week, any

_______________

1 Please read: http://www.huongsentemple.com/index.php/vn/
phat-phap/kinh-ta-ng-ca-a-cha-a-hs/6256-nghi-le-hang-ngay-20.

place and any time, or more often if we have more time. The chant will help to avoid negative thoughts, defilements, distractions-any of the myriad things that intrude into the one-pointed mind. We definitely feel the connectedness with Dharma (the Buddha's teaching), we feel the spirit being lifted up, the awakening and the settling of the mind to enter meditation. We will become bright, enduring, detached, diligent, generous, loving, understanding and so on . . . because we practice following the chanting and the role model of Buddhas.

Chanting out loud or silently listening to chanting can also be very relaxing as we go about our day. It can be used to calm our mind before work or sleeping.

For the sake of all the general practitioners, there are some changes, combinations, additions, reductions, and creations made in this English version. This is the first time that both traditions have been combined in an English version for the necessary needs at Huong Sen Buddhist Temple.

We would like to gratefully acknowledge with special thanks the Buddhas, Boddhisattvas, Sanghas, the English translators, Master Thích Nhất Hạnh, our Late Respectful Teacher - Venerable Elder Bhikkhunī Hải Triều Âm and others. You all provided us the awakening words to remind and guide us in the right way of practice. We will keep chanting, learning and practicing it until we and all beings get the enlightenment as well as realize our Buddha nature.

If there is any merit in compiling this book, may it be shared with all sentient beings. May they diligently practice and soon gain the way of love and understanding.

Reciting the sutras, practicing the way of awareness

gives rise to benefits without limit.

We vow to share the fruits with all beings.

We vow to offer tribute to parents, teachers, friends,

and numerous beings who

give guidance and support along the path.

(Thích Nhất Hạnh)

Hương Sen Temple, Riverside, California

March 7, 2023

**Bhikkhunī TN Giới Hương**

# Chapter 1
# INTRODUCTION

## 1. INTRODUCTION

Before the chanting course, the leader should announce the reason, the place, the time and members of sangha for this chanting today.

## 2.THE INCENSE OFFERING

Leader: **In gratitude, we offer this incense to all Buddhas and Bodhisattvas throughout space and time.**

**May it be fragrant as Earth herself, reflecting our careful efforts, our wholehearted mindfulness, and the fruit of understanding, slowly ripening.**

**May we and all beings be companions of Buddhas and Bodhisattvas.**

**May we awaken from forgetfulness and realize our true home. (o)**

**Namo Offering the Incense Bodhisattva Mahasattvas.** (3 times) (ooo)

# 3. SALUTATION IN GRATITUDE

(All Sangha members read)

## 3. 1. GRATITUDE THE BUDDHAS AND BODHISATTVAS

1. **Offering light in the Ten Directions, the Buddha, the Dharma, and the Sangha, to whom we bow in gratitude.** (o) (1 prostration)

2. **Teaching and living the way of awareness in the very midst of suffering and confusion, Shakyamuni Buddha, the Fully Enlightened One, to whom we bow in gratitude.** (o) (1 prostration)

3. **Cutting through ignorance, awakening our hearts and our minds, Manjushri, the Bodhisattva of Great Understanding, to whom we bow in gratitude.** (o) (1 prostration)

4. **Working mindfully, working joyfully for the sake of all beings, Samantabhadra, the Bodhisattva of Great Action, to whom we bow in gratitude.** (o) (1 prostration)

5. **Seed of awakening and loving kindness in children and all beings, Maitreya, the Buddha to-be-born, to whom we bow in gratitude.** (o) (1 prostration)

6. **Seeing the Buddha in everyone, Sadaparibhuta, the Bodhisattva of Constant Respect, to whom we bow in gratitude.** (o) (1 prostration)

7. **Showing the way fearlessly and compassionately, the stream of all our Ancestral Teachers, to whom we bow in gratitude.** (ooo) (1 prostration)

## 3.2. GRATITUDE THE BUDDHAS IN THE PAST

1. **The Buddha Vipashyin, to whom we bow in gratitude.** (o) (1 prostration)

2. **The Buddha Shikhin, to whom we bow in gratitude.** (o) (1 prostration) **The Buddha Vishvabhu, to whom we bow in gratitude.** (o) (1 prostration)

3. **The Buddha Krakkucchandha, to whom we bow in gratitude.** (o) (1 prostration)

4. **The Buddha Konagamana, to whom we**

bow in gratitude. (o) (1 prostration)

5. **The Buddha Kashyapa, to whom we bow in gratitude.** (o) (1 prostration)

6. **The Buddha Shakyamuni, to whom we bow in gratitude.** (o) (1 prostration)

7. **The Bodhisattva of Great Understanding, Manjushri, to whom we bow in gratitude.** (o) (1 prostration)

8. **The Bodhisattva of Great Action, Samantabhadra, to whom we bow in gratitude.** (o) (1 prostration)

9. **The Bodhisattva of Great Compassion, Avalokiteshvara, to whom we bow in gratitude.** (ooo) (1 prostration)

10. **The Bodhisattva of the Great Vow, Kshitigarbha, to whom we bow in gratitude.** (ooo) (1 prostration)

## 3.3. GRATITUDE THE ARAHATS

1. **The Venerable Kashyapa, to whom we bow in gratitude.** (o) (1 prostration)

2. **The Venerable Shariputra, to whom we bow in gratitude.** (o) (1 prostration)

3. **The Venerable Maudgalyayana, to whom we bow in gratitude.** (o) (1 prostration)

4. **The Venerable Upali, to whom we bow in gratitude.** (o) (1 prostration)

5. **The Venerable Ananda, to whom we bow in gratitude.** (ooo) (1 prostration)

## 3. 4. GRATITUDE THE ANCESTORS

1. **Mother of Buddhas, Bodhisattvas, and all beings, nourishing, holding, and healing all, Bodhisattva Gaia, Great Mother Earth, precious jewel of the cosmos, to whom we bow in gratitude.** (o) (1 prostration)

2. **Radiating light in all directions, source of life on Earth, Mahavairocana Tathagata, Great Father Sun, Buddha of infinite light and life, to whom we bow in gratitude.** (o) (1 prostration)

3. **Seed of awakening and loving kindness in children and all beings, Maitreya, the Buddha to-be-born, to whom we bow in gratitude.** (o) (1 prostration)

4. **Showing the way fearlessly and compassionately, the stream of all our Ancestral Teachers, to whom we bow in**

**gratitude.** (ooo) (1 prostration)

# 4. THE REPENTANCE GATHA

**All wrongdoing arises from the mind.**

**When the mind is purified, what trace of wrong is left?**

**After repentance, my heart is light like the white clouds that have always floated over the ancient forest in freedom.** (o)

**Namo the Repentance Bodhisattva Mahasattvas.** (3 times) (ooo)

# 5.OPENING VERSE

**The Dharma is deep and lovely.**

**We now have a chance to see, study, and practice it.**

**We vow to realize its true meaning.**

**Namo Shakyamunaye Buddhaya.**
(3 times) (ooo)

***

# Chapter 2
# THE BUDDHIST DISCOURSES

## 1. HEIRS IN DHAMMA

(3. Dhammadayada Sutta,
Majjhima Nikaya 1)

Translated by Bhikkhu Bodhi

Thus have i heard. On one occasion the Blessed One was living in Savatthi in Jeta's Grove, Anathapindika's Park, addressed the monks thus:

"Bhikkhus, be my heirs in Dhamma, not my heirs in material things (material wealth). If you are my heirs in Dhamma, not my heirs in material things, you will not be reproached and I will not be reproached."

Bhikkhus' will is for long conduce to his fewness of wishes (less desires), contentment, effacement, easy support, and arousal of energy. Therefore, bhikkhus, be my heirs in Dhamma, not my heirs in material things. That is what the Blessed One said. Having said this, the Sublime One rose from his seat and went into his dwelling.

Soon after he had left, the venerable Sariputta addressed the bhikkhus thus:

1. As disciples of the Teacher who lives secluded they train in seclusion.

2. They abandon what the Teacher tells them to abandon.

3. They are not luxurious and careless; they are keen to avoid backsliding and are leaders in seclusion.

It is in this way that disciples of the Teacher who lives secluded train in seclusion.

There friends, greed, anger, ill will, hypocrisy, mercilessness, envy, selfishness, deceit, craftiness, obstinacy, haughty talk, measuring, conceit, intoxication, negligence, intoxication and negligence are the evils. There is the middle path for the abandoning of all these evils, which conduces to wisdom, giving vision, giving knowledge, enlightenment and to Nibbana.

It is just this Noble Eightfold Path: right view, right intention, right speech, right action, right livelihood, right effort, right mindfulness, and right concentration. That is what the venerable Sariputta said.

**The bhikkhus were satisfied and delighted in the venerable Sariputta's words.**

**Namo Shakyamunaye Buddhaya.**
(3 times) (ooo)


***


# 2.THE DISCOURSE ON EFFACEMENT

(8. Sallekha Sutta, Majjhima Nikaya 1)

Translated and edited by Nyanaponika Thera


**Thus have I heard. Once the Blessed One was staying at Savatthi, in Jeta's Grove, Anathapindika's monastery and taught to venerable Maha-Cunda that:**

**The effacement should be practiced by you and all:**

**1. Others will be harmful; we shall not be harmful here -- thus effacement can be done.**

**2. Others will kill living beings; we shall abstain from killing living beings here -- thus effacement can be done.**

**3. Others will take what is not given; we**

shall abstain from taking what is not given here -- thus effacement can be done.

4. Others will be unchaste; we shall be chaste here -- thus effacement can be done.

5. Others will speak falsehood; we shall abstain from false speech here -- thus effacement can be done.

6. Others win speak maliciously; we shall abstain from malicious speech here -- thus effacement can be done.

7. Others will speak harshly; we shall abstain from harsh speech here -- thus effacement can be done.

8. Others will gossip; we shall abstain from gossip here -- thus effacement can be done.

9. Others will be covetous; we shall not be covetous here -- thus effacement can be done.

10.   Others will have thoughts of ill will; we shall not have thoughts of ill will here -- thus effacement can be done.

11.   Others will have wrong views; we shall have right view here -- thus

effacement can be done.

12.   Others will have wrong intention; we shall have right intention here -- thus effacement can be done.

13.   Others will use wrong speech; we shall use right speech here -- thus effacement can be done.

14.   Others will commit wrong actions; we shall do right actions here -- thus effacement can be done.

15.   Others will have wrong livelihood; we shall have right livelihood here -- thus effacement can be done.

16.   Others will make wrong effort; we shall make right effort here -- thus effacement can be done.

17.   Others will have wrong mindfulness; we shall have right mindfulness here -- thus effacement can be done.

18.   Others will have wrong concentration; we shall have right concentration here -- thus effacement can be done.

19.   Others will have wrong knowledge; we shall have right knowledge here -- thus effacement can be done.

20.   Others will have wrong deliverance; we shall have right deliverance here -- thus effacement can be done.

21.   Others will be overcome by sloth and torpor; we shall be free from sloth and torpor here -- thus effacement can be done.

22.   Others will be agitated; we shall be unagitated here -- thus effacement can be done.

23.   Others will be doubting; we shall be free from doubt here -- thus effacement can be done.

24.   Others will be angry; we shall not be angry here -- thus effacement can be done.

25.   Others will be hostile; we shall not be hostile here -- thus effacement can be done.

26.   Others will denigrate; we shall not denigrate here -- thus effacement can be done.

27.   Others will be domineering; we shall not be domineering here -- thus effacement can be done.

28.   Others will be envious; we shall not

be envious here -- thus effacement can be done.

29.   Others will be jealous; we shall not be jealous here -- thus effacement can be done.

30.   Others will be fraudulent; we shall not be fraudulent here -- thus effacement can be done.

31.   Others will be hypocrites; we shall not be hypocrites here -- thus effacement can be done.

32.   Others will be obstinate; we shall not be obstinate here -- thus effacement can be done.

33.   Others will be arrogant; we shall not be arrogant here -- thus effacement can be done.

34.   Others will be difficult to admonish; we shall be easy to admonish here -- thus effacement can be done.

35.   Others will have bad friends; we shall have noble friends here -- thus effacement can be done.

36.   Others will be negligent; we shall be heedful here -- thus effacement can be done.

37.   Others will be faithless; we shall be faithful here -- thus effacement can be done.

38.   Others will be shameless; we shall be shameful here -- thus effacement can be done.

39.   Others will be without conscience; we shall have conscience here -- thus effacement can be done.

40.   Others will have no learning; we shall be learned here -- thus effacement can be done.

41.   Others will be idle; we shall be energetic here -- thus effacement can be done.

42.   Others will be lacking in mindfulness; we shall be established in mindfulness here -- thus effacement can be done.

43.   Others will be without wisdom; we shall be endowed with wisdom -- thus effacement can be done.

44.   Others will misapprehend according to their individual views, hold on to them tenaciously and not easily discard them; we shall not misapprehend according to individual views nor hold on to them

**tenaciously, but shall discard them with ease -- thus effacement can be done.**

**Namo Shakyamunaye Buddhaya. (3 times) (ooo)**

***

# 3.THE DISCOURSE ON RIGHT VIEW

(9. Sammaditthi Sutta. Majjhima Nikaya 1)

Translated from the Pali by Ñanamoli Thera edited and revised by Bhikkhu Bodhi

**Thus have I heard. On one occasion the Blessed One was living at Savatthi in Jeta's Grove, Anathapindika's Park. There the Venerable Sariputta addressed the bhikkhus.**

## 1. THE WHOLESOME

**Abstention from killing living beings, taking what is not given, misconduct in sensual pleasures, false speech, malicious speech, harsh speech, gossip, non-covetousness, non-ill will and right**

view are wholesome.

## 2. THE UNWHOLESOME

Killing, taking what is not given, misconduct in sensual pleasures, false speech, malicious speech, harsh, gossip, covetousness, ill will and wrong view is unwholesome.

## 3. NUTRIMENT

There are these four kinds of nutriment for the maintenance of beings that already have come to be and for the support of those seeking a new existence. What four? They are physical food as nutriment, gross or subtle; contact as the second; mental volition as the third; and consciousness as the fourth. With the arising of craving there is the arising of nutriment. With the cessation of craving there is the cessation of nutriment.

## 4. THE FOUR NOBLE TRUTHS

A noble disciple understands suffering, the origin of suffering, the cessation of suffering, and the way leading to the cessation of suffering.

## 5. AGING AND DEATH

The aging of beings in the various orders of beings, their old age, brokenness of teeth, grayness of hair, wrinkling of skin, decline of life, weakness of faculties -- this is called aging.

The passing of beings out of the various orders of beings, their passing away, dissolution, disappearance, dying, completion of time, dissolution of the aggregates, laying down of the body -- this is called death.

With the arising of birth there is the arising of aging and death. With the cessation of birth there is the cessation of aging and death.

## 6. BIRTH

The birth of beings into the various orders of beings, their coming to birth, precipitation [in a womb], generation, manifestation of the aggregates, obtaining the bases for contact -- this is called birth. With the arising of being there is the arising of birth. With the cessation of being there is the cessation of birth.

## 7. BEING

There are these three kinds of being: sense-sphere being, fine-material being and immaterial being. With the arising of clinging there is the arising of being. With the cessation of clinging there is the cessation of being.

## 8. CLINGING

There are these four kinds of clinging: clinging to sensual pleasures, clinging to views, clinging to rituals and observances, and clinging to a doctrine of self. With the arising of craving there is the arising of clinging. With the cessation of craving there is the cessation of clinging.

## 9. CRAVING

There are these six classes of craving: craving for forms, craving for sounds, craving for odors, craving for flavors, craving for tangibles, craving for mind-objects. With the arising of feeling there is the arising of craving. With the cessation of feeling there is the cessation of craving.

## 10. FEELING

There are these six classes of feeling: feeling born of eye-contact, feeling born of ear-contact, feeling born of nose-contact, feeling born of tongue-contact, feeling born of body-contact, feeling born of mind-contact. With the arising of contact there is the arising of feeling. With the cessation of contact there is the cessation of feeling.

## 11. CONTACT

There are these six classes of contact: eye-contact, ear-contact, nose-contact, tongue-contact, body-contact, mind-contact. With the arising of the sixfold base there is the arising of contact. With the cessation of the sixfold base there is the cessation of contact.

## 12. THE SIXFOLD BASE

There are these six bases: the eye-base, the ear-base, the nose-base, the tongue-base, the body-base, the mind-base. With the arising of mentality-materiality there is the arising of the sixfold base. With the cessation of mentality-materiality there is the cessation of the sixfold base.

## 13. MENTALITY-MATERIALITY

Feeling, perception, volition, contact and attention -- these are called mentality. The four great elements and the material form derived from the four great elements -- these are called materiality. With the arising of consciousness there is the arising of mentality-materiality. With the cessation of consciousness there is the cessation of mentality-materiality.

## 14. CONSCIOUSNESS

There are these six classes of consciousness: eye-consciousness, ear-consciousness, nose-consciousness, tongue-consciousness,body-consciousness, ind-consciousness. With the arising of formations there is the arising of consciousness. With the cessation of formations there is the cessation of consciousness.

## 15. FORMATIONS

There are these three kinds of formations: the bodily formation, the verbal formation, the mental formation. With the arising of ignorance there is the arising of formations. With the cessation of ignorance there is the cessation of formations.

## 16. IGNORANCE

Not knowing about suffering, not knowing about the origin of suffering, not knowing about the cessation of suffering, not knowing about the way leading to the cessation of suffering -- this is called ignorance. With the arising of the taints there is the arising of ignorance. With the cessation of the taints there is the cessation of ignorance.

## 17. TAINTS

There are three taints: the taint of sensual

desire, the taint of being and the taint of ignorance. With the arising of ignorance there is the arising of the taints. With the cessation of ignorance there is the cessation of the taints.

When a noble disciple has thus understood wholesome, unwholesome, nutriment, the four noble truths, aging and death, birth, being, clinging, craving, feeling, contact, the sixfold base, the mentality-materiality, consciousness, formations, ignorance and the taints. He entirely abandons the underlying tendency to lust, he abolishes the underlying tendency to aversion, he extirpates the underlying tendency to the view and conceit 'I am,' and by abandoning ignorance and arousing true knowledge he here and now makes an end of suffering. In that way too a noble disciple is one of right view, whose view is straight, who has perfect confidence in the Dhamma and has arrived at this true Dhamma."

The way leading to the cessation of the unwholesome, nutriment, aging and death, birth, being, clinging, craving, feeling, contact, the sixfold base, the mentality-materiality, consciousness, formations, ignorance and the taints are just this Noble Eightfold Path; that is, right view, right intention, right speech, right action, right livelihood, right effort, right mindfulness and right concentration.

That is what the Venerable Sariputta said. The bhikkhus were satisfied and delighted in the Venerable Sariputta's words.

Namo Shakyamunaye Buddhaya.
(3 times) (ooo)


***


# 4. THE GREATER DISCOURSE ON WAYS OF UNDERTAKING THINGS
(46. Mahādhammasamādānasutta,
Majjhima Nikāya 1)
Translated by Bhikkhu Bodhi


Thus have I heard. On one occasion the Blessed One was living at Sāvatthī in Jeta's Grove, Anāthapiṇḍika's Park. There he addressed the bhikkhus thus:

AN UNTAUGHT ORDINARY PERSON

who has no regard for noble ones and is unskilled and undisciplined in their Dhamma, who has no regard for true men and is unskilled and undisciplined in their Dhamma, does not know what things should be cultivated and what things should not be cultivated, he does not know what things should be followed and what things should not be followed. Therefore, the unwished for, undesired, disagreeable things increase for him and wished for, desired, agreeable things diminish.

THE WELL-TAUGHT NOBLE DISCIPLE who has regard for noble ones and is skilled and disciplined in their Dhamma, who has regard for true men and is skilled and disciplined in their Dhamma, knows what things should be cultivated and what things should not be cultivated, he knows what things should be followed and what things should not be followed. Therefore, the unwished for, undesired, disagreeable things diminish for him and wished for, desired, agreeable things increase.

THERE ARE FOUR WAYS OF UNDERTAKING THINGS:

1. There is a way of undertaking things

that is painful now and ripens in the future as pain.

2. There is a way of undertaking things that is pleasant now and ripens in the future as pain.

3. There is a way of undertaking things that is painful now and ripens in the future as pleasure.

4. There is a way of undertaking things that is pleasant now and ripens in the future as pleasure.

**THE IGNORANT PERSON**

**1. THERE IS A WAY OF UNDERTAKING THINGS THAT IS PAINFUL NOW AND RIPENS IN THE FUTURE AS PAIN.**

"Now, bhikkhus, one who is ignorant, not knowing this way of undertaking things that is painful now and ripens in the future as pain, does not understand it as it actually is thus: 'This way of undertaking things is painful now and ripens in the future as pain.' The ignorant one cultivates it and does not avoid it; because he does so, unwished for, undesired, disagreeable things increase for him and wished for, desired, agreeable things diminish.

## 2. THERE IS A WAY OF UNDERTAKING THINGS THAT IS PLEASANT NOW AND RIPENS IN THE FUTURE AS PAIN.

"Now, bhikkhus, one who is ignorant, not knowing this way of undertaking things that is pleasant now and ripens in the future as pain, does not understand it as it actually is thus: 'This way of undertaking things is pleasant now and ripens in the future as pain.' The ignorant one cultivates it and does not avoid it; because he does so, unwished for, undesired, disagreeable things increase for him and wished for, desired, agreeable things diminish.

THERE IS A WAY OF UNDERTAKING THINGS THAT IS PAINFUL NOW AND RIPENS IN THE FUTURE AS PLEASURE.

(3) "Now, bhikkhus, one who is ignorant, not knowing this way of undertaking things that is painful now and ripens in the future as pleasure, does not understand it as it actually is thus: 'This way of undertaking things is painful now and ripens in the future as pleasure.' The ignorant one does not cultivate it but avoids it; because he does so, unwished for, undesired,

disagreeable things increase for him and wished for, desired, agreeable things diminish.

## 3. THERE IS A WAY OF UNDERTAKING THINGS THAT IS PLEASANT NOW AND RIPENS IN THE FUTURE AS PLEASURE.

(4) "Now, bhikkhus, one who is ignorant, not knowing the way of undertaking things that is pleasant now and ripens in the future as pleasure, does not understand it as it actually is thus: 'This way of undertaking things is pleasant now and ripens in the future as pleasure.' The ignorant one does not cultivate it but avoids it; because he does so, unwished for, undesired, disagreeable things increase for him and wished for, desired, agreeable things diminish.

## THE WISE PERSON

## 1. THERE IS A WAY OF UNDERTAKING THINGS THAT IS PAINFUL NOW AND RIPENS IN THE FUTURE AS PAIN.

"Now, bhikkhus, one who is wise, knowing this way of undertaking things that is painful now and ripens in the future as pain, understands it as it actually is thus: 'This way of undertaking things is painful now and ripens in the future as pain.' The wise one does not cultivate it but avoids it; because he does so, unwished for, undesired, disagreeable things diminish for him and wished for, desired, agreeable things increase.

## 2. THERE IS A WAY OF UNDERTAKING THINGS THAT IS PLEASANT NOW AND RIPENS IN THE FUTURE AS PAIN.

(2) "Now, bhikkhus, one who is wise, knowing this way of undertaking things that is pleasant now and ripens in the future as pain, understands it as it actually is thus: 'This way of undertaking things is pleasant now and ripens in the future as pain.' The wise one does not cultivate it but avoids it; because he does so, unwished for, undesired, disagreeable things diminish for him and wished for, desired, agreeable things increase.

## 3. THERE IS A WAY OF UNDERTAKING

## THINGS THAT IS PAINFUL NOW AND RIPENS IN THE FUTURE AS PLEASURE.

"Now, bhikkhus, one who is wise, knowing this way of undertaking things that is painful now and ripens in the future as pleasure, understands it as it actually is thus: 'This way of undertaking things is painful now and ripens in the future as pleasure.' The wise one does not avoid it but cultivates it; because he does so, unwished for, undesired, disagreeable things diminish for him and wished for, desired, agreeable things increase.

## 4. THERE IS A WAY OF UNDERTAKING THINGS THAT IS PLEASANT NOW AND RIPENS IN THE FUTURE AS PLEASURE.

(4) "Now, bhikkhus, one who is wise, knowing this way of undertaking things that is pleasant now and ripens in the future as pleasure, understands it as it actually is thus: 'This way of undertaking things is pleasant now and ripens in the future as pleasure.' The wise one does not avoid it but cultivates it; because he does so, unwished for, undesired, disagreeable things diminish for him and wished for,

desired, agreeable things increase.

## THE FOUR WAYS WITH TEN PRECEPTS

## 1. THERE IS A WAY OF UNDERTAKING THINGS THAT IS PAINFUL NOW AND RIPENS IN THE FUTURE AS PAIN.

Here, bhikkhus, someone in pain and grief commit ten precepts such as kills living beings, takes what is not given, misconducts himself in sensual pleasures, speaks falsehood, speaks maliciously, speaks harshly, gossips, covetous, ill will and wrong view. Therefore, he experiences pain and grief in the present and after death, he reappears in a state of deprivation, in an unhappy destination, in perdition, even in hell.

## 2. THERE IS A WAY OF UNDERTAKING THINGS THAT IS PLEASANT NOW AND RIPENS IN THE FUTURE AS PAIN.

Here, bhikkhus, someone in pleasure and joy kills living beings, takes what is not given, misconducts himself in sensual pleasures, speaks falsehood, speaks maliciously, speaks harshly, gossips, covetous, ill will and wrong view. Therefore, he experiences pleasure and joy in the present and after death, he reappears in a state of deprivation, in an unhappy destination, in perdition, even in hell.

## 3. THERE IS A WAY OF UNDERTAKING THINGS THAT IS PAINFUL NOW AND RIPENS IN THE FUTURE AS PLEASURE.

Here, bhikkhus, someone in pain and grief abstains from killing living beings, taking what is not given, misconduct himself in sensual pleasures, speaking falsehood, speaking maliciously, speaking harshly, gossipping, covetous, ill will and wrong view. Therefore, he experiences pain and grief in the present and after death, he reappears in a happy destination, even in the heavenly world.

## 4. THERE IS A WAY OF UNDERTAKING THINGS THAT IS PLEASANT NOW AND RIPENS IN THE FUTURE AS PLEASURE.

Here, bhikkhus, someone in pleasure and joy abstains from killing living beings, taking what is not given, misconduct himself in sensual pleasures, speaking falsehood, speaking maliciously, speaking harshly, gossipping, covetous, ill will and wrong view. Therefore, he experiences pleasure and joy in the present and after death, he reappears in a happy destination, even in the heavenly world.

That is what the Blessed One said. The bhikkhus were satisfied and delighted in the Blessed One's words.

**Namo Shakyamunaye Buddhaya.**
(3 times) (ooo)


***


# 5. THE WAYS OF THE FOREST

(17. Vanapattha Sutta, Majjhima Nikaya 1)

Translation by Bhikkhu Thanissaro


**I heard thus:**

At one time the Blessed One lived in the monastery offered by Anathapindika in Jeta's grove in Savatthi, taught about the Ways of the Forest.

## DON'T STAY IN A PLACE WITHOUT THE CONDITION FOR PRACTICE

Bhikkhu abides in a certain forest stretch, when abiding there un-established mindfulness, un-concentrated mind, not destroyed desires and the not attained noble even it has the good accommodation as robes, morsel food, dwellings and medicine, he should not abide in that stretch of forest, he should leave it by night or by day.

## STAY FOREVER IN A PLACE WITH THE GOOD CONDITION FOR PRACTICE EVEN KICKED OUT

Bhikkhu abides in a certain forest stretch, village, hamlet, town, or any place or any person when abiding there, un-established mindfulness gets established, the un-concentrated mind concentrates, the not destroyed desires get destroyed and the not attained noble end of the yoke is attained even it lacks or has full the good accommodation as robes, morsel food, dwellings and medicine. That Bhikkhu considering should not leave that place as long as life lasts, even if chased should follow.

The Blessed One said thus and those Bhikkhus delighted in the words of the Blessed One.

**Namo Shakyamunaye Buddhaya.**
(3 times) (ooo)

***

# 6. TWO SORTS OF THINKING

(19. Dvedhavitakka Sutta, Majjhima Nikaya 1)
Translation by Bhikkhu Thanissaro

I have heard that on one occasion the Blessed One was staying at Savatthi, in Jeta's Grove, Anathapindika's monastery and He taught about the two sorts of thinks.

Monks, before my self-awakening, when I was still just an unawakened Bodhisatta, the thoughts occurred to me: the thinking imbued with sensuality, ill will, and harmfulness and the thinking imbued with renunciation, non-ill will, and with harmlessness.

And as I remained thus heedful, ardent, and resolute, thinking imbued with sensuality arose. I discerned that 'Thinking imbued with sensuality, ill will, and harmfulness lead to my own affliction, the affliction of others, the affliction of both; it obstructs discernment, promotes vexation, and does not lead to Unbinding, it subsided. I simply abandoned it, destroyed it, dispelled it, wiped it out of existence.

And as I remained thus heedful, ardent, and resolute, thinking imbued with renunciation, non-ill and harmlessness arose. I discerned that 'Thinking imbued with renunciation, non-ill and harmlessness has arisen in me; and that lead neither to my own affliction, nor to the affliction of others, nor to the affliction of both. It fosters discernment, promotes lack of vexation, and leads to Unbinding. I simply steadied my mind right within, settled, unified, and concentrated in it.

Unflagging persistence was aroused in me, and unmuddled mindfulness established. My body was calm and unaroused, my mind concentrated and single. Quite withdrawn from sensuality, withdrawn from unskillful mental qualities, I entered and remained in THE FIRST JHANA: rapture and pleasure born from withdrawal, accompanied by directed thought and evaluation.

With the stilling of directed thought and evaluation, I entered and remained in THE SECOND JHANA: rapture and pleasure born of composure, unification of awareness free from directed thought and evaluation -- internal assurance.

With the fading of rapture I remained in equanimity, mindful and alert, and physically sensitive of pleasure. I entered and remained in THE THIRD JHANA, of which the Noble Ones declare, 'Equanimous and mindful, he has a pleasurable abiding.'

With the abandoning of pleasure and pain -- as with the earlier disappearance of elation and distress -- I entered and remained in THE FOURTH JHANA: purity of equanimity and mindfulness, neither pleasure nor pain.

"When the mind was thus concentrated, purified, bright, unblemished, rid of defilement, pliant, malleable, steady, and attained to imperturbability, I directed it to the **KNOWLEDGE OF RECOLLECTING MY PAST LIVES.** I recollected my manifold past lives, i.e., one birth, two...five, ten...fifty, a hundred, a thousand, a hundred thousand, many eons of cosmic contraction, many eons of cosmic expansion, many eons of cosmic contraction and expansion: 'There I had such a name, belonged to such a clan, had such an appearance. Such was my food, such my experience of pleasure and pain, such the end of my life. Passing away from that state, I re-arose there. There too I had such a name, belonged to such a clan, had such an appearance. Such was my food, such my experience of pleasure and pain, such the end of my life. Passing away from that state, I re-arose here.' Thus I remembered my manifold past lives in their modes and details.

This was THE FIRST KNOWLEDGE I attained in the first watch of the night. Ignorance was destroyed; knowledge arose; darkness was destroyed; light arose -- as happens in one who is heedful, ardent, and resolute.

When the mind was thus concentrated, purified, bright, unblemished, rid of defilement, pliant, malleable, steady, and attained to imperturbability, I directed it to THE KNOWLEDGE OF THE PASSING AWAY AND REAPPEARANCE OF BEINGS. I saw -- by means of the divine eye, purified and surpassing the human -- beings passing away and re-appearing, and I discerned how they are inferior and superior, beautiful and ugly, fortunate and unfortunate in accordance with their kamma: 'These beings -- who were endowed with bad conduct of body, speech and mind, who reviled the Noble Ones, held wrong views and undertook actions under the influence of wrong views -- with the break-up of the body, after death, have re-appeared in the plane of deprivation, the bad destination, the lower realms, in hell. But these beings -- who were endowed with good conduct of body, speech, and mind, who did not revile the Noble Ones, who held right views and undertook actions under the influence of right views -- with the break-up of the body, after death, have re-appeared in the good destinations, in the heavenly world.' Thus -- by means of the divine eye, purified and surpassing the human -- I saw beings passing away and re-appearing, and I discerned how they are inferior and superior, beautiful and ugly, fortunate and unfortunate in accordance with their kamma.

This was THE SECOND KNOWLEDGE I attained in the second watch of the night. Ignorance was destroyed; knowledge arose; darkness was destroyed; light arose -- as happens in one who is heedful, ardent, and resolute.

When the mind was thus concentrated, purified, bright, unblemished, rid of defilement, pliant, malleable, steady, and attained to imperturbability, I directed it to the KNOWLEDGE OF THE ENDING OF THE MENTAL FERMENTATIONS. I discerned, as it was actually present, that 'This is stress...This is the origination of stress...This is the cessation of stress... This is the way leading to the cessation of stress...These are fermentations... This is the origination of fermentations... This is the cessation of fermentations... This is the way leading to the cessation of fermentations.' My heart, thus knowing, thus seeing, was released from the fermentation of sensuality, released from the fermentation of becoming, released from the fermentation of ignorance. With release, there was the knowledge, 'Released.' I discerned that 'Birth is ended, the holy life fulfilled, the task done. There is nothing further for this world.'

This was THE THIRD KNOWLEDGE I attained in the third watch of the night. Ignorance was destroyed; knowledge arose; darkness was destroyed; light arose -- as happens in one who is heedful, ardent, and resolute.

So, monks, I have opened up the safe, restful path, closed off the false path, removed the male decoy, destroyed the female. Whatever a teacher should do -- seeking the welfare of his disciples, out of sympathy for them -- that have I done for you. Over there are the roots of trees; over there, empty dwellings. Practice jhana, monks. Don't be heedless. Don't later fall into regret. This is our message to you."

That is what the Blessed One said. Gratified, the monks delighted in the Blessed One's words.

Namo Shakyamunaye Buddhaya.

(3 times) (ooo)

# 7. THE SIMILE OF THE SNAKE

(22.Alagaddupama Sutta, Majjhima Nikaya 1)

Translated by Bhikkhu Nanamoli
and Bhikkhu Bodhi

**Thus I Have Heard. On one occasion the Blessed One was living at Savatthi in Jeta's Grove, Anathapindika's Park, taught bhikkhu Arittha about the harm of desire as the poison of a snake.**

**The sensual pleasure provides little gratification, much suffering, and much despair, and how great the danger in them. With the simile of the skeleton, the piece of meat, the grass torch, the pot of coals, the dream, the borrowed goods, the tree laden with fruit, the slaughterhouse, the sword stake, the snake's head."**

## THE HARM OF DESIRE AS THE POISON OF A SNAKE

## 1. LEARN DHARMA WITH THE INCORRECT WAY IS HARMFUL AS WRONGLY GRASP OF THE SNAKE

**Some misguided men learn the Dhamma,**

only for the sake of criticising others and for winning debates. Those teachings, being wrongly grasped by them, conduce to their harm and suffering for a long time. Just like a man searched of a snake, saw a large snake and grasped its coils or its tail. It would turn back on him and bite him, because of his wrong grasp of the snake.

## 2. LEARN DHARMA WITH THE CORRECT WAY IS BENIFIT AS RIGHTLY GRASP OF THE SNAKE'S NECK

Some clansmen learn the Dhamma with wisdom. They gain a reflective acceptance and experience the good for the sake of which they learned the Dhamma. Those teachings, being rightly grasped by them, conduce to their welfare and happiness for a long time. It is like a man who searched of a snake and grasped it rightly by the neck. It would not turn back on him and bite him, because of his right grasp of the snake.

## DHARMA IS AS THE SIMILE OF THE RAFT

"Bhikkhus, I shall show you how the

Dhamma is similar to a raft, being for the purpose for crossing over, not for the purpose grasping.

A man used a raft to get across and had arrived at the far shore, he might think thus: 'This raft has been very helpful to me, but I must left it behind because I donot need it anymore."

Now, bhikkhus, it is by so doing that that man would be doing what should be done with that raft. So, I have shown you how the Dhamma is similar to a raft, being for the purpose of crossing over, not for the purpose of grasping. After liberated, Dhamma is left beind, otherwise illegal.

Bhikkhus, the Dhamma well proclaimed by me thus is clear, open, evident, and free of patchwork. In the Dhamma well proclaimed by me thus, which is clear, open, evident, and free of patchwork, those who have sufficient faith in me, sufficient love for me, are all headed for heaven.

That is what the Blessed One said. The bhikkhus were satisfied and delighted in the Blessed One's words.

**Namo Shakyamunaye Buddhaya.**
(3 times) (ooo)


***


# 8. THE IGNOBLE AND NOBLE SEARCHS

(26. Ariyapariyesana Sutta,
Majjhima Nikaya 1)

Translated from the Pali by Thanissaro Bhikkhu


**I have heard that on one occasion the Blessed One was staying at Savatthi, in Jeta's Grove, Anathapindika's monastery, taught about the ignoble search & noble search.**


## THE IGNOBLE SEARCH

**There is the case where a person, being subject himself to birth, seeks [happiness in] what is likewise subject to birth. Being subject himself to aging... illness... death... sorrow... defilement, he seeks [happiness in] what is likewise subject to illness... death... sorrow... defilement.**

And what may be said to be subject to birth? Spouses & children are subject to birth. Men & women slaves... goats & sheep... fowl & pigs... elephants, cattle, horses, & mares... gold & silver are subject to birth. Subject to birth are these acquisitions, and one who is tied to them, infatuated with them, who has totally fallen for them, being subject to birth, seeks what is likewise subject to birth.

And what may be said to be subject to aging... illness... death... sorrow... defilement? Spouses & children... men & women slaves... goats & sheep... fowl & pigs... elephants, cattle, horses, & mares... gold & silver are subject to aging... illness... death... sorrow... defilement. Subject to aging... illness... death... sorrow... defilement are these acquisitions, and one who is tied to them, infatuated with them, who has totally fallen for them, being subject to birth, seeks what is likewise subject to aging... illness... death... sorrow... defilement. This is ignoble search.

## THE NOBLE SEARCH

Monks, being subject myself to birth, seeing the drawbacks of birth, seeking the unborn, unexcelled rest from the yoke, Unbinding, I reached the unborn, unexcelled rest from the yoke: Unbinding. Being subject myself to aging... illness... death... sorrow... defilement, seeing the drawbacks of aging... illness... death... sorrow... defilement, seeking the aging-less, illness-less, deathless, sorrow-less, unexcelled rest from the yoke, Unbinding, I reached the aging-less, illness-less, deathless, sorrow-less, unexcelled rest from the yoke: Unbinding. Knowledge & vision arose in me: 'Unprovoked is my release. This is the last birth. There is now no further becoming.'

This Dhamma that I have attained is deep, hard to see, hard to realize, peaceful, refined, beyond the scope of conjecture, subtle, to-be-experienced by the wise.

That is what the Blessed One said. Gratified, the monks delighted in the Blessed One's words.

Namo Shakyamunaye Buddhaya.

(3 times) (ooo)

# 9. THE SHORTER SIMILE OF THE ELEPHANT'S FOOTPRINT

(27. Cūḷahatthipadopamasutta,
Majjhima Nikaya 1)

Translated by Bhikkhu Sujato

So I have heard. At one time the Buddha was staying near Sāvatthī in Jeta's Grove, Anāthapiṇḍika's monastery, talked with brahmin Jāṇussoṇi and thewanderer Pilotika as follows,

"Suppose that an elephant tracker were to enter an elephant wood. There they'd see a large elephant's footprint, long and broad. A skilled elephant tracker wouldn't yet come to the conclusion, 'This must be a big bull elephant.' Why not? Because in an elephant wood there are dwarf she-elephants with big footprints, and this footprint might be one of theirs.

They keep following the track until they see a big footprint, long and broad, and, high up, signs of usage. A skilled elephant tracker wouldn't yet come to the conclusion, 'This must be a big bull elephant.' Why not? Because in an elephant wood there are tall she-elephants with long trunks and big footprints, and this footprint might be one of theirs.

They keep following the track until they see a big footprint, long and broad, and, high up, signs of usage, tusk-marks, and broken branches. And they see that bull elephant walking, standing, sitting, or lying down at the root of a tree or in the open. Then they'd come to the conclusion, 'This is that big bull elephant.'

In the same way, brahmin, a Realized One arises in the world, perfected, a fully awakened Buddha, accomplished in knowledge and conduct, holy, knower of the world, supreme guide for those who wish to train, teacher of gods and humans, awakened, blessed. He realizes with his own insight this world-with its gods, Māras and Brahmās, this population with its ascetics and brahmins, gods and humans-and he makes it known to others. He teaches Dhamma that's good in the beginning, good in the middle, and good in the end, meaningful and well-phrased. And he reveals a spiritual practice that's entirely complete and pure.

The householders hear that teaching and gain faith in the Realized One, and after some time they shave off hair and beard, dress in ocher robes, and go forth from the lay life to homelessness.

Once they've gone forth, they take up the training and livelihood of the mendicants. They give up killing living creatures, stealing, lying, avoid injuring plants and seeds snd they attain THE ENTIRE SPECTRUM OF NOBLE ETHICS, they experience a blameless happiness inside themselves.

When their six sense bases face to six worldly objects, they don't get caught up in the features and details. They practice restraint, protecting the faculty of mind, and ACHIEVING ITS RESTRAINT. When they have this noble sense restraint, they experience an unsullied bliss inside themselves.

They act with situational awareness when going out and coming back; when looking ahead and aside; when bending and extending the limbs; when bearing the outer robe, bowl and robes; when eating, drinking, chewing, and tasting;

when urinating and defecating; when walking, standing, sitting, sleeping, waking, speaking, and keeping silent. The achieve THE NOBLE MINDFULNESS AND SITUATIONAL AWARENESS, they frequent a secluded lodging-a wilderness, the root of a tree, a hill, a ravine, a mountain cave, a charnel ground, a forest, the open air, a heap of straw.

After the meal, they meditate with a heart rid of desire, cleansing the ill will, malevolence. five hindrances, corruptions that weaken wisdom. Then, quite secluded from sensual pleasures, secluded from unskillful qualities, they enter and remain in THE FIRST ABSORPTION, which has the rapture and bliss born of seclusion.

Furthermore, as the placing of the mind and keeping it connected are stilled, a mendicant enters and remains in THE SECOND ABSORPTION, which has the rapture and bliss born of immersion, with internal clarity and confidence, and unified mind, without placing the mind and keeping it connected.

Furthermore, with the fading away of rapture, a mendicant enters and remains in THE THIRD ABSORPTION, where they meditate with equanimity, mindful and aware.

Furthermore, giving up pleasure and pain, and ending former happiness and sadness, a mendicant enters and remains in THE FOURTH ABSORPTION, without pleasure or pain, with pure equanimity and mindfulness.

When their mind has become immersed in samādhi like this-purified, bright, flawless, rid of corruptions, pliable, workable, steady, and imperturbable-they extend it toward RECOLLECTION OF PAST LIVES. They recollect many kinds of past lives, that is, one, two, three, four, five, ten, twenty, thirty, forty, fifty, a hundred, a thousand, a hundred thousand rebirths; many eons of the world contracting, many eons of the world expanding, many eons of the world contracting and expanding.

When their mind has become immersed in samādhi like this-purified, bright, flawless, rid of corruptions, pliable, workable, steady, and imperturbable-they extend it TOWARD KNOWLEDGE OF THE DEATH AND REBIRTH OF SENTIENT BEINGS.

With clairvoyance that is purified and surpasses the human, they understand how sentient beings are reborn according to their deeds.

When their mind has become immersed in samādhi like this-purified, bright, flawless, rid of corruptions, pliable, workable, steady, and imperturbable-they extend it toward knowledge of THE ENDING OF DEFILEMENTS. They truly understand: 'This is suffering'... 'This is the origin of suffering'... 'This is the cessation of suffering'... 'This is the practice that leads to the cessation of suffering.' They truly understand: 'These are defilements'... 'This is the origin of defilements'... 'This is the cessation of defilements'... 'This is the practice that leads to the cessation of defilements.' This, brahmin, is called 'a footprint of the Realized One' and also 'used by the Realized One' and also 'marked by the Realized One'.

Knowing and seeing like this, their mind is freed from the defilements of sensuality, desire to be reborn, and ignorance. When they're freed, they know they're freed.

They understand: 'Rebirth is ended, the

spiritual journey has been completed, what had to be done has been done, there is no return to any state of existence.' This, brahmin, is called 'a footprint of the Realized One' and also 'used by the Realized One' and also 'marked by the Realized One'. At this point a noble disciple has come to the conclusion, 'The Blessed One is a fully awakened Buddha. The teaching is well explained. The Saṅgha is practicing well.' And it is at this point that the simile of the elephant's footprint has been completed in detail."

When he had spoken, the brahmin Jāṇussoṇi said to the Buddha, "Excellent, Master Gotama! Excellent! As if he were righting the overturned, or revealing the hidden, or pointing out the path to the lost, or lighting a lamp in the dark so people with good eyes can see what's there, Master Gotama has made the teaching clear in many ways. I go for refuge to Master Gotama, to the teaching, and to the mendicant Saṅgha. From this day forth, may Master Gotama remember me as a lay follower who has gone for refuge for life."

**Namo Shakyamunaye Buddhaya.**
(3 times) (ooo)

***

# 10. THE SHORTER DISCOURSE ON THE SIMILE OF THE HEARTWOOD

(30. Culasaropama Sutta, Majjhima Nikaya 1)

Thus have i heard.

On one occasion, at Savatthi in Jeta's Grove, Anathapindika's Park, the Blessed One taught brahmin Pingalakoccha as follows:

A man needing heartwood, seeking heartwood, wandering in search of heartwood, came to a great tree standing possessed of heartwood. Passing over its heartwood, its sapwood, its inner bark, and its outer bark, he would cut off its twigs and leaves and take them away thinking they were heartwood.

Then a man with good sight, seeing him, might say: 'This good man did not know the heartwood, the sapwood, the inner bark, the outer bark, or the twigs and leaves. Thus, while needing heartwood, seeking heartwood, wandering in search of heartwood, he came to a great tree standing possessed of heartwood, and passing over its heartwood, its sapwood, its inner bark, and its outer bark, he cut off its twigs and leaves and took them away thinking they were heartwood. Whatever it was this good man had to make with heartwood, his purpose will not be served.'

## FIVE EXAMPLES

1. He would cut off its twigs and leaves and take it away thinking it was heartwood.

2. He would cut off its outer bark and take it away thinking it was heartwood.

3. He would cut off its inner bark and take it away thinking it was heartwood.

4. He would cut off its sapwood and take it away thinking it was heartwood.

5. He would cut off only its heartwood, he would take it away knowing it was heartwood.

6.

# FIVE KINDS OF MONASTICS

1. **Similarly brahmin, here some clansman goes forth out of faith from the home life into homelessness, considering: 'I am a victim of birth, ageing, and death, of sorrow, lamentation, pain, grief, and despair; I am a victim of suffering, a prey to suffering. Surely an ending of this whole mass of suffering can be known.'**

   **When he has gone forth thus, he acquires gain, offerings and fame. He is pleased with that gain, OFFERINGS AND FAME, and his intention is fulfilled. On account of it he lauds himself and disparages others thus: 'I have gain, offerings and fame, but these other bhikkhus just like a man cuts off its twigs and leaves and took them away thinking they were heartwood; his purpose will not have been served."**

2. **Some clansman goes forth out of faith from the home life into homelessness, considering: 'I am a victim of birth, ageing, and death, of sorrow, lamentation, pain, grief, and despair; I am a victim of suffering, a prey to**

suffering. Surely an ending of this whole mass of suffering can be known.'

When he has gone forth thus, he acquires gain, offerings and fame. He is not pleased with that and his intention is not fulfilled. He does not, on account of it, laud himself and disparage others. He achieves the attainment of VIRTUE. He is pleased with that attainment of virtue and his intention is fulfilled and makes no effort for the realization of those other states that are higher and more sublime than the attainment of virtue; he hangs back and slackens. Just like a man cuts off the outer bark and took them away thinking they were heartwood; his purpose will not have been served."

3. Some clansman goes forth out of faith from the home life into homelessness, considering: 'I am a victim of birth, ageing, and death, of sorrow, lamentation, pain, grief, and despair; I am a victim of suffering, a prey to suffering. Surely an ending of this whole mass of suffering can be known.' When he has gone forth thus, he acquires gain, honour, and

renown. He is not pleased with that and his intention is not fulfilled. He achieves the attainment of virtue and CONCENTRATION. He is pleased with that attainment of concentration and his intention is fulfilled. He hangs back and slackens, just like the person cuts off its inner bark and took it away thinking it was heartwood; his purpose will not have been served."

4. Some clansman goes forth out of faith from the home life into homelessness, considering: 'I am a victim of birth, ageing, and death, of sorrow, lamentation, pain, grief, and despair; I am a victim of suffering, a prey to suffering. Surely an ending of this whole mass of suffering can be known.' When he has gone forth thus, he acquires gain, honour, and renown. He is not pleased with that and his intention is not fulfilled...He achieves the attainment of virtue, concentration and KNOWLEDGE AND VISION. He is pleased with that knowledge and vision and his intention is fulfilled. On account of it he lauds himself and disparages

others just like the person cuts off its sapwood and took it away thinking it was heartwood; his purpose will not have been served."

5. Some clansman goes forth out of faith from the home life into homelessness, considering: 'I am a victim of birth, ageing, and death, of sorrow...; I am a victim of suffering, a prey to suffering. Surely an ending of this whole mass of suffering can be known.' When he has gone forth thus ,he acquires gain, honor, and renown. He is not pleased with that and his intention is not fulfilled... He achieves the attainment of virtue, concentration, knowledge and vision. He is pleased with that knowledge and vision, but his intention is not fulfilled. He does not, on account of it, laud himself and disparage others. He arouses desire to act and he makes an effort for the realization of those other states that are higher and more sublime than knowledge and vision he does not hang back and slacken."

There are the states that are higher and more sublime than knowledge and vision?

Here, brahmin, quite secluded from sensual pleasures, secluded from unwholesome states, a bhikkhu enters upon and abides in THE FIRST JHANA, which is accompanied by applied and sustained thought, with rapture and pleasure born of seclusion.

Again, with the stilling of applied and sustained thought, a bhikkhu enters upon and abides IN THE SECOND JHANA, which has self-confidence and singleness of mind without applied and sustained thought, with rapture and pleasure born of concentration.

Again, with the fading away as well of rapture, a bhikkhu abides in equanimity, and mindful and fully aware, still feeling pleasure with the body, he enters upon and abides in THE THIRD JHANA, on account of which noble ones announce: 'He has a pleasant abiding who has equanimity and is mindful.'

"Again, with the abandoning of pleasure and pain, and with the previous disappearance of joy and grief, a bhikkhu enters upon and abides in THE FOURTH JHANA, which has neither-pain-nor pleasure and purity of mindfulness due to equanimity. This too is a state higher and more sublime than knowledge and vision.

Again, with the complete surmounting of perceptions of form, with the disappearance of perceptions of sensory impact, with non-attention to perceptions of diversity, aware that 'space is infinite', a bhikkhu enters upon and abides in the base of INFINITE SPACE. This too is a state higher and more sublime than knowledge and vision.

Again, by completely surmounting the base of infinite space, aware that 'Consciousness Is Infinite', a bhikkhu enters upon and abides in the base of infinite consciousness.

Again, by completely surmounting the base of infinite consciousness, aware that 'there is nothing,' a bhikkhu enters upon and abides in the base of NOTHINGNESS.

"Again, by completely surmounting the base of nothingness, a bhikkhu enters upon and abides in the base of NEITHER PERCEPTION-NOR-NON-PERCEPTION.

Again, by completely surmounting the base of neither perception-nor-non-perception, a bhikkhu enters upon and abides in THE CESSATION OF PERCEPTION AND FEELING. And his taints are destroyed by seeing with wisdom. This too is a state higher and more sublime than knowledge and vision. These are the states that are higher and more sublime than knowledge and vision."

Just like a man needing heartwood, seeking heartwood,who came to a great tree standing possessed of heartwood, and cutting off its heartwood, took it away knowing it was heartwood; and so whatever it was he had to make with heartwood, his purpose will have been served.

"So this holy life, brahmin, does not have gain, honor, and renown for its benefit, or the attainment of virtue or the attainment of concentration or knowledge and vision for its benefit. But it is this un-shake-able deliverance of mind that is the goal of this holy life, its heartwood, and its end."

When this was said, the brahmin Pingalakoccha said to the Blessed One: "Magnificent, Master Gotama! Magnificent, Master Gotama! Master Gotama has made the Dhamma clear in many ways, as though he were turning upright what had been overthrown, revealing what was hidden, showing the way to one who was lost, or holding up a lamp in the dark for those with eyesight to see forms. I go to Master Gotama for refuge and to the Dhamma and to the Sangha of bhikkhus. From today let Master Gotama remember me as a lay follower who has gone to him for refuge for life."

**Namo Shakyamunaye Buddhaya.**
(3 times) (ooo)


***


# 11. THE GREATER COWHERD DISCOURSE

(32. Maha-gopalaka Sutta,
Majjhima Nikaya 1, AN 11.18.)

Translated from the Pali
by Thanissaro Bhikkhu


I have heard that on one occasion the Blessed One was staying near Savatthi in Jeta's Grove, Anathapindika's monastery.

There he addressed the monks:

## A. ELEVEN FACTORS IS INCAPABLE

"Monks, a cowherd endowed with eleven factors is incapable of looking after a herd so that it prospers & grows.

Which eleven?

There is the case where a cowherd is not well-versed in forms (appearances), unskilled in characteristics, doesn't pick out flies' eggs, doesn't dress wounds, doesn't fumigate [the cattle pen], doesn't know fords, doesn't know what it is [for the cattle] to have drunk, doesn't know the road, is not skilled in pastures, milks dry, and shows no extra respect for the bulls who are fathers & leaders of the herd. A cowherd endowed with these eleven factors is incapable of looking after a herd so that it prospers & grows.

"A monk endowed with these eleven factors is incapable of attaining growth, increase, & abundance in this Dhamma-Vinaya.

Which eleven?

1. There is the case where a monk does

not discern, as it actually is, that every form whatsoever is composed of the four great existents (earth, water, fire, & wind) and the forms dependent on them. This is how a monk is not well-versed in forms.

2. There is the case where a monk does not discern, as it actually is, that a fool is characterized by his actions, a wise person is characterized by his actions. This is how a monk is unskilled in characteristics.

3. There is the case where a monk acquiesces with an arisen thought of sensuality. He does not abandon it, dispel it, or wipe it out of existence. He acquiesces with an arisen thought of ill will... an arisen thought of harmfulness. He does not abandon it, dispel it, or wipe it out of existence. He acquiesces with arisen evil, unskillful qualities. He doesn't abandon them, dispel them demolish them, or wipe the out of existence. This is how a monk doesn't pick out flies' eggs.

4. There is the case where a monk, on seeing a form with the eye, hearing a

sound with the ear, smelling an odor with the nose, tasting a flavor with the tongue, touching a tactile sensation with the body and cognizing an idea with the intellect, he grasps at themes or details and he doesn't practice with restraint. This is how a monk doesn't dress wounds.

5. There is the case where a monk does not teach others in detail the Dhamma as he has heard and mastered it. This is how a monk doesn't fumigate.

6. There is the case where a monk goes time & again to the monks who are learned, well-versed in the tradition, the monk nether learn nor ask to resolve his doubts about the many teachings. This is how a monk doesn't know fords.

7. There is the case where a monk, when the Dhamma-Vinaya proclaimed by the Tathagata is being taught, doesn't gain knowledge of the meaning, doesn't gain knowledge of the Dhamma, doesn't gain joy connected with the Dhamma. This is how a monk doesn't know what it is to have drunk.

8. There is the case where a monk does not discern, as it actually is, the noble eightfold path. This is how a monk doesn't know the road.

9. There is the case where a monk does not discern, as they actually are, the four frames of reference. This is how a monk is unskilled in pastures.

10. There is the case where a monk - when faithful householders invite him to accept gifts of cloth, alms food, lodgings, and medicinal requisites for curing the sick - knows no moderation in taking. This is how a monk milks dry.

11. There is the case where a monk does not respect at the elder monks. He does not establish himself in verbal acts of goodwill.

A monk endowed with these eleven factors is incapable of attaining growth, increase, & abundance in this Dhamma-Vinaya.

## B. ELEVEN FACTORS IS CAPABLE

"Monks, a cowherd endowed with eleven factors is capable of looking after a herd so that it prospers & grows.

Which eleven?

There is the case where a cowherd is well-versed in forms (appearances), skilled in characteristics, picks out flies' eggs, dresses wounds, fumigates, knows fords, knows what it is to have drunk, knows the road, is skilled in pastures, doesn't milk dry, and shows extra respect for the bulls who are fathers & leaders of the herd. A cowherd endowed with these eleven factors is capable of looking after a herd so that it prospers & grows.

"A monk endowed with these eleven factors is capable of attaining growth, increase, & abundance in this Dhamma-Vinaya.

Which eleven?

1. There is the case where a monk discerns, as it actually is, that every form whatsoever is composed of the four great existents (earth, water, fire, & wind) and the forms dependent on them. This is how a monk is well-versed in forms.

2. There is the case where a monk

discerns, as it actually is, that a fool is characterized by his actions, a wise person is characterized by his actions. This is how a monk is skilled in characteristics.

3. There is the case where a monk does not acquiesce with an arisen thought of sensuality. He doesn't acquiesce with arisen evil, unskillful qualities. He abandons them, dispels them, demolishes them, & wipes them out of existence. This is how a monk pick outs flies' eggs.

4. There is the case where a monk, on seeing a form with the eye, hearing a sound with the ear, smelling an odor with the nose, tasting a flavor with the tongue, touching a tactile sensation with the body, cognizing an idea with the intellect, he does not grasp at any theme or details by which. He practices for its restraint. He protects the faculty of the intellect. This is how a monk dresses wounds.

5. There is the case where a monk teaches others in detail the Dhamma as he has heard and mastered it. This is how a

monk fumigates.

6. There is the case where a monk goes time & again to the monks who are learned, well-versed in the tradition, he learns and resolve his doubts about the many teachings. This is how a monk knows fords.

7. There is the case where a monk, when the Dhamma-Vinaya proclaimed by the Tathagata is being taught, gains knowledge of the meaning, gains knowledge of the Dhamma, gains joy connected with the Dhamma. This is how a monk knows what it is to have drunk.

8. There is the case where a monk discerns, as it actually is, the noble eightfold path. This is how a monk knows the roads.

9. There is the case where a monk discerns, as they actually are, the four frames of reference. This is how a monk is skilled in pastures.

10. There is the case where a monk - when faithful householders invite him to accept gifts of cloth, alms food, lodgings, and medicinal requisites for

curing the sick - knows moderation in taking. This is how a monk does not milk dry.

11. There is the case where a monk respect to the elder monks. He establishes himself in verbal acts of goodwill.

A monk endowed with these eleven factors is capable of attaining growth, increase, & abundance in this Dhamma-Vinaya.

That is what the Blessed One said. Gratified, the monks delighted in the Blessed One's words.

**Namo Shakyamunaye Buddhaya.**
(3 times) (ooo)

***

# 12. THE SHORTER DISCOURSE ON THE COWHERD

(34. Cūḷagopālakasutta, Majjhima Nikaya 1)

Translated from the Pali by Bhikkhu Sujato

So, I have heard. At one time the Buddha

was staying in the land of the Vajjis near Ukkacelā on the bank of the Ganges River. There the Buddha addressed the mendicants,

There are ascetics and brahmins who are skilled in this world and the other world, skilled in Māra's domain and its opposite, and skilled in Death's domain and its opposite. If anyone thinks they are worth listening to and trusting, it will be for their lasting welfare and happiness.

Just like the bulls, fathers and leaders of the herd, who crossed the Ganges to safety are the mendicants who are perfected, who have ended the defilements, completed the spiritual journey, done what had to be done, laid down the burden, achieved their own goal, utterly ended the fetters of rebirth, and are rightly freed through enlightenment. Having breasted Māra's stream, they have safely crossed over to the far shore.

Just like the strong and tractable cattle who crossed the Ganges to safety are the mendicants who, with the ending of the five lower fetters, are reborn spontaneously. They're extinguished there, and are not liable to return from that world. They too, having breasted Māra's stream, will safely cross over to the far shore.

Just like the bullocks and heifers who crossed the Ganges to safety are the mendicants who, with the ending of three fetters, and the weakening of greed, hate, and delusion, are once-returners. They come back to this world once only, then make an end of suffering. They too, having breasted Māra's stream, will safely cross over to the far shore.

Just like the calves and weak cattle who crossed the Ganges to safety are the mendicants who, with the ending of three fetters are stream-enterers, not liable to be reborn in the underworld, bound for awakening. They too, having breasted Māra's stream, will safely cross over to the far shore.

Just like the baby calf who had just been born, but, urged on by its mother's lowing, still managed to cross the Ganges to safety are the mendicants who are followers of principles, followers by faith. They too, having breasted Māra's stream, will safely cross over to the far shore.

Mendicants, I am skilled in this world and the other world, skilled in Māra's domain and its opposite, and skilled in Death's domain and its opposite. If anyone thinks I am worth listening to and trusting, it will be for their lasting welfare and happiness."

That is what the Buddha said. Then the Holy One, the Teacher, went on to say:

"This world and the other world

have been clearly explained by one who knows;

as well as Māra's reach,

and what's out of Death's reach.

Directly knowing the whole world,

The Buddha who understands has flung

open the door of the deathless,

for realizing the sanctuary, extinguishment.

The Wicked One's stream has been cut,

it's blown away and mown down.

Be full of joy, mendicants,

set your heart on the sanctuary!"

Namo Shakyamunaye Buddhaya.

(3 times) (ooo)

# 13. THE LONGER DISCOURSE ON THE ENDING OF CRAVING

(38. Mahātaṇhāsaṅkhayasutta, Majjhima Nikaya 1)

Translated by Bhikkhu Sujato

So I have heard. At one time the Buddha was staying near Sāvatthī in Jeta's Grove, Anāthapiṇḍika's monastery gave the lecture to Reverend Sāti as follows:

## 1. CONSCIOUSNESS THAT ARISES DEPENDENT

Consciousness is reckoned according to the specific conditions dependent upon which it arises.

Consciousness that arises dependent on the eye and sights is reckoned as eye consciousness.

Consciousness that arises dependent on the ear and sounds is reckoned as ear consciousness.

Consciousness that arises dependent on the nose and smells is reckoned as nose consciousness.

Consciousness that arises dependent on the tongue and tastes is reckoned as tongue consciousness.

Consciousness that arises dependent on the body and touches is 4. reckoned as body consciousness.

Consciousness that arises dependent on the mind and thoughts is reckoned as mind consciousness.

## 2. THESE FOUR FUELS & 12 DEPENDENT ORIGINATION

"Mendicants, there are these four fuels. They maintain sentient beings that have been born and help those that are about to be born. What four? Solid food, whether coarse or fine; contact is the second, mental intention the third, and consciousness the fourth.

What is the source, origin, birthplace, and inception of these four fuels? CRAVING.

And what is the source of craving? FEELING.

And what is the source of feeling? CONTACT.

And what is the source of contact? THE SIX SENSE FIELDS.

And what is the source of the six sense fields? NAME AND FORM.

And what is the source of name and form? CONSCIOUSNESS.

And what is the source of consciousness? CHOICES.

And what is the source of choices? IGNORANCE.

## 3. A CONDITION FOR CHOICES

So, ignorance is a condition for choices. Choices are a condition for consciousness. Consciousness is a condition for name and form. Name and form are conditions for the six sense fields. The six sense fields are conditions for contact. Contact is a condition for feeling. Feeling is a condition for craving. Craving is a condition for grasping. Grasping is a condition for continued existence. Continued existence is a condition for rebirth. Rebirth is a condition for old age and death, sorrow, lamentation, pain, sadness, and distress to come to be. That is how this entire mass of suffering originates.

## 4. THE PROCESS OF ARISES

"Good, mendicants! So both you and I say this. When this exists, that is; due to the arising of this, that arises. That is: Ignorance is a condition for choices. Choices are a condition for consciousness. Consciousness is a condition for name and form. Name and form are conditions for the six sense fields. The six sense fields are conditions for contact. Contact is a condition for feeling. Feeling is a condition for craving. Craving is a condition for grasping. Grasping is a condition for continued existence. Continued existence is a condition for rebirth. Rebirth is a condition for old age and death, sorrow, lamentation, pain, sadness, and distress to come to be. That is how this entire mass of suffering originates.

## 5. THE CEASES FOR CHOICES

When ignorance fades away and ceases with nothing left over, choices cease. When choices cease, consciousness ceases.

When consciousness ceases, name and form cease. When name and form cease, the six sense fields cease. When the six sense fields cease, contact ceases. When contact ceases, feeling ceases. When feeling ceases, craving ceases. When craving ceases, grasping ceases. When grasping ceases, continued existence ceases. When continued existence ceases, rebirth ceases. When rebirth ceases, old age and death, sorrow, lamentation, pain, sadness, and distress cease. That is how this entire mass of suffering ceases.

## 6. THE PROCESS OF CEASES

"Good, mendicants! When this doesn't exist, that is not; due to the cessation of this, that ceases. That is: When ignorance ceases, choices cease. When choices cease, consciousness ceases. When consciousness ceases, name and form cease. When name and form cease, the six sense fields cease. When the six sense fields cease, contact ceases. When contact ceases, feeling ceases. When feeling ceases, craving ceases. When craving ceases, grasping ceases. When grasping ceases, continued existence ceases. When continued existence ceases, rebirth ceases. When rebirth ceases, old age and death, sorrow, lamentation, pain, sadness, and distress cease. That is how this entire mass of suffering ceases.

When they see a sight with their eyes, if it's pleasant they desire it, but if it's unpleasant they dislike it. They live with mindfulness of the body unestablished and their heart restricted. And they don't truly understand the freedom of heart and freedom by wisdom where those arisen bad, unskillful qualities cease without anything left over.

Being so full of favoring and opposing, when they experience any kind of feeling-pleasant, unpleasant, or neutral-they approve, welcome, and keep clinging to it. This gives rise to relishing. Relishing feelings is grasping. Their grasping is a condition for continued existence. Continued existence is a condition for rebirth. Rebirth is a condition for old age and death, sorrow, lamentation, pain, sadness, and distress to come to be. That is how this entire mass of suffering originates.

They give up these five hindrances, corruptions of the heart that weaken wisdom. Then, quite secluded from sensual pleasures, secluded from unskillful qualities, they enter and remain in the first absorption, which has the rapture and bliss born of seclusion, while placing the mind and keeping it connected. Furthermore, as the placing of the mind and keeping it connected are stilled, a mendicant enters and remains in the second absorption... third absorption... fourth absorption.

## 7. THIS ENTIRE MASS OF SUFFERING CEASES

When they see a sight with their eyes, if it's pleasant they don't desire it, and if it's unpleasant they don't dislike it. They live with mindfulness of the body established and a limitless heart. And they truly understand the freedom of heart and freedom by wisdom where those arisen bad, unskillful qualities cease without anything left over.

Having given up favoring and opposing, when they experience any kind of feeling-pleasant, unpleasant, or neutral-they don't approve, welcome, or keep clinging to it. As a result, relishing of feelings ceases. When their relishing ceases, grasping ceases. When grasping ceases, continued existence ceases. When continued existence ceases, rebirth ceases. When rebirth ceases, old age and death, sorrow, lamentation, pain, sadness, and distress cease. That is how this entire mass of suffering ceases.

When they hear a sound with their ears...

When they smell an odor with their nose...

When they taste a flavor with their tongue...

When they feel a touch with their body...

When they know a thought with their mind, if it's pleasant they don't desire it, and if it's unpleasant they don't dislike it. They live with mindfulness of the body established and a limitless heart. And they truly understand the freedom of heart and freedom by wisdom where those arisen bad, unskillful qualities cease without anything left over.

Having given up favoring and opposing, when they experience any kind of feeling-pleasant, unpleasant, or neutral-they don't approve, welcome, or keep clinging to it. As a result, relishing of feelings ceases. When their relishing ceases, grasping ceases. When grasping ceases, continued existence ceases. When continued existence ceases, rebirth ceases. When rebirth ceases, old age and death, sorrow, lamentation, pain, sadness, and distress cease. That is how this entire mass of suffering ceases.

Mendicants, you should memorize that brief statement on freedom through the ending of craving. But the mendicant Sāti, the fisherman's son, is caught in a vast net of craving, a tangle of craving."

That is what the Buddha said. Satisfied, the mendicants were happy with what the Buddha said.

**Namo Shakyamunaye Buddhaya.** (3 times) (ooo)

***

# 14. THE GREAT CLASSIFICATION

(43. Mahāvedallasutta, Majjhima Nikaya 1)

Tranlated byBhikkhu Sujato

So I have heard. At one time the Buddha was staying near Sāvatthī in Jeta's Grove, Anāthapiṇḍika's monastery.

Then in the late afternoon, Venerable Mahākoṭṭhita came out of retreat, went to Venerable Sāriputta, and exchanged greetings with him. When the greetings and polite conversation were over, he sat down to one side and said to Sāriputta:

"Reverend, they speak of 'a witless person'. How is a witless person defined?"

"Reverend, they're called witless because they don't understand. And what don't they understand? They don't understand: 'This is suffering'... 'This is the origin of suffering'... 'This is the cessation of suffering'... 'This is the practice that leads to the cessation of suffering.' They're called witless because they don't understand."

Saying "Good, reverend," Mahākoṭṭhita approved and agreed with what Sāriputta said. Then he asked another question:

"They speak of 'a wise person'. How is a wise person defined?"

"They're called wise because they understand. And what do they understand? They understand: 'This is suffering'... 'This is the origin of suffering'... 'This is the cessation of suffering'... 'This is the practice that leads to the cessation of suffering.' They're called wise because they understand."

"They speak of 'consciousness'. How is consciousness defined?"

"It's called consciousness because it cognizes. And what does it cognize? It cognizes 'pleasure' and 'pain' and 'neutral'. It's called consciousness because it cognizes."

"Wisdom and consciousness-are these things mixed or separate? And can we completely dissect them so as to describe the difference between them?"

"Wisdom and consciousness-these things are mixed, not separate. And you can never completely dissect them so as to describe the difference between them. For you understand what you cognize, and you cognize what you understand. That's why these things are mixed, not separate. And you can never completely dissect them so as to describe the difference between them."

"Wisdom and consciousness-what is the difference between these things that are mixed, not separate?"

"The difference between these things is that wisdom should be developed, while consciousness should be completely understood."

"They speak of this thing called 'feeling'. How is feeling defined?"

"It's called feeling because it feels. And what does it feel? It feels pleasure, pain, and neutral. It's called feeling because it feels."

"They speak of this thing called 'perception'. How is perception defined?"

"It's called perception because it perceives. And what does it perceive? It perceives blue, yellow, red, and white. It's called perception because it perceives."

"Feeling, perception, and consciousness-are these things mixed or separate? And can we completely dissect them so as to describe the difference between them?"

"Feeling, perception, and consciousness-these things are mixed, not separate. And you can never completely dissect them so as to describe the difference between them. For you perceive what you feel, and you cognize what you perceive. That's why these things are mixed, not separate. And you can never completely dissect them so as to describe the difference between them."

"What can be known by purified mind consciousness released from the five senses?"

"Aware that 'space is infinite' it can know the dimension of infinite space. Aware that 'consciousness is infinite' it can know the dimension of infinite consciousness. Aware that 'there is nothing at all' it can know the dimension of nothingness."

"How do you understand something that can be known?"

"You understand something that can be known with the eye of wisdom."

"What is the purpose of wisdom?"

"The purpose of wisdom is direct knowledge, complete understanding, and giving up."

"How many conditions are there for the arising of right view?"

"There are two conditions for the arising of right view: the words of another and proper attention. These are the two conditions for the arising of right view."

"When right view is supported by how many factors does it have freedom of heart and freedom by wisdom as its fruit and benefit?"

"When right view is supported by five factors it has freedom of heart and freedom by wisdom as its fruit and benefit. It's when right view is supported by ethics, learning, discussion, serenity, and discernment. When right view is supported by these five factors it has freedom of heart and freedom by wisdom as its fruit and benefit."

"How many states of existence are there?"

"Reverend, there are these three states of existence. Existence in the sensual realm, the realm of luminous form, and the formless realm."

"But how is there rebirth into a new state of existence in the future?"

"It's because of sentient beings-shrouded by ignorance and fettered by craving-chasing pleasure in various realms. That's how there is rebirth into a new state of existence in the future."

"But how is there no rebirth into a new state of existence in the future?"

"It's when ignorance fades away, knowledge arises, and craving ceases. That's how there is no rebirth into a new state of existence in the future."

"But what, reverend, is the first absorption?"

"Reverend, it's when a mendicant, quite secluded from sensual pleasures, secluded from unskillful qualities, enters and remains in the first absorption, which has the rapture and bliss born of seclusion, while placing the mind and keeping it connected. This is called the first absorption."

"But how many factors does the first absorption have?"

"The first absorption has five factors. When a mendicant has entered the first absorption, placing the mind, keeping it connected, rapture, bliss, and unification of mind are present. That's how the first absorption has five factors."

"But how many factors has the first absorption given up and how many does it possess?"

"The first absorption has given up five factors and possesses five factors. When a mendicant has entered the first absorption, sensual desire, ill will, dullness and drowsiness, restlessness and remorse, and doubt are given up. Placing the mind, keeping it connected, rapture, bliss, and unification of mind are present. That's how the first absorption has given up five factors and possesses five factors."

"Reverend, these five faculties have different scopes and different ranges, and don't experience each others' scope and range. That is, the faculties of the eye, ear, nose, tongue, and body. What do these five faculties, with their different scopes and ranges, have recourse to? What experiences their scopes and ranges?"

"These five faculties, with their different scopes and ranges, have recourse to the mind. And the mind experiences their scopes and ranges."

"These five faculties depend on what to continue?"

"These five faculties depend on life to continue."

"But what does life depend on to continue?"

"Life depends on warmth to continue."

"But what does warmth depend on to continue?"

"Warmth depends on life to continue."

"Just now I understood you to say: 'Life depends on warmth to continue.' But I also understood you to say: 'Warmth depends on life to continue.' How then should we see the meaning of this statement?"

"Well then, reverend, I shall give you a simile. For by means of a simile some sensible people understand the meaning of what is said. Suppose there was an oil lamp burning. The light appears dependent on the flame, and the flame appears dependent on the light. In the same way, life depends on warmth to continue, and warmth depends on life to continue."

"Are the life forces the same things as the phenomena that are felt? Or are they different things?"

"The life forces are not the same things as the phenomena that are felt. For if the life forces and the phenomena that are felt were the same things, a mendicant who had attained the cessation of perception and feeling would not emerge from it. But because the life forces and the phenomena that are felt are different things, a mendicant who has attained the cessation of perception and feeling can emerge from it."

"How many things must this body lose before it lies forsaken, tossed aside like an insentient log?"

"This body must lose three things before it lies forsaken, tossed aside like an insentient log: vitality, warmth, and consciousness."

"What's the difference between someone who has passed away and a mendicant who has attained the cessation of perception and feeling?"

"When someone dies, their physical, verbal, and mental processes have ceased and stilled; their vitality is spent; their warmth is dissipated; and their faculties have disintegrated. When a mendicant has attained the cessation of perception and feeling, their physical, verbal, and mental processes have ceased and stilled. But their vitality is not spent; their warmth is not dissipated; and their faculties are very clear. That's the difference between someone who has passed away and a mendicant who has attained the cessation of perception and feeling."

"How many conditions are necessary to attain the neutral release of the heart?"

"Four conditions are necessary to attain the neutral release of the heart. Giving up pleasure and pain, and ending former happiness and sadness, a mendicant enters and remains in the fourth absorption, without pleasure or pain, with pure equanimity and mindfulness. These four conditions are necessary to attain the neutral release of the heart."

"How many conditions are necessary to

attain the signless release of the heart?"

"Two conditions are necessary to attain the signless release of the heart: not focusing on any signs, and focusing on the signless. These two conditions are necessary to attain the signless release of the heart."

"How many conditions are necessary to remain in the signless release of the heart?"

"Three conditions are necessary to remain in the signless release of the heart: not focusing on any signs, focusing on the signless, and a previous determination. These three conditions are necessary to remain in the signless release of the heart."

"How many conditions are necessary to emerge from the signless release of the heart?"

"Two conditions are necessary to emerge from the signless release of the heart: focusing on all signs, and not focusing on the signless. These two conditions are necessary to emerge from the signless release of the heart."

"The limitless release of the heart, and the release of the heart through nothingness, and the release of the heart through emptiness, and the signless release of the heart: do these things differ in both meaning and phrasing? Or do they mean the same thing, and differ only in the phrasing?"

"There is a way in which these things differ in both meaning and phrasing. But there's also a way in which they mean the same thing, and differ only in the phrasing.

And what's the way in which these things differ in both meaning and phrasing?

Firstly, a mendicant meditates spreading a heart full of love to one direction, and to the second, and to the third, and to the fourth. In the same way above, below, across, everywhere, all around, they spread a heart full of love to the whole world-abundant, expansive, limitless, free of enmity and ill will. They meditate spreading a heart full of compassion... They meditate spreading a heart full of rejoicing... They meditate spreading a heart full of equanimity to one direction, and to the second, and to the third, and to the fourth. In the same way above, below, across, everywhere, all around, they spread a heart full of equanimity to the whole world-abundant, expansive, limitless, free of enmity and ill will. This is called the limitless release of the heart.

And what is the release of the heart through nothingness? It's when a mendicant, going totally beyond the dimension of infinite consciousness, aware that 'there is nothing at all', enters and remains in the dimension of nothingness. This is called the heart's release through nothingness.

And what is the release of the heart through emptiness? It's when a mendicant has gone to a wilderness, or to the root of a tree, or to an empty hut, and reflects like this: 'This is empty of a self or what belongs to a self.' This is called the release of the heart through emptiness.

And what is the signless release of the heart? It's when a mendicant, not focusing on any signs, enters and remains in the signless immersion of the heart. This is called the signless release of the heart.

This is the way in which these things differ in both meaning and phrasing.

And what's the way in which they mean the same thing, and differ only in the phrasing?

Greed, hate, and delusion are makers of limits. A mendicant who has ended the defilements has given these up, cut them off at the root, made them like a palm stump, and obliterated them, so they are unable to arise in the future. The unshakable release of the heart is said to be the best kind of limitless release of the heart. That unshakable release of the heart is empty of greed, hate, and delusion.

Greed is something, hate is something, and delusion is something. A mendicant who has ended the defilements has given these up, cut them off at the root, made them like a palm stump, and obliterated them, so they are unable to arise in the future. The unshakable release of the heart is said to be the best kind of release of the heart through nothingness. That unshakable release of the heart is empty of greed, hate, and delusion.

Greed, hate, and delusion are makers of signs. A mendicant who has ended the defilements has given these up, cut them off at the root, made them like a palm stump, and obliterated them, so they are unable to arise in the future. The unshakable release of the heart is said to be the best kind of signless release of the heart. That unshakable release of the heart is empty of greed, hate, and delusion.

This is the way in which they mean the same thing, and differ only in the phrasing."

This is what Venerable Sāriputta said. Satisfied, Venerable Mahākoṭṭhita was happy with what Sāriputta said.

**Namo Shakyamunaye Buddhaya.** (3 times) (ooo)

***

# 15. THE SHORTER SET OF QUESTIONS-AND-ANSWERS

(44. Culavedalla Sutta. Majjhima Nikaya 1)

Translated by Bhikkhu Thanissaro

*(The Buddha praised Dhammadinna the nun as the foremost Dhamma teacher among his nun disciples. In this discourse she answers questions put to her by a layman -- Visakha*

*-- who, according to the commentary, was her former husband, a merchant of Rajagaha, and a non-returner.)*

**I have heard that on one occasion the Blessed One was staying near Rajagaha in the Bamboo Grove, the Squirrels' Sanctuary. Then Visakha the lay follower went to Dhammadinna the nun to raise questions. She answered it as follows.**

## 1. SELF-IDENTIFICATION

**Friend Visakha: form as a clinging-aggregate, feeling as a clinging-aggregate, perception as a clinging-aggregate, fabrications as a clinging-aggregate, consciousness as a clinging-aggregate. These five clinging-aggregates are the self-identification described by the Blessed One.**

**The craving that makes for further becoming -- accompanied by passion and delight, relishing now here and now there -- i.e., craving for sensual pleasure, craving for becoming, craving for non-becoming are the origination of self-identification described by the Blessed One.**

The remainderless fading and cessation, renunciation, relinquishment, release, and letting go of that very craving, are the cessation of self-identification described by the Blessed One.

Precisely this noble eightfold path -- right view, right resolve, right speech, right action, right livelihood, right effort, right mindfulness, right concentration are the way of practice leading to the cessation of self-identification described by the Blessed One."

Neither is clinging the same thing as the five clinging-aggregates, nor is it something separate. Whatever desire and passion there is with regard to the five clinging-aggregates, that is the clinging there.

## 2. THE VIEW ON SELF-IDENTIFICATION

There is the case, friend Visakha, where an uninstructed, run-of-the-mill person -- who has no regard for noble ones, is not well-versed or disciplined in their Dhamma; who has no regard for men of integrity, is not well-versed or disciplined in their

Dhamma – assumes the five aggregates (form/body, feeling, perception, mental/fabrications and consciousness) to be the self, or the self as the five aggregates. This is how self-identification comes about.

There is the case where a well-instructed noble disciple -- who has regard for noble ones, is well-versed and disciplined in their Dhamma; who has regard for men of integrity, is well-versed and disciplined in their Dhamma -- does not assumes the five aggregates (form/body, feeling, perception, mental/fabrications and consciousness) to be the self, or the self as the five aggregates. This is how self-identification does not come about."

## 3. THE NOBLE EIGHTFOLD PATH

This is the noble eightfold path, friend Visakha: right view, right resolve, right speech, right action, right livelihood, right effort, right mindfulness, right concentration.

The noble eightfold path is included under the three aggregates. Right speech, right action, and right livelihood come under the aggregate of virtue. Right effort, right mindfulness, and right concentration come under the aggregate of concentration. Right view and right resolve come under the aggregate of discernment.

## 4. THE FABRICATION

These three fabrications, friend Visakha: bodily-fabrications, verbal fabrications, and mental fabrications."

In-and-out breaths are bodily fabrications. Directed thought and evaluation are verbal fabrications. Perceptions and feelings are mental fabrications."

## 5. THE CESSATION OF THE PERCEPTIONS AND FEELINGS MENTAL FABRICATIONS

In-and-out breaths are bodily; these are things tied up with the body. That's why in-and-out breaths are bodily fabrications. Having first directed one's thoughts and made an evaluation, one then breaks out into speech. That's why directed thought and evaluation are verbal fabrications. Perceptions and feelings are mental; these are things tied up with the mind. That's why perceptions and feelings are mental fabrications.

The thought does not occur to a monk as he is attaining the cessation of perception and feeling that 'I am about to attain the cessation of perception and feeling' or that 'I am attaining the cessation of perception and feeling' or that 'I have attained the cessation of perception and feeling.' Instead, the way his mind has previously been developed leads him to that state."

When a monk is attaining the cessation of perception and feeling, friend Visakha, verbal fabrications cease first, then bodily fabrications, then mental fabrications.

## 6. THE FEELING

These three kinds of feeling: pleasant feeling, painful feeling, and neither-pleasant-nor-painful feeling.

Whatever is experienced physically or mentally as pleasant and gratifying is pleasant feeling. Whatever is experienced physically or mentally as painful and hurting is painful feeling. Whatever is experienced physically or mentally as neither gratifying nor hurting is neither-pleasant-nor-painful feeling.

Pleasant feeling is pleasant in remaining, and painful in changing, friend Visakha. Painful feeling is painful in remaining and pleasant in changing. Neither-pleasant-nor-painful feeling is pleasant in occurring together with knowledge, and painful in occurring without knowledge.

The latent tendency to passion lies latent in pleasant feeling. The latent tendency to irritation lies latent in painful feeling. The latent tendency to ignorance lies latent in neither-pleasant-nor-painful feeling.

## 7. THE LATENT TENDENCY

The latent tendency to passion is to be abandoned in pleasant feeling. The latent tendency to irritation is to be abandoned in painful feeling. The latent tendency to ignorance is to be abandoned in neither-pleasant-nor-painful feeling.

There is the case where a monk -- quite withdrawn from sensuality, withdrawn from unskillful qualities -- enters and remains in the first jhana: rapture and pleasure born from withdrawal, accompanied by directed thought and evaluation. With that he abandons passion. No latent tendency to passion lies latent there.

There is the case where a monk considers, 'O when will I enter and remain in the sphere that those who are noble now enter and remain in?' And as he thus nurses this yearning for the unexcelled liberations, there arises within him sorrow based on that yearning. With that he abandons irritation. No latent tendency to irritation lies latent there.

There is the case where a monk, with the abandoning of pleasure and pain -- as with the earlier disappearance of elation and distress -- enters and remains in the fourth jhana: purity of equanimity and mindfulness, neither pleasure nor pain. With that he abandons ignorance. No latent tendency to ignorance lies latent there."

## 8. THE OBJECT

Passion lies on the other side of pleasant

feeling.

Irritation lies on the other side of painful feeling.

Ignorance lies on the other side of neither-pleasant-nor-painful feeling.

Clear knowing lies on the other side of ignorance.

Release lies on the other side of clear knowing.

Unbinding lies on the other side of release.

For the holy life plunges into Unbinding, culminates in Unbinding, has Unbinding as its final end. If you wish, go to the Blessed One and ask him the meaning of these things. Whatever he says, that's how you should remember it."

## 9. CONCLUSION

Then Visakha the lay follower, delighting and rejoicing in what Dhammadinna the nun had said, bowed down to her and, keeping her to his right, went to the Blessed One. On arrival, having bowed down to the Blessed One, he sat to one side. As he was sitting there he told the Blessed

One the full extent of the conversation he had had with Dhammadinna the nun. When this was said, the Blessed One said to him, "Dhammadinna the nun is wise, Visakha, a woman of great discernment. If you had asked me those things, I would have answered you in the same way she did. That is the meaning of those things. That is how you should remember it."

That is what the Blessed One said. Gratified, Visakha the lay follower delighted in the Blessed One's words.

**Namo Shakyamunaye Buddhaya.** (3 times) (ooo)

***

# 16. THE DIAMOND THAT CUTS THROUGH ILLUSION

(Vajracchedika Prajñaparamita Sutra, Taisho Revised Tripitaka 335)

## OPENING GATHA

How may we overcome the fear of birth and death

and arrive at the state that is as indestructible as a diamond?

What way can direct us in our practice

to sweep away our thousands of illusions? If the awakened mind shows its compassion and opens up for us the treasure store,

then we may bring into our lives

the wonderful diamond teachings.


## DISCOURSE

This is what I heard one time when the Buddha was staying in the monastery in Anathapindika's park in the Jeta Grove near Shravasti with a community of 1,250 bhikshus, fully ordained monks.

That day, when it was time to make the almsround, the Buddha put on his sanghati robe and, holding his bowl, went into the city of Shravasti to beg for food, going from house to house. When the almsround was completed, he returned to the monastery to eat the midday meal. Then he put away his sanghati robe and his bowl, washed his feet, arranged his cushion, and sat down.

At that time, the Venerable Subhuti stood up, bared his right shoul- der, put his knee on the ground, and, folding his palms respectfully, said to the Buddha, "World-Honored One, it is rare to find someone like you. You always support and show special confidence in the Bodhisattvas.

"World-Honored One, if sons and daughters of good families want to give rise to the highest, most fulfilled, awakened mind, what should they rely on and what should they do to master their thinking?"

The Buddha said to Subhuti, "This is how the Bodhisattva Mahasat- tvas master their thinking: 'However many species of living beings there are

- whether born from eggs, from the womb, from moisture, or spontaneously; whether they have form or do not have form; whether they have perceptions or do not have perceptions; or whether it cannot be said of them that they have perceptions or that they do not have perceptions, we must lead all these beings to nirvana so that they can be liberated. Yet when this innumerable, immeasurable, infinite number of beings has become liberated, we do not, in truth, think that a single being has been liberated.'

"Why is this so? If, Subhuti, a bodhisattva holds on to the idea that a self, a person, a living being, or a life span exists, that person is not a true bodhisattva.

"Moreover, Subhuti, when a bodhisattva practices generosity, he does not rely on any object - any form, sound, smell, taste, tactile object, or dharma - to practice generosity. That, Subhuti, is the spirit in which a bo- dhisattva practices generosity, not relying on signs. Why? If a bodhisattva practices generosity without relying on signs, the happiness that results can- not be conceived of or measured. Subhuti, do you think that the space in the Eastern Quarter can be measured?

No, World-Honored One."

"Subhuti, can space in the Western, Southern, or Northern Quarters, above or below be measured?"

"No, World-Honored One."

"Subhuti, if a bodhisattva does not rely on any concept while practic- ing generosity, the happiness that results from that virtuous act is as great as space. It cannot be measured. Subhuti, the bodhisattvas should let their minds dwell in the teachings I have just given.

"What do you think, Subhuti? Is it possible to grasp the Tathagata by means of bodily signs?"

"No, World-Honored One. When the Tathagata speaks of bodily signs, there are no signs being talked about."

The Buddha said to Subhuti, "In a place where there is something

that can be distinguished by signs, in that place there is deception. If you can see the signless nature of signs, you can see the Tathagata."

The Venerable Subhuti said to the Buddha, "In times to come, will there be people who, when they hear these teachings, have real faith and con- fidence in them?"

The Buddha replied, "Do not speak that way, Subhuti. Five hundred years after the Tathagata has passed away, there will still be people who ap- preciate the joy and happiness that come from observing the precepts. When such people hear these words, they will have faith and confidence that this is the truth. Know that such people have sown seeds not only during the lifetime of one Buddha, or even two, three, four, or five Buddhas, but have, in fact, planted wholesome seeds during the lifetimes of tens of thousands of Buddhas. Anyone who, for even a moment, gives rise to a pure and clear confidence upon hearing these words of the Tathagata, the Tathagata sees and knows that person, and he or she will attain immeasurable happiness because of this understanding. Why?

"Because that person is not caught in the idea of a self, a person, a liv- ing being, or a life span. He or she is not caught in the idea of a dharma or the idea of a non-dharma. He or she is not caught in the notion that this is a sign and that is not a sign. Why? If you are caught in the idea of a dharma, you are also caught in the ideas of a self, a person, a living being, and a life span. If you are caught in the idea that there is no dharma, you are still caught in the ideas of a self, a person, a living being, and a life span. That is why we should not get caught in dharmas or in the idea that dharmas do not exist. This is the hidden meaning when the Tathagata says, 'Bhikshus, you should know that all of the teachings I give to you are a raft.' All teachings must be abandoned, not to mention non-teachings."

The Buddha asked Subhuti, "In ancient times when the Tathagata practiced under the guidance of the Buddha Dipankara, did the Tathagata at- tain anything?"

Subhuti answered, "No, World-Honored One. In ancient times when the Tathagata practiced under the guidance of the Buddha Dipankara, he did not attain anything."

"What do you think, Subhuti? Does a bodhisattva create a serene and beautiful Buddha Field?"

"No, World-Honored One. Why? To create a serene and beautiful Buddha Field is not in fact to create a serene and beautiful Buddha Field. That is why it is called creating a serene and beautiful Buddha Field."

The Buddha said, "So, Subhuti, all the

## Bodhisattva Mahasattvas

should give rise to a pure and clear intention in this spirit. When they give rise to this intention, they should not rely on forms, sounds, smells, tastes,

tactile objects, or objects of mind. They should give rise to an intention with their minds not dwelling anywhere."

"So, Subhuti, when a bodhisattva gives rise to the unequaled mind of awakening, he has to give up all ideas. He cannot rely on forms when he gives rise to that mind, nor on sounds, smells, tastes, tactile objects, or objects of mind. He can only give rise to the mind that is not caught in anything.

"The Tathagata has said that all notions are not notions and that all living beings are not living beings. Subhuti, the Tathagata is one who speaks of things as they are, speaks what is true, and speaks in accord with reality. He does not speak deceptively or to please people. Subhuti, if we say that the Tathagata has realized a teaching, that teaching is neither graspable nor deceptive.

"Subhuti, a bodhisattva who still depends on notions to practice gen- erosity is like someone walking in the dark. She will not see anything. But when a bodhisattva does not

depend on notions to practice generosity, she is like someone with good eye- sight walking under the bright light of the sun. She can see all shapes and colors.

"Subhuti, do not say that the Tathagata has the idea, 'I will bring liv- ing beings to the shore of liberation.' Do not think that way, Subhuti. Why? In truth there is not one single being for the Tathagata to bring to the other shore. If the Tathagata were to think there was, he would be caught in the idea of a self, a person, a living being, or a life span. Subhuti, what the Tathagata calls a self essentially has no self in the way that ordinary persons think there is a self. Subhuti, the Tathagata does not regard anyone as an ordinary person. That is why he can call them ordinary persons.

"What do you think, Subhuti? Can someone meditate on the Tathagata by means of the thirty-two marks?"

Subhuti said, "Yes, World-Honored One.

We should use the thirty- two marks to meditate on the Tathagata."

The Buddha said, "If you say that you can use the thirty-two marks to see the Tathagata, then the Cakravartin is also a Tathagata?"

Subhuti said, "World-Honored One, I understand your teaching. One should not use the thirty-two marks to meditate on the Tathagata."

Then the World-Honored One spoke this verse:

"Someone who looks for me in form or

seeks me in sound

is on a mistaken path

and cannot see the Tathagata."

"Subhuti, if you think that the Tathagata realizes the highest, most fulfilled, awakened mind and does not need to have all the marks, you are wrong. Subhuti, do not think in that way. Do not think that when one gives rise to the highest, most fulfilled, awakened mind, one needs to see all objects of mind as nonexistent, cut off from life. Do not think in that way. One who gives rise to the highest, most fulfilled, awakened mind does not say that all objects of mind are nonexistent and cut off from life."

After they heard the Lord Buddha deliver this discourse, the Vener- able Subhuti, the bhikshus and bhikshunis, laymen and laywomen, and gods and asuras, filled with joy and confidence, began to put these teachings into practice.

**Namo Shakyamunaye Buddhaya.** (3 times) (ooo)

***

# 17. DISCOURSE ON LOVE

(Mettā Sutta, Sutta Nipāta 1.8)

Translated by Thích Nhất Hạnh

He or she who wants to attain peace should practice being upright, humble, and capable of using loving speech. He or she will know how to live simply and happily, with senses calmed, without being covetous and carried away by the emotions of the majority. Let him or her not do anything that will be disapproved of by the wise ones.

And this is what he or she contemplates:

May everyone be happy and safe, and may all hearts be filled with joy.

May all beings live in security and in peace – beings who are frail or strong, tall or short, big or small, invisible or visible, near or faraway, already born, or yet to be born. May all of them dwell in perfect tranquility.

Let no one do harm to anyone. Let no one put the life of anyone in danger. Let no one, out of anger or ill will, wish anyone any harm.

Just as a mother loves and protects her only child at the risk of her own life, cultivate boundless love to offer to all living beings in the entire cosmos.

Let our boundless love pervade the whole universe, above, below, and across. Our love will know no obstacles. Our heart will be absolutely free from hatred and enmity. Whether standing or walking, sitting or lying, as long as we are awake, we should maintain this mindfulness of love in our own heart. This is the noblest way of living.

Free from wrong views, greed, and sensual desires, living in beauty and realizing Perfect Understanding, those who practice boundless love will certainly transcend birth and death.

By the firm determination of this truth, may you ever be well.

**Namo Shakyamunaye Buddhaya.** (3 times) (ooo)


***


# 18. THE TEN GREAT ASPIRATIONS OF SAMANTABHADRA BODHISATTVA

(Avatamsaka Sutra - Flower Garland Discourse 36, Taishō Revised Tripiṭaka 279)

Translated by Thích Nhất Hạnh from


Body, speech and mind, purified, in oneness,

I bow deeply to touch limitless Buddhas

of the past, present, and future

throughout all worlds in the Ten Directions.

The power of Samantabhadra's vow
enables me to be present everywhere.
Where there is a Buddha, I am there.
As Buddhas are countless, so too am I.

In a particle of dust are countless Buddhas,
all of them present with their own assembly.
The strength of my faith penetrates deeply
into every atom of all Dharma realms.

I aspire to use the Great Ocean of Sound,
giving rise to words of wonderful effect
that praise the Buddha's oceans of virtues,
in the past, present, and future.

I bring these offerings:
garlands of the most beautiful flowers,
incense, music, perfumes, and parasols,
all to adorn the Tathagatas and their lands.

Bringing food, robes, and fragrant flowers,
torches, sandalwood, sitting mats,

the finest adornments here in abundance
–an offering to the Tathagatas.

Inspired by Samantabhadra's vow,

I bring my heart, wide with deep
understanding,

with loving faith in the Buddhas of the
Three Times,

as an offering to the Tathagatas everywhere.

From beginningless time I have acted
unskillfully

with craving, hatred, and ignorance

in actions of body, speech, and mind.

Determined now to begin anew, I repent.

I rejoice in every virtuous action

by anyone, in any direction,

by learners and by those who need learn
no more,

of Buddhas and Bodhisattvas.

All beings who are Lamps for the world

and those who have just attained enlightenment,

I beg that you will think lovingly of us,

turning the Wheel of the Dharma to help the world.

With sincerity, I make a humble request

of the Buddhas and those who are about to enter nirvana:

remain forever in the world,

for the benefit and the welfare of all.

I humbly make offerings inviting all Buddhas

to stay with us and guide all beings to the other shore.

All the merit of joyous praise and repenting

I offer to the Path of Awakening.

This merit is transferred to the Three Jewels,

to their nature and form in the Dharma realms.

The Two Truths are perfectly woven together

into the Samadhi Seal.

The ocean of merit is measureless.

I vow to transfer it and not hold anything for myself.

If any human, out of discrimination and prejudice,

tries to do harm to the path of liberation

may their obstacles be fully removed.

In each moment, wisdom envelops the Dharma realms,

welcoming all to the place of non-regression.

Space and living beings are without limit,

the same with afflictions and results of past actions.

These four are fully and truly immeasurable.

So, too, is my offering of merit.

Namo Samantabhadra Boddhisattva.

(3 times) (ooo)

# 19. DISCOURSE ON THE FIVE WAYS OF PUTTING AN END TO ANGER

*(Madhyama Agama 25 Corresponds
with Aghata Vinaya Sutta
[Discourse on Water as an Example],
Anguttara Nikaya 5.162.)*

I heard these words of the Buddha one time when he was staying in the Anathapindika Monastery in the Jeta Grove near the town of Shravasti.

One day the Venerable Shariputra said to the monks, "Friends, today I want to share with you five ways of putting an end to anger. Please listen carefully and put into practice what I teach."

The bhikshus agreed and listened carefully.

The Venerable Shariputra then said, "What are these five ways of put- ting an end to anger?

"This is the first way. My friends, if there is someone whose bodily actions are not kind but whose words are kind, if you feel anger toward that person but you are wise, you will know how to meditate in order to put an end to your anger.

"My friends, say there is a bhikshu practicing asceticism who wears a patchwork robe. One day he is going past a garbage pile filled with excrement, urine, mucus, and many other filthy things, and he sees in the pile one piece of cloth still intact. Using his left hand, he picks up the piece of cloth, and he takes the other end and stretches it out with his right hand. He observes that this piece of cloth is not torn and has not been stained by excrement, urine, sputum, or other kinds of filth. So he folds it and puts it away to take home, wash, and sew into his patchwork robe. My friends, if we are wise, when someone's bodily actions are not kind but his words are kind, we should not pay attention to his unkind bodily actions, but only be attentive to his kind words. This will help us put an end to our anger.

"My friends, this is the second method. If you become angry with someone whose words are not kind but whose bodily actions are kind, if you are wise, you will know how to meditate in order to put an end to your an- ger.

"My friends, say that not far from the village there is a deep lake, and the surface of that lake is covered with algae and grass. There is someone who comes near that lake who is very thirsty, suffering greatly from the heat. He takes off his clothes, jumps into the water, and using his hands to clear away the algae and grass, enjoys bathing and drinking the cool water of the lake. It is the same, my friends, with someone whose words are not kind but whose bodily actions are kind. Do not pay attention to that person's words. Only be attentive to his bodily actions in order to be able to put an end to your anger. Someone who is wise should practice in this way.

"Here is the third method, my friends. If there is someone whose bodily actions and words are not kind, but who still has a little kindness in his heart, if you feel anger toward that person and are wise, you will know how to meditate to put an end to your anger.

"My friends, say there is someone going to a crossroads. She is weak, thirsty, poor, hot, deprived, and filled with sorrow. When she arrives at the crossroads, she sees a buffalo's footprint with a little stagnant rainwater in it. She thinks to herself, 'There is very little water in this buffalo's footprint. If I use my hand or a leaf to scoop it up, I will stir it up and it will become muddy and undrinkable. Therefore, I will have to kneel down with my arms and knees on the earth, put my lips right to the water, and drink it directly.' Straightaway, she does just that. My friends, when you see someone whose bodily actions and words are not kind, but where there is still a little kindness in her heart, do not pay attention to her actions and words, but to the little kindness that is in her heart so that you may put an end to your anger. Someone who is wise should practice in that way.

"This is the fourth method, my friends. If there is someone whose words and bodily actions are not kind, and in whose heart there is nothing that can be called kindness, if you are angry with that person and you are wise, you will know how to meditate in order to put an end to your anger.

"My friends, suppose there is someone on

a long journey who falls sick. He is alone, completely exhausted, and not near any village. He falls into despair, knowing that he will die before completing his journey. If at that point, someone comes along and sees this man's situation, she immediately takes the man's hand and leads him to the next village, where she takes care of him, treats his illness, and makes sure he has everything he needs by way of clothes, medicine, and food. Because of this compassion and loving kindness, the man's life is saved. Just so, my friends, when you see some- one whose words and bodily actions are not kind, and in whose heart there is nothing that can be called kindness, give rise to this thought: 'Someone whose words and bodily actions are not kind and in whose heart is nothing that can be called kindness, is someone who is undergoing great suffering. Unless he meets a good spiritual friend, there will be no chance for him to transform and go to realms of happiness.' Thinking like this, you will be able to open your heart with love and compassion toward that person. You will be able to put an end to your anger and help that person. Someone who is wise should practice like this.

"My friends, this is the fifth method. If there is someone whose bodily actions are kind, whose words are kind, and whose mind is also kind, if you are angry with that person and you are wise, you will know how to meditate in order to put an end to your anger.

"My friends, suppose that not far from the village there is a very beau- tiful lake. The water in the lake is clear and sweet, the bed of the lake is even, the banks of the lake are lush with green grass, and all around the lake, beauti- ful fresh trees give shade. Someone who is thirsty, suffering from heat, whose body is covered in sweat, comes to the lake, takes off his clothes, leaves them on the shore, jumps down into the water, and finds great comfort and enjoy- ment in drinking and bathing in the pure water. His heat, thirst, and suffering disappear immediately. In the same way, my friends, when you see someone whose bodily actions are kind, whose words are kind, and whose mind is also kind, give your attention to all his kindness of body, speech, and mind, and do not allow anger or jealousy to overwhelm you. If you do not know how to live happily with someone who is as fresh as that, you cannot be called someone who has wisdom.

"My dear friends, I have shared with you the five ways of putting an end to anger."

When the bhikshus heard the Venerable Shariputra's words, they were

happy to receive them and put them into practice.

**Namo Shakyamunaye Buddhaya.** (3 times) (ooo)

***

# 20. DISCOURSE ON THE FULL AWARENESS OF BREATHING
## (*Anapanasati Sutta*)

I. I heard these words of the Buddha one time when he was staying in Savatthi in the Eastern Park, with many well-known and accomplished disciples, including Sariputta, Mahamoggallana,

Mahakassapa, Mahakacchayana, Mahakotthita, Mahakappina, Mahachunda, Anuradha, Revata, and Ananda. The senior bhikkhus in the community were diligently instructing bhikkhus who were new to the practice - some instructing ten bhikkhus, some twenty, some thirty, and some forty; and in this way the bhikkhus who were new to the practice gradually made great progress.

That night the moon was full, and the Pavarana Ceremony was held to mark the end of the rainy-season retreat. Lord Buddha, the Awakened One, was sitting in the open air, and his disciples were gathered around him. After looking over the assembly, he began to speak:

"O bhikkhus, I am pleased to observe the fruit you have attained in your practice. Yet I know you can make even more progress. What you have not yet attained, you can attain. What you have not yet realized, you can real- ize perfectly. [To engage your efforts,] I will remain here until the next full- moon day."

When they heard that the Lord Buddha was going to remain in Savatthi for another month, bhikkhus throughout the country began traveling there to study with him. The senior bhikkhus continued teaching the bhikkhus new to the practice even more ardently. Some were instructing ten bhikkhus, some twenty, some thirty, and some forty. With this help, the newer bhikkhus were able, little by little, to continue their progress in understanding.

When the next full-moon day arrived, the Buddha, seated under the open sky, looked over the assembly of bhikkhus and began to speak:

"O bhikkhus, our community is pure and good. At its heart, it is with- out useless and boastful talk, and therefore it deserves to receive offerings and be considered a field of merit. Such a community is rare, and any pilgrim who seeks it, no matter how far he must travel, will find it worthy.

"O bhikkhus, there are bhikkhus in this assembly who have realized the fruit of Arhatship, destroyed every root of affliction, laid aside every bur- den, and attained right understanding and emancipation. There are also bhik- khus who have cut off the first five internal knots and realized the fruit of never returning to the cycle of birth and death.

"There are those who have thrown off the first three internal knots and realized the fruit of returning once more. They have cut off the roots of greed, hatred, and ignorance, and will only need to return to the cycle of birth and death one more time. There are those who have thrown off the three internal knots and attained the fruit of stream-enterer, coursing steadily to the Awakened State. There are those who practice the Four Establishments of Mindfulness. There are those who practice the Four Right Efforts, and those who practice the Four Bases of Success. There are those who practice the Five Faculties, those who practice the Five Powers, those who practice the Seven Factors of Awakening, and those who practice the Noble Eightfold Path. There are those who practice loving kindness, those who practice com- passion, those who practice joy, and those who practice equanimity. There are those who practice the Nine Contemplations, and those who practice the Ob- servation of Impermanence. There are also bhikkhus who are already practicing Full Awareness of Breathing."

II. "O bhikkhus, the Full Awareness of Breathing, if developed and practiced continuously, will be rewarding and bring great advantages. It will lead to success in practicing the Four Establishments of Mindfulness. If the method of the Four Establishments of Mindfulness is developed and practiced contin- uously, it will lead to success in the practice of the Seven Factors of Awaking.

The Seven Factors of Awakening, if developed and practiced continuously,

will give rise to understanding and liberation of the mind.

"What is the way to develop and practice continuously the method of Full Awareness of Breathing so that the practice will be rewarding and offer great benefit?

"It is like this, bhikkhus: the practitioner goes into the forest or to the foot of a tree, or to any deserted place, sits stably in the lotus position, holding his or her body quite straight, and practices like this:

'Breathing in, I know I am breathing in. Breathing out, I know I am breathing out.'

1. 'Breathing in a long breath, I know I am breathing in a long breath. Breathing out a long breath, I know I am breathing out a long breath.

2. 'Breathing in a short breath, I know I am breathing in a short breath. Breathing out a short breath, I know I am breathing out a short breath.

3. 'Breathing in, I am aware of my whole body. Breathing out, I am aware of my whole body.' He or she practices like this.

4. 'Breathing in, I calm my whole body.

   Breathing out, I calm my whole body.' He or she practices like this.

5. 'Breathing in, I feel joyful. Breathing out, I feel joyful.' He or she practices like this.

6. 'Breathing in, I feel happy. Breathing out, I feel happy.' He or she practices like this.

7. 'Breathing in, I am aware of my mental formations. Breathing out, I am aware of my mental formations.' He or she

practices like this.

8. 'Breathing in, I calm my mental formations. Breathing out, I calm my mental formations.' He or she practices like this.

9. 'Breathing in, I am aware of my mind. Breathing out, I am aware of my mind.' He or she practices like this.

10. 'Breathing in, I make my mind happy. Breathing out, I make my mind happy.' He or she practices like this.

11. 'Breathing in, I concentrate my mind. Breathing out, I concentrate my mind.' He or she practices like this.

12. 'Breathing in, I liberate my mind. Breathing out, I liberate my mind.' He or she practices like this.

13. 'Breathing in, I observe the impermanent nature of all dharmas. Breathing out, I observe the impermanent nature of all dharmas.' He or she practices like this.

14. 'Breathing in, I observe the disappearance of desire. Breathing out, I observe the disappearance of desire.'

He or she practices like this.

15.    'Breathing in, I observe the no-birth, no-death nature of all phenomena. Breathing out, I observe the no birth, no-death nature of all phenomena.' He or she practices like this.

16.    'Breathing in, I observe letting go.

Breathing out, I observe letting go.' He or she practices like this.

"The Full Awareness of Breathing, if developed and practiced continuously according to these instructions, will be rewarding and of great benefit."

III. "In what way does one develop and continuously practice the Full Awareness of Breathing, in order to succeed in the practice of the Four Establishments of Mindfulness?

"When the practitioner breathes in or out a long or a short breath, aware of his breath or his whole body, or aware that he is making his whole body calm and at peace, he abides peacefully in the observation of the body in the body, persevering, fully awake, clearly understanding his state, gone beyond all attachment and aversion to this life. These exercises of breathing with Full Awareness belong to the First Establishment of Mindfulness, the body.

"When the practitioner breathes in or out aware of joy or happiness, of the mental formations, or to make the mental formations peaceful, he abides peacefully in the observation of the feelings in the feelings, persevering, fully awake, clearly understanding his state, gone beyond all attachment and aver-sion to this life. These exercises of breathing with Full Awareness belong to the Second Establishment of Mindfulness, the feelings.

"When the practitioner breathes in or out with the awareness of the mind, or to make the mind happy, to collect the mind in concentration, or to free and liberate the mind, he abides peacefully in the observation of the mind in the mind, persevering, fully awake, clearly understanding his state, gone beyond all attachment and aversion to this life. These exercises of breathing with Full Awareness belong to the Third Establishment of Mindfulness, the mind. Without Full

Awareness of Breathing, there can be no development of meditative stability and understanding.

"When the practitioner breathes in or breathes out and contemplates the essential impermanence or the essential disappearance of desire or the no-birth, no-death nature of all phenomena or letting go, he abides peacefully in the observations of the objects of mind in the objects of mind, persevering, fully awake, clearly understanding his state, gone beyond all attachment and aversion to this life. These exercises of breathing with Full Awareness belong to the Fourth Establishment of Mindfulness, the objects of mind.

"The practice of Full Awareness of Breathing, if developed and practiced continuously, will lead to perfect accomplishment of the Four Establishments of Mindfulness."

IV. "Moreover, if they are developed and continuously practiced, the Four Establishments of Mindfulness will lead to perfect abiding in the Seven Factors of

**Awakening. How is this so?**

**"When the practitioner can maintain, without distraction, the practice of observing the body in the body, the feelings in the feelings, the mind in the mind, and the objects of mind in the objects of mind, persevering, fully awake, clearly understanding her state, gone beyond all attachment and aver- sion to this life, with unwavering, steadfast, imperturbable meditative stabil- ity, she will attain the First Factor of Awakening, namely mindfulness. When this factor is developed, it will come to perfection.**

**"When the practitioner can abide in meditative stability without being distracted and can investigate every dharma, every object of mind that arises, then the Second Factor of Awakening will be born and developed in her, the factor of investigating dharmas. When this factor is developed, it will come to perfection.**

**"When the practitioner can observe and investigate every dharma in a sustained, persevering, and steadfast way, without being distracted, the Third Factor of Awakening will be born and developed in**

her, the factor of energy. When this factor is developed, it will come to perfection.

"When the practitioner has reached a stable, imperturbable abiding in the stream of practice, the Fourth Factor of Awakening will be born and developed in her, the factor of joy. When this factor is developed, it will come to perfection.

"When the practitioner can abide undistractedly in the state of joy, she will feel her body and mind light and at peace. At this point the Fifth Factor of Awakening will be born and developed, the factor of ease. When this factor is developed, it will come to perfection.

"When both body and mind are at ease, the practitioner can easily enter into concentration. At this point the Sixth Factor of Awakening will be born and developed in her, the factor of concentration. When this factor is developed, it will come to perfection.

"When the practitioner is abiding in concentration with deep calm, she will cease discriminating and comparing. At this point the Seventh Factor of Awakening is released, born, and developed in her, the factor of letting go. When this factor is developed, it will come to perfection.

"This is how the Four Establishments of Mindfulness, if developed and practiced continuously, will lead to perfect abiding in the Seven Factors of Awakening."

V. "How will the Seven Factors of Awakening, if developed and practiced con- tinuously, lead to the perfect accomplishment of true understanding and com- plete liberation?

"If the practitioner follows the path of the Seven Factors of Awaken-ing, living in quiet seclusion, observing and contemplating the disappearance of desire, he will develop the capacity of letting go. This will be a result of following the path of the Seven Factors of Awakening and will lead to the perfect accomplishment of true understanding and complete liberation."

This is what the Lord, the Awakened One, said; and everyone in the assembly felt gratitude and delight at having heard his teachings.

**Namo Shakyamunaye Buddhaya.**
(3 times) (ooo)

# 21. DISCOURSE THE UNIVERSAL DOOR (THE LOTUS OF THE WONDERFUL DHARMA)

*(Saddharmapundarika Sutra, Chapter 25, Taisho Revised Tripitaka 262)*

Buddha of ten thousand beautiful aspects,
may I ask you this question:
"Why did they give that bodhisattva the
name Avalokita?"

The World-Honored One, beautifully adorned,
offered this reply to Akshayamati:

"Because actions founded on her deep aspiration
can respond to the needs of any being in
any circumstance.

"Aspirations as wide as the oceans
were made for countless lifetimes.
She has attended to billions of Buddhas,

her great aspiration purified by mindfulness.

"Whoever calls her name or sees her image, if their mind be perfectly collected and pure, they will then be able to overcome the suffering of all the worlds.

"When those with cruel intent

push us into a pit of fire,

invoking the strength of Avalokita,

the fire becomes a refreshing lake. "Adrift on the waters of the great ocean, threatened by monsters of the deep, invoking the strength of Avalokita, we are saved from the storm waves.

"Standing atop Mount Meru,

should someone desire to push us down, invoking the strength of Avalokita,

we dwell unharmed like the sun hanging in space.

"Chased by a cruel person down the Diamond Mountain,

invoking the strength of Avalokita,

not even a hair of our body will be in danger.

"Encircled and assaulted by bandits holding swords to wound and to kill, invoking the strength of Avalokita,

sword blades shatter into millions of pieces.

"Imprisoned or bound in iron chains, with hands and feet placed in a yoke, invoking the strength of Avalokita, we are released into freedom. "Poisons, curses, and bewitchings putting us into

danger,

invoking the strength of Avalokita, harmful things return to their source. "Attacked by a fierce and cruel yaksha, a poisonous naga, or unkind spirit, invoking the strength of Avalokita,

they will do us no harm.

"With wild animals all around baring their teeth, tusks, and claws, invoking the strength of Avalokita will cause them to run far away.

"Confronted with scorpions and poisonous snakes, breathing fire and smoke of poisonous gas,invoking the strength of Avalokita, they depart, the air clears.

"Caught beneath lightning, thunder, and clouds,with hail pouring down in torrents,

invoking the strength of Avalokita,

the storm ends, the sunlight appears.

"All living beings caught in distress, oppressed by immeasurable suffering are rescued in ten thousand ways

by the wonderful power of her understanding.

"Miraculous power with no shortcoming,

wisdom and skillful means so vast -

in the Ten Directions of all the worlds,

there is no place she does not appear.

"The paths to realms of suffering,

the pain of birth, old age, sickness, and
death,
hells, hungry spirits, or animals
are all purified, brought to an end.

"Look of truth, look of purity, look
of boundless understanding,
look of love, look of compassion -
the look to be always honored and
practiced.
"Look of immaculate light and purity,
the Sun of Wisdom destroying darkness,

master of fire, wind, and disaster
illuminating the whole world.

"Heart of compassion like rolling thunder,
heart of love like gentle clouds,
water of Dharma nectar raining upon us,
extinguishing the fire of afflictions.

"In the courtroom, the place of lawsuits,

on the fields in the midst of war, invoking
the strength of Avalokita,
our enemies become our friends.

"Sound of wonder, noble sound,
sound of one looking deeply into the world,
extraordinary sound, sound of the rising tide,
the sound to which we will always listen.

"With mindfulness, free from doubts, in
moments of danger and affliction, our
faith in the purity of Avalokita
is where we go for refuge.

"We bow in gratitude to the one who
has all the virtues, regarding the world
with compassionate eyes,
an Ocean of Well-Being beyond measure."
Namo the Great Compassionate
Avalokiteshvara Bodhisattva.
(3 times) (ooo)

# 22. DISCOURSE ON THE EIGHT REALIZATIONS OF THE GREAT BEINGS

*(Taisho Revised Tripitaka 779)*

Wholeheartedly, day and night, disciples of the Awakened One should recite and meditate on the Eight Realizations discovered by the Great Beings.

The First Realization is the awareness that the world is impermanent. Political regimes are subject to fall. Things composed of the four elements are empty, containing within them the seeds of suffering. Human beings are com- posed of Five Aggregates and are without a separate self. They are always in the process of change - constantly being born and constantly dying. They are empty of self and without a separate existence. The mind is the source of all confusion, and the body the forest of all unwholesome actions. Meditating on this, you can be released from the round of birth and death.

The Second Realization is the awareness that more desire brings more suffering. All hardships in daily life arise from greed and desire. Those with little desire and ambition are able to relax, their body and mind free from entanglement.

The Third Realization is the awareness that the human mind is always searching outside itself and never feels fulfilled. This brings about unwhole- some activity. Bodhisattvas, on the other hand, know the value of having few desires. They live simply and peacefully, so they can devote themselves to practicing the Way. They regard the realization of perfect understanding to be their only career.

The Fourth Realization is the awareness that indolence is an obstacle to practice. You must practice diligently to transform unwholesome mental states that bind you, and you must conquer the four kinds of Mara in order to free yourself from the prisons of the Five Aggregates and the three worlds.

The Fifth Realization is the awareness that ignorance is the cause of the endless round of birth and death. Bodhisattvas always listen to and learn from others so their understanding and skillful means can develop, and so they can teach living beings and bring them great joy.

The Sixth Realization is the awareness that poverty creates hatred and anger, which creates a vicious cycle of negative thoughts and actions. When practicing generosity, bodhisattvas consider everyone - friends and enemies alike - to be equal. They do not condemn anyone's past wrongdoings or hate even those presently causing harm.

The Seventh Realization is the awareness that the five categories of sensual desire - money, sex, fame, overeating, and oversleeping - lead to problems. Although you are in the world, try not to be caught in worldly matters. A monk, for example, has in his possession only three robes and one bowl. He lives simply in order to practice the Way. His precepts keep him free of attachment to worldly things, and he treats everyone equally and with compassion.

The Eighth Realization is the awareness that the fire of birth and death is raging, causing endless suffering everywhere. Take the Great Vow to help all beings, to suffer with all beings, and to guide all beings to the Realm of Great Joy.

These Eight Realizations are the discoveries of great beings, Buddhas and Bodhisattvas who have practiced diligently the way of understanding and love. They have sailed the Dharmakaya boat to the shore of nirvana, and have then returned to the ordinary world, free of the five sensual desires, their minds and hearts directed toward the Noble Way. Using these Eight Realiza- tions, they help all beings recognize the suffering in the world. If disciples of the Buddha recite and meditate on these Eight Realizations, they will put an end to countless misunderstandings and difficulties and progress toward enlightenment, leaving behind the world of birth and death, dwelling forever in peace.

**Namo Shakyamunaye Buddhaya.**
(3 times) (ooo)

***

# 23. FIVE PRACTICES
# FOR  NURTURING HAPPINESS
## (Thích Nhất Hạnh)

## I. READING NURTURING HAPPINESS

"The essence of our practice can be described as transforming suffering into happiness," says Thích Nhất Hạnh. Here, he offers five practices to nourish our happiness daily.

We all want to be happy and there are many books and teachers in the world that try to help people be happier. Yet we all continue to suffer.

Therefore, we may think that we're "doing it wrong." Somehow we are "failing at happiness." That isn't true. Being able to enjoy happiness doesn't require that we have zero suffering. In fact, the art of happiness is also the art of suffering well. When we learn to acknowledge, embrace, and understand our suffering, we suffer much less. Not only that, but we're also able to go further and transform our suffering into understanding, compassion, and joy for ourselves and for others.

One of the most difficult things for us to accept is that there is no realm where there's only happiness and there's no suffering. This doesn't mean that we should despair. Suffering can be transformed. As soon as we open our mouth to say "suffering," we know that the opposite of suffering is already there as well. Where there is suffering, there is happiness.

According to the creation story in the biblical book of Genesis, God said, "Let there be light." I like to imagine that light replied, saying, "God, I have to wait for my twin brother, darkness, to be with me. I can't be there without the darkness." God asked, "Why do you need to wait? Darkness is there." Light answered, "In that case, then I am also already there."

One of the most difficult things for us to accept is that there is no realm where there's only happiness and there's no suffering. This doesn't mean that we should despair. Suffering can be transformed.

If we focus exclusively on pursuing happiness, we may regard suffering as something to be ignored or resisted. We think of it as something that gets in the way of happiness. But the art of happiness is also the art of knowing how to suffer well. If we know how to use our suffering, we can transform it and suffer much less. Knowing how to suffer well is essential to realizing true happiness.

## Healing Medicine

The main affliction of our modern civilization is that we don't know how to handle the suffering inside us and we try to cover it up with all kinds of consumption. Retailers peddle a plethora of devices to help us cover up the suffering inside. But unless and until we're able to face our suffering, we can't be present and available to life, and happiness will continue to elude us.

There are many people who have enormous suffering, and don't know how to handle it. For many people, it starts at a very young age. So why don't schools teach our young people the way to manage suffering? If a student is very unhappy, he can't concentrate and he can't learn. The suffering of each of us affects others. The more we learn about the art of suffering well, the less suffering there will be in the world.

Mindfulness is the best way to be with our suffering without being overwhelmed by it. Mindfulness is the capacity to dwell in the present moment, to know what's happening in the here and now. For example, when we're lifting our two arms, we're conscious of the fact that we're lifting our arms. Our mind is with our lifting of our arms, and we don't think about the past or the future, because lifting our arms is what's happening in the present moment.

To be mindful means to be aware. It's the energy that knows what is happening in the present moment. Lifting our arms and knowing that we're lifting our arms-that's mindfulness, mindfulness of our action. When we breathe in and we know we're breathing in, that's mindfulness. When we make a step and we know that the steps are taking place, we are mindful of the steps. Mindfulness is always mindfulness of something. It's the energy that helps us be aware of what is happening right now and right here-in our body, in our feelings, in our perceptions, and around us.

With mindfulness we are no longer afraid of pain. We can even go further and make good use of suffering to generate the energy of understanding and compassion that heals us and we can help others to heal and be happy as well.

With mindfulness, you can recognize the presence of the suffering in you and in the world. And it's with that same energy that you tenderly embrace the suffering. By being aware of your in-breath and out-breath you generate the energy of mindfulness, so you can continue to cradle the suffering. Practitioners of mindfulness can help and support each other in recognizing, embracing, and transforming suffering. With mindfulness we are no longer afraid of pain. We can even go further and make good use of suffering to generate the energy of understanding and compassion that heals us and we can help others to heal and be happy as well. Generating Mindfulness

The way we start producing the medicine of mindfulness is by stopping and taking a conscious breath, giving our complete attention to our in-breath and our out-breath. When we stop and take a breath in this way, we unite body and mind and come back home to ourselves. We feel our bodies more fully. We are truly alive only when the mind is with the body. The great news is that oneness of body and mind can be realized just by one in-breath. Maybe we have not been kind enough to our body for some time. Recognizing the tension, the pain, the stress in our body, we can bathe it in our mindful awareness, and that is the beginning of healing.

If we take care of the suffering inside us, we have more clarity, energy, and strength to help address the suffering of our loved ones, as well as the suffering in our community and the world. If, however, we are preoccupied with the fear and despair in us, we can't help remove the suffering of others. There is an art to suffering well. If we know how to take care of our suffering, we not only suffer much, much less, we also create more happiness around us and in the world.

## Why the Buddha Kept Meditating

When I was a young monk, I wondered why the Buddha kept practicing mindfulness and meditation even after he had already become a buddha. Now I find the answer is plain enough to see. Happiness is impermanent, like everything else. In order for happiness to be extended and renewed, you have to learn how to feed your happiness. Nothing can survive without food, including happiness; your happiness can die if you don't know how to nourish it. If you cut a flower but you don't put it in some water, the flower will wilt in a few hours.

We can condition our bodies and minds to happiness with the five practices of letting go, inviting positive seeds, mindfulness, concentration, and insight.

Even if happiness is already manifesting, we have to continue to nourish it. This is sometimes called conditioning, and it's very important. We can condition our bodies and minds to happiness with the five practices of letting go, inviting positive seeds, mindfulness, concentration, and insight.

## 1. LETTING GO

The first method of creating joy and happiness is to cast off, to leave behind.

There is a kind of joy that comes from letting go. Many of us are bound to so many things. We believe these things are necessary for our survival, our security, and our happiness. But many of these things-or more precisely, our beliefs about their utter necessity-are really obstacles for our joy and happiness.

Sometimes you think that having a certain career, diploma, salary, house, or partner is crucial for your happiness. You think you can't go on without it. Even when you have achieved that situation, or are with that person, you continue to suffer. At the same time, you're still afraid that if you let go of that prize you've attained, it will be even worse; you will be even more miserable without the object you are clinging to. You can't live with it, and you can't live without it.

If you come to look deeply into your fearful attachment, you will realize that it is in fact the very obstacle to your joy and happiness. You have the capacity to let it go. Letting go takes a lot of courage sometimes. But once you let go, happiness comes very quickly. You won't have to go around searching for it.

Imagine you're a city dweller taking a weekend trip out to the countryside. If you live in a big metropolis, there's a lot of noise, dust, pollution, and odors, but also a lot of opportunities and excitement. One day, a friend coaxes you into getting away for a couple of days. At first you may say, "I can't. I have too much work. I might miss an important call."

But finally he convinces you to leave, and an hour or two later, you find yourself in the countryside. You see open space. You see the sky, and you feel the breeze on your cheeks. Happiness is born from the fact that you could leave the city behind. If you hadn't left, how could you experience that kind of joy? You needed to let go.

## 2. INVITING POSITIVE SEEDS

We each have many kinds of "seeds" lying deep in our consciousness. Those we water are the ones that sprout, come up into our awareness, and manifest outwardly.

So in our own consciousness there is hell,

and there is also paradise. We are capable of being compassionate, understanding, and joyful. If we pay attention only to the negative things in us, especially the suffering of past hurts, we are wallowing in our sorrows and not getting any positive nourishment. We can practice appropriate attention, watering the wholesome qualities in us by touching the positive things that are always available inside and around us. That is good food for our mind.

One way of taking care of our suffering is to invite a seed of the opposite nature to come up. As nothing exists without its opposite, if you have a seed of arrogance, you have also a seed of compassion. Every one of us has a seed of compassion. If you practice mindfulness of compassion every day, the seed of compassion in you will become strong. You need only concentrate on it and it will come up as a powerful zone of energy.

Naturally, when compassion comes up, arrogance goes down. You don't have to fight it or push it down. We can selectively water the good seeds and refrain from watering the negative seeds. This doesn't mean we ignore our suffering; it just means that we allow the positive seeds that are naturally there to get attention and nourishment.

## 3. MINDFULNESS-BASED JOY

Mindfulness helps us not only to get in touch with suffering, so that we can embrace and transform it, but also to touch the wonders of life, including our own body. Then breathing in becomes a delight, and breathing out can also be a delight. You truly come to enjoy your breathing.

A few years ago, I had a virus in my lungs that made them bleed. I was spitting up blood. With lungs like that, it was difficult to breathe, and it was difficult to be happy while breathing. After treatment, my lungs healed and my breathing became much better. Now when I breathe, all I need to do is to remember the time when my lungs were infected with this virus. Then every breath I take becomes really delicious, really good.

When we practice mindful breathing or mindful walking, we bring our mind home to our body and we are established in the here and the now. We feel so lucky; we have so many conditions of happiness that are already available. Joy and happiness come right away. So mindfulness is a source of joy. Mindfulness is a source of happiness.

Mindfulness is an energy you can generate all day long through your practice. You can wash your dishes in mindfulness. You can cook your dinner in mindfulness. You can mop the floor in mindfulness. And with mindfulness you can touch the many conditions of happiness and joy that are already available. You are a real artist. You know how to create joy and happiness any time you want. This is the joy and the happiness born from mindfulness.

## 4. CONCENTRATION

Concentration is born from mindfulness. Concentration has the power to break through, to burn away the afflictions that make you suffer and to allow joy and happiness to come in.

To stay in the present moment takes concentration. Worries and anxiety about the future are always there, ready to take us away. We can see them, acknowledge them, and use our concentration to return to the present moment.

When we have concentration, we have a lot of energy. We don't get carried away by visions of past suffering or fears about the future. We dwell stably in the present moment so we can get in touch with the wonders of life, and generate joy and happiness.

Concentration is always concentration on something. If you focus on your breathing in a relaxed way, you are already cultivating an inner strength. When you come back to feel your breath, concentrate on your breathing with all your heart and mind. Concentration is not hard labor. You don't have to strain yourself or make a huge effort. Happiness arises lightly and easily.

## 5. INSIGHT

With mindfulness, we recognize the tension in our body, and we want very much to release it, but sometimes we can't. What we need is some insight.

Insight is seeing what is there. It is the clarity that can liberate us from afflictions such as jealousy or anger, and allow true happiness to come. Every one of us has insight, though we don't always make use of it to increase our happiness.

The essence of our practice can be described as transforming suffering into happiness. It's not a complicated practice, but it requires us to cultivate mindfulness, concentration, and insight.

We may know, for example, that something (a craving, or a grudge) is an obstacle for our happiness, that it brings us anxiety and fear. We know this thing is not worth the sleep we're losing over it. But still we go on spending our time and energy obsessing about it. We're like a fish who has been caught once before and knows there's a hook inside the bait; if the fish makes use of that insight, he won't bite, because he knows he'll get caught by the hook.

Often, we just bite onto our craving or grudge, and let the hook take us. We get caught and attached to these situations that are not worthy of our concern. If mindfulness and concentration are there, then insight will be there and we can make use of it to swim away, free.

In springtime when there is a lot of pollen in the air, some of us have a hard time breathing due to allergies. Even when we aren't trying to run five miles and we just want to sit or lie down, we can't breathe very well. So in wintertime, when there's no pollen, instead of complaining about the cold, we can remember how in April or May we couldn't go out at all. Now our lungs are clear, we can take a brisk walk outside and we can breathe very well. We consciously call up our experience of the past to help ourselves treasure the good things we are having right now.

In the past we probably did suffer from one thing or another. It may even have felt like a kind of hell. If we remember that suffering, not letting ourselves get carried away by it, we can use it to remind ourselves, "How lucky I am right now. I'm not in that situation. I can be happy"-that is insight; and in that moment, our joy, and our happiness can grow very quickly.

The essence of our practice can be

described as transforming suffering into happiness. It's not a complicated practice, but it requires us to cultivate mindfulness, concentration, and insight.

It requires first of all that we come home to ourselves, that we make peace with our suffering, treating it tenderly, and looking deeply at the roots of our pain. It requires that we let go of useless, unnecessary sufferings and take a closer look at our idea of happiness.

Finally, it requires that we nourish happiness daily, with acknowledgment, understanding, and compassion for ourselves and for those around us. We offer these practices to ourselves, to our loved ones, and to the larger community. This is the art of suffering and the art of happiness. With each breath, we ease suffering and generate joy. With each step, the flower of insight blooms.

## I. CHANTING: NOURISHING HAPPINESS

Sitting here in this moment, protected by the Sangha,

my happiness is clear and alive.

What a great fortune to have been born a human, to encounter the Dharma,
to be in harmony with others, and
to water the Mind of Love
in this beautiful garden of practice. (o)

The energies of the Sangha and mindfulness trainings are protecting and helping me not make mistakes
or be swept along in darkness by unwholesome seeds. With kind spiritual friends, I am on the path of goodness, illumined by the light of Buddhas and Bodhisattvas.Although seeds of suffering are still in me in the form of afflictions and habit energies, mindfulness is also there, helping me touch
what is most wonderful within and around me.

I can still enjoy mindfulness of the six senses: my eyes look peacefully upon the clear blue sky, my ears listen with wonder to the songs of birds, my nose smells the rich scent of sandalwood, my tongue tastes the nectar of the Dharma,

my posture is upright, stable, and relaxed,

and my mind is one with my body.

If there were not a World-Honored One, if there were not the wonderful Dharma, if there were not a harmonious Sangha,

I would not be so fortunate

to enjoy this Dharma happiness today.

My resources for practice are my own peace and joy.

I vow to cultivate and nourish them with daily mindfulness.

For my ancestors, family, future generations,

and the whole of humanity, I vow to practice well.

In my society I know that there are countless people suffering,

drowned in sensual pleasure, jealousy, and hatred.

I am determined to take care of my own mental formations, to learn the art of deep

listening and using loving speech
in order to encourage communication and understanding
and to be able to accept and love.

Practicing the actions of a bodhisattva,
I vow to look with eyes of love and a heart of understanding. I vow to listen with a clear mind and ears of compassion, bringing peace and joy into the lives of others,
to lighten and alleviate the suffering of living beings.

I am aware that ignorance and wrong perceptions
can turn this world into a fiery hell.
I vow to walk always upon the path of transformation.
Producing understanding and loving kindness.
I will be able to cultivate a garden of awakening.
Although there are birth, sickness, old age, and death,

now that I have a path of practice, I have nothing more to fear.
It is a great happiness to be alive in the

Sangha
with the practice of mindfulness trainings
and concentration, to live every moment
in stability and freedom,
to take part in the work of relieving others'
suffering,
the career of Buddhas and Bodhisattvas.

In each precious moment,
I am filled with deep gratitude.
I bow before the World-Honored One.
Please bear witness to my wholehearted
gratitude, embracing all beings with arms
of great compassion. (ooo)
**Namo Shakyamunaye Buddhaya.** (3
times) (ooo)

***

# 24. THE FOUR ESTABLISHMENTS OF MINDFULNESS

(Satipatthana Sutta, Majjhima Nikaya 10)

I heard these words of the Buddha one
time when he was living at Kammas-

sadhamma, a market town of the Kuru people. The Buddha addressed the bhikkhus, "O bhikkhus."

And the bhikkhus replied, "Venerable Lord."

The Buddha said, "Bhikkhus, there is a most wonderful way to help living beings realize purification, overcome directly grief and sorrow, end pain and anxiety, travel the right path, and realize nirvana. This way is the Four Establishments of Mindfulness.

## WHAT ARE THE FOUR ESTABLISHMENTS?

1. Bhikkhus, a practitioner remains established in the observation of the body in the body, diligent, with clear understanding, mindful, having abandoned every craving and every distaste for this life.

2. He remains established in the observation of the feelings in the feelings, diligent, with clear understanding, mindful, having abandoned every craving and every distaste for this life.

3. He remains established in the

**observation of the mind in the mind, diligent, with clear understanding, mindful, having abandoned every craving and every distaste for this life.**

**4. He remains established in the observation of the objects of mind in the objects of mind, diligent, with clear understanding, mindful, having abandoned every craving and every distaste for this life.**

## I. THE OBSERVATION OF THE BODY IN THE BODY

**And how does a practitioner remain established in the observation of the body in the body?**

**She goes to the forest, to the foot of a tree, or to an empty room, sits down cross-legged in the lotus position, holds her body straight, and estab- lishes mindfulness in front of her. She breathes in, aware that she is breath- ing in. She breathes out, aware that she is breathing out. When she breathes in a long breath, she knows, 'I am breathing in a long breath.' When she breathes out a long breath, she knows, 'I**

am breathing out a long breath.' When she breathes in a short breath, she knows, 'I am breathing in a short breath.' When she breathes out a short breath, she knows, 'I am breathing out a short breath.'

She uses the following practice: 'Breathing in, I am aware of my whole body. Breathing out, I am aware of my whole body. Breathing in, I calm my body. Breathing out, I calm my body.'

Just as a skilled potter knows when he makes a long turn on the wheel, 'I am making a long turn,' and knows when he makes a short turn, 'I am making a short turn,' so a practitioner, when she breathes in a long breath, knows, 'I am breathing in a long breath,' and when she breathes in a short breath, knows, 'I am breathing in a short breath,' when she breathes out a long breath, knows, 'I am breathing out a long breath,' and when she breathes out a short breath, knows, 'I am breathing out a short breath.'

She uses the following practice: 'Breathing in, I am aware of my whole body. Breathing out, I am aware of my whole body. Breathing in, I calm my body. Breathing out, I calm my body.'

Moreover, when a practitioner walks, he is aware, 'I am walking.' When he is standing, he is aware, 'I am standing.' When he is sitting, he is aware, 'I am sitting.' When he is lying down, he is aware, 'I am lying down.' In whatever position his body happens to be, he is aware of the position of his body.

Moreover, when the practitioner is going forward or backward, he applies full awareness to his going forward or backward. When he looks in front or looks behind, bends down or stands up, he also applies full awareness to what he is doing. He applies full awareness to wearing the sanghati robe

or carrying the alms bowl. When he eats or drinks, chews, or savors the food, he applies full awareness to all this. When passing excrement or urinating, he applies full awareness to this. When he walks, stands, lies down, sits, sleeps or wakes up, speaks or is silent, he shines his awareness on all this. "Further, the practitioner meditates on her very own body from the soles of the feet upwards and then from the hair on top of the head downwards, a body contained inside the skin and full of all the impurities which belong to the body: 'Here is the hair of the head, the hairs on the body, the nails, teeth, skin, flesh, sinews, bones, bone marrow, kidneys, heart, liver, diaphragm, spleen, lungs, intestines, bowels, excrement, bile, phlegm, pus, blood, sweat, fat, tears, grease, saliva, mucus, synovial fluid, urine.'

Bhikkhus, imagine a sack which can be opened at both ends, contain- ing a variety of grains - brown rice, wild rice, mung beans, kidney beans, sesame, white rice. When someone with good eyesight opens the bags, he will review it like this: 'This is brown rice, this is wild rice, these are mung beans, these are kidney beans, these are sesame seeds, this is white rice.' Just so the practitioner passes in review the whole of his body from the soles of the feet to the hair on the top of the head, a body enclosed in a layer of skin and full of all the impurities which belong to the body: 'Here is the hair of the head, the hairs on the body, nails, teeth, skin, flesh, sinews, bones, bone marrow, kidneys, heart, liver, diaphragm, spleen, lungs, intestines, bowels, excrement, bile, phlegm, pus, blood, sweat, fat, tears, grease, saliva, mucus, synovial fluid, urine.'

Further, in whichever position her body happens to be, the practitio- ner passes in review the elements which constitute the body: 'In this body is the earth element, the water element, the fire element, and the air element.'

As a skilled butcher or an apprentice butcher, having killed a cow, might sit at the crossroads to divide the cow into many parts, the practitioner passes in review the elements which comprise her very own body: 'Here in this body are the earth element, the water element, the fire element, and the air element.'

Further, the practitioner compares his own body with a corpse which he visualizes thrown onto a charnel ground and lying there for one, two, or three days - bloated, blue in color, and festering, and he observes, 'This body of mine is of the same nature. It will end up in the same way; there is no way it can avoid that state.'

Further, the practitioner compares his own body with a corpse which he visualizes thrown onto a charnel ground, pecked at by crows, eaten by hawks, vultures, and jackals, and infested with maggots and worms, and he observes, 'This body of mine is of the same nature, it will end up in the same way, there is no way it can avoid that state.'

Further, the practitioner compares his own body with a corpse which he visualizes thrown onto a charnel ground; it is just a skeleton with a little flesh and blood sticking to it, and the bones are held together by the liga- ments.

"Further, the practitioner compares his own body with a corpse which he vi-sualizes thrown onto a charnel ground; it is just a skeleton, no longer adhered to by any flesh, but still smeared by a little blood, the bones still held together by the ligaments.

Further, the practitioner compares his own body with a corpse which he visualizes thrown onto a charnel ground; it is just a skeleton, no longer adhered to by any flesh nor smeared by any blood, but the bones are still held together by the ligaments.

Further, the practitioner compares his own body with a corpse which he visualizes thrown onto a charnel ground; all that is left is a collection of bones scattered here and there; in one place a hand bone, in another a shin bone, a thigh bone, a pelvis, a spinal column, a skull.

Further, the practitioner compares his own body with a corpse which he visualizes thrown onto a charnel ground; all that is left is a collection of bleached bones, the color of shells.

Further, the practitioner compares his own body with a corpse which he visualizes thrown onto a charnel ground; it has been lying there for more than one year and all that is left is a collection of dried bones.

Further, the practitioner compares his own body with a corpse which he visualizes thrown onto a charnel ground; all that is left is the dust which comes from the rotted bones, and he observes, 'This body of mine is of the same nature, it will end up in the same way. There is no way it can avoid that state.'

This is how the practitioner remains established in the observation of the body in the body, observation of the body from within or from without, or both from within or from without. He remains established in the observation of the process of coming-to-be in the body or the process of dissolution in the body or both in the process of coming-to-be and the process of dissolution. Or he is mindful of the fact, 'There is a body here,' until understanding and full awareness come about. He remains established in the observation, free, not caught in any worldly consideration. That is how to practice observation of the body in the body, O bhikkhus."

## II. THE OBSERVATION OF THE FEELINGS IN THE FEELINGS

Bhikkhus, how does a practitioner remain established in the observation of the feelings in the feelings?

Whenever the practitioner has a pleasant feeling, she is aware, 'I am experiencing a pleasant feeling.' The practitioner practices like this for all the feelings, whether they are pleasant, painful, or neutral, observing when they belong to the body and when they belong to the mind.

This is how the practitioner remains established in the observation of the feelings in the feelings, observation of the feelings from within or from without, or observation of the feelings both from within and from without. She remains established in the observation of the process of coming-to-be in the feelings or the process of dissolution in the feelings or both in the process of coming-to-be and the process of dissolution. Or she is mindful of the fact, 'There is feeling here,' until understanding and full awareness come about. She remains established in the observation, free, not caught in any worldly consideration. That is how to practice observation of the feelings in the feel- ings, O bhikkhus."

## III. THE OBSERVATION OF THE MIND IN THE MIND

Bhikkhus, how does a practitioner remain established in the observation of the mind in the mind?

When his mind is desiring, the practitioner is aware, 'My mind is desiring.' When his mind is not desiring, he is aware, 'My mind is not desir- ing.' He is aware in the same way concerning a hating mind, a confused mind, a collected mind, a dispersed mind, an expansive mind, a narrow mind, the highest mind, and a concentrated and liberated mind.

This is how the practitioner remains established in the observation of the mind in the mind, observation of the mind from within or from without, or observation of the mind both from within and from without. He remains es- tablished in the observation of the process of coming-to-be in the mind or the process of dissolution in the mind or both in the process of coming-to-be and the process of dissolution. Or he is mindful of the fact, 'There is mind here,' until understanding and full awareness come about. He remains established in the observation, free, not caught in any worldly consideration. This is how to practice observation of the mind in the mind, O bhikkhus."

# IV. IN THE OBSERVATION OF THE OBJECTS OF MIND IN THE OBJECTS OF MIND

Bhikkhus, how does a practitioner remain established in the observation of the objects of mind in the objects of mind?

First of all, she observes the objects of mind in the objects of mind with regard to the Five Hindrances. How does she observe this?

When sensual desire is present in her, she is aware, 'Sensual desire is present in me.' Or when sensual desire is not present in her, she is aware, 'Sensual desire is not present in me.' When sensual desire begins to arise, she is aware of it. When sensual desire that has already arisen is abandoned, she is aware of it. When sensual desire that has already been abandoned will not arise again in the future, she is aware of it.

She practices in the same way concerning anger, dullness and drowsiness, agitation and remorse, and doubt.

Further, the practitioner observes the objects of mind in the objects of mind with regard to the Five Aggregates of Clinging. How does she ob- serve this?

She observes like this: 'Such is form. Such is the arising of form. Such is the disappearance of form. Such is feeling. Such is the arising of feeling. Such is the disappearance of feeling. Such is perception. Such is the arising of perception. Such is the disappearance of perception. Such are mental formations. Such is the arising of mental formations. Such is the dis- appearance of mental formations. Such is consciousness. Such is the arising of consciousness. Such is the disappearance of consciousness.

Further, bhikkhus, the practitioner observes the objects of mind in the objects of mind with regard to the six sense organs and the six sense ob- jects. How does she observe this?

She is aware of the eyes and aware of the form, and she is aware of the internal formations which are produced in dependence on these two things. She is aware of the birth of a new internal formation and is aware of abandoning an already produced internal formation, and she is aware when an already abandoned internal formation will not arise again.

She is aware in the same way of the ears and sound, the nose and smell, the tongue and taste, the body and touch, the mind and objects of mind.

Further, bhikkhus, the practitioner remains established in the obser- vation of the objects of mind in the objects of mind with regard to the Seven Factors of Awakening.

How does he remain established in the practice of observation of the Seven Factors of Awakening?

When the factor of awakening, mindfulness, is present in him, he is aware, 'Mindfulness is present in me.' When mindfulness is not present in him, he is aware, 'Mindfulness is not present in me.' He is aware when not-yet-born mindfulness is being born and when already-born mindfulness is perfectly developed.

In the same way, he is aware of the factors of investigation, dili-gence, joy, ease, concentration, and equanimity.

Further, bhikkhus, a practitioner remains established in the observa- tion of objects of mind in the objects of mind with regard to the Four Noble Truths.

How, bhikkhus, does the practitioner remain established in the ob- servation of the Four Noble Truths?

A practitioner is aware 'This is suffering,' as it arises. She is aware, 'This is the cause of the suffering,' as it arises. She is aware, 'This is the end of suffering,' as it arises. She is aware, 'This is the path which leads to the end of suffering,' as it arises.

This is how the practitioner remains established in the observation of the objects of mind in the objects of mind either from within or from without, or both from within and from without. She remains established in the obser- vation of the process of coming-to-be in any of the objects of mind or the process of dissolution in the objects of mind or both in the process of coming- to-be and the process of dissolution. Or she is mindful of the fact, 'There is an object of mind here,' until understanding and full awareness come about. She remains established in the observation, free, not caught in any worldly consideration. That is how to practice observation of the objects of mind in the objects of mind, O bhikkhus."

Bhikkhus, he who practices the Four Establishments of Mindfulness for seven years can expect one of two fruits - the highest understanding in this very life or, if there remains some residue of affliction, he can attain the fruit of no-return.

Let alone seven years, bhikkhus, whoever practices the Four Estab- lishments of Mindfulness for six, five, four, three, two years or one year, for seven, six, five, four, three, or two months, one month or half a month, can also expect one of two fruits - either the highest understanding in this very life or, if there remains some residue of affliction, he can attain the fruit of no-return.

That is why we said that this path, the path of the four grounds for the estab- lishment of mindfulness, is the most wonderful path, which helps beings real- ize purification, transcend grief and sorrow, destroy pain and anxiety, travel the right path, and realize nirvana.

The bhikkhus were delighted to hear the teaching of the Buddha. They took it to heart and began to put it into practice.

Namo Shakyamunaye Buddhaya.

(3 times) (ooo)

***

# 25. THE PROTECTING AND TRANSFORMING

(Thích Nhất Hạnh)

We, your disciples, who from beginningless time

have made ourselves unhappy out of confusion and ignorance,

being born and dying with no direction,

have now found confidence in the highest awakening.

However much we may have drifted on the ocean of suffering,

today we see clearly that there is a beautiful path.

We turn toward the light of loving kindness to direct us.

We bow deeply to the Awakened One and

to our spiritual ancestors

who light up the path before us, guiding every step. (o)

The wrongdoings and sufferings that imprison us

are brought about by craving, hatred, ignorance, and pride.

Today we begin anew to purify and free our hearts.

With awakened wisdom, bright as the sun and the full moon,

and immeasurable compassion to help humankind,

we resolve to live beautifully.

With all our heart, we go for refuge to the Three Precious Jewels.

With the boat of loving kindness,

we cross over the ocean of suffering.

With the torch of wisdom, we leave behind the forest of confusion.

With determination, we learn, reflect, and practice.

Right View is the ground of our actions, in body, speech, and mind.

Right Mindfulness embraces us,

walking, standing, lying down, and sitting,

speaking, smiling, coming in, and going out. (o)

Whenever anger or anxiety enter our heart,

we are determined to breathe mindfully and come back to ourselves.

With every step, we will walk in the Pure Land.

With every look, the Dharmakaya is revealed.

We are careful and attentive as sense organs touch sense objects

so mindfulness will protect us all day,

so all habit energies can be observed and easily transformed.

May our heart's garden of awakening

bloom with hundreds of flowers.

May we bring the feelings of peace and joy into every household.

May we plant wholesome seeds on the ten thousand paths.

May we never have the need to leave the Sangha body.

May we never attempt to escape the suffering of the world,

always being present wherever beings need our help.

May mountains and rivers be our witness in this moment

as we bow our heads and request the Lord of Compassion to embrace us all. (o)

**Namo Shakyamunaye Buddhaya.**
(3 times) (ooo)


***


# 26. THE MIDDLE WAY

(Samyukta Agama 301)


I heard these words of the Buddha one time when the Lord was staying at the guest house in a forest of the district of Nala. At that time, the Venerable Kacchayana came to visit him and asked, "The Tathagata has spoken of Right View. How would the Tathagata describe Right View?"

The Buddha told the venerable monk,

"People in the world tend to be- lieve in one of two views: the view of being or the view of nonbeing. That is because they are bound to wrong perception. It is wrong perception that leads to the concepts of being and nonbeing. Kaccayana, most people are bound to the internal formations of discrimination and preference, grasping and at- tachment. Those who are not bound to the internal knots of grasping and at- tachment no longer imagine and cling to the idea of a self. They understand, for example, that suffering comes to be when conditions are favorable, and that it fades away when conditions are no longer favorable. They no longer have any doubts. Their understanding has not come to them through others; it is their own insight. This insight is called Right View, and this is the way the Tathagata would describe Right View.

"How is this so? When a person who has correct insight observes the coming to be of the world, the idea of nonbeing does not arise in her, and when she observes the fading away of the world, the idea of being does not arise in her mind. Kaccayana, viewing the world as being is an extreme; viewing it as nonbeing is another extreme. The Tathagata avoids these two extremes and teaches the Dharma dwelling in the Middle Way.

"The Middle Way says that this is, because that is; this is not, because

that is not. Because there is ignorance, there are impulses; because there are impulses, there is consciousness; because there is consciousness, there is the psyche-soma; because there is the psyche-soma, there are the six senses; be- cause there are the six senses, there is contact; because there is contact, there is feeling; because there is feeling, there is craving; because there is craving, there is grasping; because there is grasping, there is becoming; because there is becoming, there is birth; because there is birth, there are old age, death, grief, and sorrow. That is how this entire mass of suffering arises. But with the fading away of ignorance, impulses cease; with the fading away of im- pulses, consciousness ceases;...and finally birth, old age, death, grief, and sorrow will fade away. That is how this entire mass of suffering ceases."

After listening to the Buddha, the Venerable Kaccayana was enlight- ened and liberated from sorrow. He was able to untie all of his internal knots and attain Arhatship.

**Namo Shakyamunaye Buddhaya.**
(3 times) (ooo)


***


# 27. MEASURING AND REFLECTING
(15.Anumana Sutta, Majjhima Nikaya)


I heard these words of the Buddha one time when he was staying with the Bhagga people in Sumsumaragiri, in the Deer Park in the Bhesakala Grove. The Venerable Mahamoggallana addressed the bhikkhus, "My friends."

"Yes, friend," they replied to the Venerable Mahamoggallana.

The Venerable Mahamoggallana spoke as follows:

"My friends, suppose there is a bhikkhu

who says to the other bhik- khus: 'Please talk to me, Reverend Bhikkhus. I want you to offer me guid- ance.' If he is difficult to talk to, endowed with qualities that make him dif- ficult to deal with, impatient, intolerant, not good at accepting constructive criticism or the words of advice and instruction from friends in the practice, then those who practice the path of sublime conduct with him will think, 'He is not one to be spoken to, he is not one to be instructed, he is not someone to have confidence in.' What are the qualities that make someone difficult to approach?

"My friends, a bhikkhu who is attached to wrong desires and is controlled by wrong desires is difficult to approach and talk to.

"These are other reasons that make it difficult to approach and talk to him: a person praises himself and despises others; he is easily angered and mastered by his anger; because he is angry, he bears a grudge; because he is angry, he is bad-tempered; because he is angry, he speaks in a bad-tempered way; he accuses one who has corrected him; he disparages one who has corrected him; he corrects in turn one who has corrected him; he evades the criticism by asking another question; he changes the subject; he manifests ill-temper, anger, and sulkiness; he does not succeed in explaining his behavior when corrected; he is unmindful and ill-willed; he is jealous and greedy; he is hypocritical and deceitful; he is stubborn and arrogant; or he is worldly and clings to things that belong to this world and finds it difficult to let go. These, my friends, are the habit energies that make it difficult to approach and talk to him.

"My friends, suppose there is a bhikkhu who requests of other bhik- khus: 'Please talk to me, Reverend Bhikkhus. I want you to offer me guid- ance.' If he is easy to talk to, endowed with qualities that make him easy to deal with, patient, tolerant, open and able to accept constructive criticism or the words of advice and instruction from friends in the practice, then those who practice the path of sublime conduct with him will think, 'He is someone we can talk to, someone we can instruct, someone we can have confidence in.' What are the qualities that make someone easy to approach?

"My friends, a bhikkhu who is not caught in wrong desires and is not controlled by wrong desires is easy to approach and talk to. He does not praise himself and despise others; he is not easily angered or mastered by his anger; because he is not angry, he does not bear a grudge; because he is not angry, he is not bad-tempered; because he is not angry, he does not speak in a bad-tempered way; he does not accuse one who has corrected him; he does not disparage one who has corrected him; he does not correct in turn one who has corrected him; he does not evade the criticism by asking another ques- tion; he does not change the subject; he does not manifest ill-temper, anger, and sulkiness; he succeeds in explaining his behavior when corrected; he is not jealous and greedy; he is not hypocritical and deceitful; he is not stubborn and arrogant; he is not worldly nor does he cling to things that belong to this world and he does not find it difficult to let go. These, my friends, are the qualities that make it easy to approach and talk to him.

"My friends, one should infer one's own state by considering the state of others in the following way: 'That person has wrong desires and is con- trolled by his wrong desires; therefore, I do not find him easy to approach. If I had wrong desires and were controlled by those wrong desires, others would not find me easy to approach.' When one sees this clearly, one should make the following determination: 'May I not be attached to wrong desires or be controlled by those wrong desires.'

"This method of reflection needs to be practiced in other cases, such as praising oneself and despising others, being easily angered and mastered by anger, and so on.

"My friends, this is how a bhikkhu should reflect on himself: 'At this moment, am I attached to wrong desires and controlled by wrong desires?' If when a bhikkhu reflects in this way, he knows, 'At this moment, I am at- tached to wrong desires and controlled by wrong desires,' then he should practice diligently to put an end to these unwholesome mental formations. If, on the other hand, when he reflects, he knows, 'At this moment, I am not at- tached to wrong desires and not controlled by wrong desires,' then a bhikkhu should live with a feeling of happiness, and he should practice diligently to nourish and increase these wholesome mental formations.

"This method of reflection needs to be practiced in other cases, such as praising oneself and despising others, becoming easily angered and mas- tered by anger, and so on.

"If, my friends, when he reflects, a bhikkhu sees clearly that he has not yet given up all these unbeneficial qualities, then he should practice dili- gently to give them all up. If, when he reflects, a bhikkhu sees clearly that he has given up all these unwholesome mental formations, then he should live with a feeling of happiness, and he should practice diligently to nourish and increase these wholesome mental formations.

"It is like when a young person who is fond of adorning himself con- templates his face in the mirror or a bowl of clear water. If he sees dirt or a blemish on his face, he tries to clean it. If he does not see dirt or a blemish, he thinks to himself, 'It is good, my face is clean.'

"So, my friends, if a bhikkhu reflects and sees that all these unwhole- some mental formations have not yet been given up, then he practices dili- gently to give them all up. If he sees that he has given them all up, he feels happy about this and knows that he needs to practice diligently in order to nourish and increase these wholesome mental formations."

The Venerable Mahamoggallana had spoken. The bhikkhus were de- lighted, had confidence in, and accepted their teacher's words.

**Namo Shakyamunaye Buddhaya.**
(3 times) (ooo)


***


## 28. KNOWING THE BETTER WAY TO LIVE ALONE

(131. Bhaddekaratta Sutta, Majjhima Nikaya)


I heard these words of the Buddha one time when the Lord was staying at the monastery in the Jeta Grove, in the town of Savatthi. He called all the monks to him and instructed them, "Bhikkhus!"

And the bhikkhus replied, "We are here."

The Blessed One taught, "I will teach you what is meant by 'knowing the better way to live alone.' I will begin with an outline of the teaching, and then I will give a detailed explanation. Bhikkhus, please listen carefully."

"Blessed One, we are listening."

The Buddha taught:

"Do not pursue the past.

Do not lose yourself in the future. The past no longer is.

The future has not yet come. Looking deeply at life as it is in the very here and now,

the practitioner dwells

in stability and freedom. We must be diligent today.

To wait till tomorrow is too late.

Death comes unexpectedly. How can we bargain with it? The sage calls a person who dwells in mindfulness night and day 'the one who knows the better way to live alone.'

"Bhikkhus, what do we mean by 'pursuing the past'? When someone considers the way her body was in the past, the way her feelings were in the past, the way her perceptions were in the past, the way her mental formations were in the past, the way her consciousness was in the past; when she con- siders these things and her mind is burdened by and attached to these things which belong to the past, then that person is pursuing the past.

"Bhikkhus, what is meant by 'not pursuing the past'? When someone considers the way her body was in the past, the way her feelings were in the past, the way her perceptions were in the past, the way her mental formations were in the past, the way her consciousness was in the past; when she con- siders these things but her mind is neither enslaved by nor attached to these things which belong to the past, then that person is not pursuing the past.

"Bhikkhus, what is meant by 'losing yourself in the future'? When someone considers the way his body will be in the future, the way his feelings will be in the future, the way his perceptions will be in the future, the way his mental formations will be in the future, the way his consciousness will be in the future; when he considers these things and his mind is burdened by and daydreaming about these things which belong to the future, then that person is losing himself in the future.

"Bhikkhus, what is meant by 'not losing yourself in the future'? When someone considers the way his body will be in the future, the way his feelings will be in the future, the way his perceptions will be in the future, the way his mental formations will be in the future, the way his consciousness will be in the future; when he considers these things but his mind is not burdened by or daydreaming about these things which belong to the future, then he is not losing himself in the future.

"Bhikkhus, what is meant by 'being swept away by the present'? When someone does not study or learn anything about the Awakened One, or the teachings of love and understanding, or the community that lives in harmony and awareness; when that person knows nothing about the noble teachers and their teachings, and does not practice these teachings, and thinks, 'This body is myself; I am this body. These feelings are myself; I am these feelings. This perception is myself; I am this perception. This mental formation is myself; I am this mental formation. This consciousness is myself; I am this consciousness,' then that person is being swept away by the present.

"Bhikkhus, what is meant by 'not being swept away by the present'? When someone studies and learns about the Awakened One, the teachings of love and understanding, and the community that lives in harmony and aware- ness; when that person knows about noble teachers and their teachings, prac- tices these teachings, and does not think, 'This body is myself; I am this body. These feelings are myself; I am these feelings. This perception is myself; I am this perception. This mental formation is myself; I am this mental formation. This consciousness is myself; I am this consciousness,' then that person is not being swept away by the present.

"Bhikkhus, I have presented the outline and the detailed explanation of knowing the better way to live alone."

Thus the Buddha taught, and the bhikkhus were delighted to put his teachings into practice.

**Namo Shakyamunaye Buddhaya.**
(3 times) (ooo)


***


# 29. TAKING REFUGE
# IN AMITABHA BUDDHA


Taking refuge in the Amitabha Buddha

In the wondrous ultimate dimension,

I devote my heart to returning to myself

And holding to the source of mindfulness.

I have vowed to go for refuge to the Amitabha Buddha. (o)


I bow my head and ask the Buddha

To receive us in his embrace.
As the Pure Land manifests,
Please bring your torch of light
To shine onto my thoughts.
Please bring the boat of long lifespan
To carry my body through life
So I live with peace and joy,
So my aspiration can be fully realized.
Buddha, please always protect me. (o)

Not letting my mind grow slack,
So that I end wrong perceptions
And the affliction fall away.
In the present moment
Buddha can be found in this world.
Taking every step with solidity and freedom
We walk in the Pure Land.
When we live the present moment mindfully,
The Pure Land is already a reality.
So whatever form we take in the future,
We can be assured of peace and joy. (o)

If we are able to recollect the Amitabha

With undispersed, one-pointed mind,

The nine lotus grades will appear.

May we enjoy life for ourselves and others

And know in advance our time of death.

At death may our mind not flinch,

Our body not be sick and in pain,

Our thoughts not waiver. (o)

May the Amitabha and his holy assembly

Holding up the golden lotuses

Be present without delay.

Together may we set out in freedom

May we see the Buddha in the opening lotus.

May the Pure Land be our home.

I bow my head to ask Buddha to be my witness

To my never slackening practice. (o)

**Namo Amitabha Buddha** (3 times) (ooo)

***

# 30. STORE OF PRECIOUS VIRTUES DISCOURSE: PRACTICE OF THE HIGHEST UNDERSTANDING

(Prajñaparamita Ratnaguna Samcaya Gāthā, Taishō Revised Tripiṭaka 229)

Translated by Thích Nhất Hạnh

Bodhisattvas, who in this life endeavor to remove

all obstacles and afflictions,

giving rise to a peaceful mind with confidence,

dwelling in awakened calm-

rely on the Practice of the Highest Understanding.


All the rivers on Roseapple Island,

producing the healing herbs, fresh fruits and flowers,

derive their power from the Naga King

who dwells in the cool Manasarowara Lake.

If all the hearer-disciples of the Buddha use skillful means to teach the Dharma,

help people experience joy, taste the fruit of happiness, and practice the holy life,

it is due to the sacred power of the Tathagata. The Buddha transmits the Eyes of the Dharma. His disciples, training according to it, practice, realize, and teach it to others.

All that is due to the power and strength of the Buddha.

The incomparable understanding is not to be grasped.

It is not an object of realization. There is no awakening.

Someone who hears this without feeling terror

is a bodhisattva who has the capacity to understand the Buddha.

Form, feelings, perceptions, mental formations,

and consciousness are all empty.

The bodhisattva is not the least bit caught

in anything.

He does not settle or abide in any dharma
and realizes the unattainable awakened
mind.

When the bodhisattva would leave the
shelter of afflictions
and shine her insight on the Five
Aggregates, she sees they are without
true nature,
she does not seek the peace of nirvana.
That is to realize the wisdom of a
bodhisattva.

What is the object realized by this
understanding?
It is to shine the light of insight and see
that all is empty. With this insight, there is
no longer any terror.
The bodhisattva awakens himself and
others.

Treating the Five Aggregates as real
is not to understand their true nature.

The bodhisattva sees the aggregates as empty

and practices without being caught in the form and in the word.


The Five Aggregates are empty.

Because she does not get caught in the form,

her practice is called "signless."

Where there is practice, there is not the Highest Understanding.

There is nothing that can be called concentration,

signlessness, and nirvana.


If he can practice this silent awakening,

all the Buddhas of the past empower him.

He knows the true nature of causes and conditions. Neither suffering nor delight can touch him.


If she practices with no object of her practice,

she practices in accord with the wisdom

of the Sugata.

If she practices with the spirit of non-practice,

this is the Highest Understanding.


The practice without object cannot be grasped.

Foolish people are caught in the signs "being" and "nonbeing." Neither "being" nor "nonbeing" can express the truth.

The bodhisattva of Awakened Understanding transcends both.


The bodhisattva, free of signs,

knows that the Five Aggregates are a magic show.

His practice is silent awakening,

which is the Practice of the Highest Understanding.


Taught by good teachers and spiritual friends, there is no fear of hearing the Mother of All Buddhas' Discourses.

But with deluded teachers and friends

traveling the wrong path, he is like a clay pot that has not been fired.

**Whom do we call a bodhisattva?**

She who is no longer caught by sensual desire, she who aspires to the fruit of awakening without being caught by it

is thus called a bodhisattva.

**Whom do we call a mahasattva?**

He who has comprehended the absolute truth and cuts through all wrong views in the world, he is thus called a mahasattva, a great being.

With great generosity, great wisdom, and virtuous power, she sits aboard the highest vehicle of the Buddhas

and gives rise to the awakened mind to save all beings. Thus she is called a great being.

Like a magician at the crossroads,

giving rise to an illusory crowd and cutting off their heads, all worlds are just as illusory. Knowing this, he feels no fear.

The Five Aggregates are ropes that bind.

Knowing they are not real, she needs no more dwelling.

She practices with her awakened mind not caught in anything. That is why she is called the highest bodhisattva.

Whom do we call a bodhisattva? -

the one who rides on the great vehicle to rescue all beings. The Great Vehicle is as vast as space.

All beings can ride on it in joy and safety.

The great vehicle cannot be grasped by ideas. It goes to nirvana, but nirvana is everywhere.

We cannot recognize the destination. It is like a fire gone out. That is why it is said he "enters nirvana."

The object of her practice cannot be

grasped. It cannot be found in the Three Times.

It is silence of ideas, fearless and beyond speculation. It is Practice of the Highest Understanding.

When a bodhisattva engages in the Practice of the Highest Understanding

and gives rise to great love and compassion to help beings,

never does he think in terms of "living beings." This is the Highest Understanding in action.

When a bodhisattva gives rise to the notion "living beings" and practices austerities, caught in the sign "suffering," she is caught in the signs "self" and "living being."

This is not the Highest Understanding in action.

When he knows clearly his own nature and that of other living beings,

and knows that all dharmas are of the same nature, that birth and death are not in opposition,

but are not distinguishable from birthless and deathless,

it is the Highest Understanding in action.


Abandoning all names and words,

abandoning all things that are born and die in the world,

there is the nectar of deathless and incomparable wisdom.


This is the Highest Understanding in action.

When the bodhisattva practices like this, and knows which skillful means to use, does not pursue anything,

and knows that these means have no separate existence,

this is the Practice of the Highest Understanding.


If she does not rely on form, feelings, perceptions, mental formations, and consciousness, and only relies on the perfect teachings,

this is the Practice of the Highest Understanding.


Permanent and impermanent, suffering and joy,

self and selfless, all are empty.

He does not abide in a world of conditioned or unconditioned elements.

Like the Buddha, he abides in the practice of signlessness.


If you aspire to attain the career of a hearer,

the self-enlightened one, or Buddha enlightenment; if you do not have endurance of the above practice, you cannot arrive.

It is like crossing the great river; you cannot see the other shore.


If you hear these teachings and are determined

to realize the highest awakening, witness the awakened mind, and see that the nature of all things is your own nature,

that is the great wisdom the Tathagata is describing.


A bodhisattva who practices great wisdom this way

does not train in the way of a hearer or a self-awakened Buddha. She trains only in the boundless knowledge of the Tathagata.

True learning is the learning of no-learning.

He trains in the non-increase and non-decrease of forms. He does not train in any other way.

His only joy is to train according to boundless knowledge. The same is true of feelings, perceptions, mental formations, and consciousness.

Form is neither wisdom nor the absence of wisdom.


Feelings, perceptions, mental formations, and consciousness are also like that.

The nature of form is like empty space - equality, nonduality, and nondiscrimination.

The basic nature of wrong perception is without limits,

as is the basic nature of all living beings.

The nature of space is without obstructions,

so is the wisdom of the one who perfectly understands the world.

The Buddha has said that wisdom is not form.

When clinging to perceptions is released, nirvana is there.

Whoever has given up clinging to perceptions,

her mind and speech are said to dwell in suchness.

For as many lifetimes as there are grains of sand in the Ganges,

he will not hear the Buddha utter the words "living beings."

Living beings are birthless, pure, and silent from the very beginning. This is the

**Practice of the Highest Understanding.**

**Since every word I have ever uttered contains the meaning of the Highest Understanding, the last Buddha transmitted to me the prediction that I would awaken in this very life.**

**The actions of one who receives and practices this understanding, are not less than that of the Buddha.**

**Swords, poison, fire, and water, and all the efforts of Mara will not touch him.**

**Mastering Anger**

**I bow my head and touch the Earth**

**before the highest charioteer who trains humankind.**

**Stretch out your arms of compassion;**

**bring us to the shore of peace and solidity.**

**For so long, confusion has inhabited us**

**so that we have not had the chance to learn, and we have often acted foolishly, allowed seeds of anger and violence to be watered in our deep consciousness.**

Whenever seeds of irritation or fury arise and operate in my mind,

They always cause wounds and resentment in myself and in so many others.

Listening to Avalokita's teaching,

I begin right now with a deep aspiration: Whenever anger arises,

I shall come back to myself,

taking refuge in my mindful breathing and steps so as to look after and embrace, to protect and recognize

the painful mental formations in me.

I shall remember to look deeply to see the true nature and source of hatred and anger.

Heeding the Buddha's teachings,

I shall know how to guard my mind.

When anger arises in me

I shall not do or say anything

until I have mastered it.

I shall look deeply to see

the real nature of my pain.

The seed of ignorance

is the cause of my suffering, and the reason why the seed of

anger in me has grown so strong.

The person who makes me angry

has so much suffering himself, herself.

Such a person has had no chance

to learn how to protect, to come home to himself or herself to take care and to transform the deep-seated habit energies within.

Contemplating in this way,

I will be able to bring about understanding and acceptance, and help the other person

to practice and to transform

the suffering within him or her.

The Blessed One has said,

When we are capable of conquering our anger,

we bring a double victory to ourself and to the other person.

I want to practice with all my heart
in order to respond to the Great Grace.

May the Three Jewels give me energy and blessing so that we can reach promptly the shore of peace and happiness.

**Namo Shakyamunaye Buddhaya.**
(3 times) (ooo)

***

# 31. THE DHARMA SEAL
(Taisho Revised Tripitaka 104)

I heard these words of the Buddha one time when the Lord was residing at Vaishali with his community of bhikshus. One day, he told the community, "Do you know of the wonderful Dharma Seal? Today I would like to tell you about it and explain it to you. Please use your pure mind to listen and receive it with care, and make the best effort to remember and practice it." The com- munity of bhikshus replied, "Wonderful, World-Honored One! Please teach us. We will listen carefully."

The Buddha said, "Emptiness is neither being nor nonbeing. It is free from all wrong views. It is neither produced nor destroyed, and it cannot be grasped by views. Why is this so? Because emptiness cannot be located in space. It has no form. It is not an object of perception. It has never been born, and the intellect cannot grasp it. Because it cannot be grasped, it embraces all dharmas and dwells only in non-discursive, nondiscriminative wisdom. This is the only true and right understanding, bhikshus! You should know that not only emptiness, but all dharmas are like that. This is the Dharma Seal.

"The Dharma Seal is also called the Three Doors of Liberation. It is the basic teaching of all Buddhas, the eye of all Buddhas, the destination of all Buddhas. Listen and receive it with care. Memorize it well and practice it right in the heart of reality.

"Bhikshus, find a quiet place to meditate, such as in a forest under a tree. There you can see that form is painful, empty, and impermanent, and as a result, you will not be attached to form. You will reach the nondiscrimi- native understanding of form. Then do the same for feelings, perceptions, mental formations, and consciousnesses. See that they are painful, empty, and impermanent, and rise above wrong views about them. Realize the nondis- criminative understanding of feelings, perceptions, mental formations, and consciousness. Bhikshus, the Five Aggregates are empty. They are produced from the mind. Once the mind stops operating in its usual way, the aggregates stop operating as well. When you see this, you will be liberated, free from all views. This is emptiness, the First Door of Liberation.

"Bhikshus, dwelling in concentration, see the dissolution of form, and be free from the illusory nature of perception vis-à-vis form. See the dissolu- tion of sound, smell, taste, touch, and mental formations, and be free from the illusory nature of perceptions vis-à-vis sound, smell, taste, touch, and mental formations. This meditation is called signlessness, the Second Door of Libera- tion. Once you have entered this door, your knowledge will be pure. Because of this purity of understanding, the three defiling qualities of mind - greed, hatred, and delusion - will be uprooted. With these uprooted, you will dwell in the realm of nondiscursive, nondiscriminative knowledge. When you are dwelling in this knowledge, views concerning 'me and mine,' and thus all views, no longer have the bases and the occasions to arise.

"Bhikshus, once you are free from the view 'I am,' you no longer con- sider what you see, hear, feel, and perceive as realities independent of your own consciousness. Why? Because you know that consciousness also arises from conditions and is impermanent. Because of its impermanent nature, it cannot be grasped either. This meditation is called wishlessness, the Third Door of Liberation. Once you enter this door, you experience fully the true nature of all dharmas, and you no longer cling to any dharma because you have seen the unconditioned nature of all dharmas."

The Buddha told the community of bhikshus, "This is the wonderful Seal of the Dharma, the Three Doors of Liberation. If you learn and practice it, you will certainly attain pure knowledge."

The monks were very happy to hear the teaching of the World-Hon- ored One. They paid respect to him and promised to learn and practice this wonderful teaching.

***

# 32. VENERABLE ANURADHA

22. Anurādha Sutta, Samyutta Nikāya.
86. Identical to SN 44.2

(Pali Text Society: 4.381–4.384,
Chinese Canon: SA 106.)

Translated by Thích Nhất Hạnh

I heard these words of the Buddha one time when the Lord was staying in the gabled house in the Great Forest near the town of Vesali. At that time, the Venerable

Anuradha was staying in a hermitage in the forest not far from where the Buddha was. One day a group of recluses came to see the Venerable Anuradha, and after exchanging greetings and courtesies, asked the venerable monk, "Venerable Anuradha, the Tathagata is often praised for having reached the highest fruit of awakening. He must have explained to you his understanding of these four propositions:

1. "After death, the Tathagata continues to exist.

2. "After death, the Tathagata ceases to exist.

3. "After death, the Tathagata both continues and ceases to exist.

4. "After death, the Tathagata neither continues nor ceases to exist.

"Please tell us which of these propositions is true."

The Venerable Anuradha replied, "Friends, the Tathagata, the World-Honored One, the one who has realized the highest fruit of awakening, has never proposed or spoken about these four propositions.

When they heard the Venerable Anuradha's reply, the recluses said, "It is possible that this monk has just been ordained, or if he was ordained some time ago, he must be of slow wits." Not satisfied with Venerable Anuradha's answer, they left him, thinking that he was either newly ordained or of little intelligence.

When the recluses had gone, the Venerable Anuradha thought, "If recluses continue to ask me these questions, how should I answer so as to speak the truth and not misrepresent the teachings of the Buddha? How should I answer so as to be in harmony with the right Dharma and not to be criticized by the adherents of the Buddhas path?" Then Anuradha went to where the Buddhawas staying, bowed to the Buddha, spoke words of greeting, and then told the Buddha what had happened.

The Buddha asked him, "What do you think, Anuradha? Can you find the Tathagata in form?"

"No, World-Honored One."

"Can you find the Tathagata outside of form?"

"No, World-Honored One."

"Can you find the Tathagata in feelings, perceptions, mental formations, or consciousness?"

"No, World-Honored One."

"Can you find the Tathagata outside of feelings, perceptions, mental formations, or consciousness?"

"No, World-Honored One."

"Well then, Anuradha, do you think that the Tathagata transcends form, feelings, perceptions, mental formations, and consciousness?"

"No, World-Honored One."

"Anuradha, if you cannot find the Tathagata even while he is still alive, can you find the Tathagata within these four propositions:

1. "After death, the Tathagata continues to exist.

2. "After death, the Tathagata ceases to exist.

3. "After death, the Tathagata both continues and ceases to exist.

4. "After death, the Tathagata neither continues nor ceases to exist."

"No, World-Honored One."

"Quite so, Anuradha. The Tathagata has only spoken and taught in relation to one thing: suffering and the end of suffering."

**Namo Shakyamunaye Buddhaya.**
(3 times) (ooo)

***

# 33. AWAKENING THE SOURCE OF LOVE

Thích Nhất Hạnh

We bow respectfully to Avalokiteshvara,

to your great vow always to be there for all beings,

your capacity to look deeply at the world with compassionate eyes,

listen deeply to understand and to relieve suffering,

and with your holy willow branch, to sprinkle the nectar of immortality,

cleansing my mind from all impurities.

I vow to take refuge in you with all my heart

Respectfully, I offer you my vow in thousands of words:

Namo Avalokiteshvara, I vow to look deeply into the Five Skandhas.

I vow to see the true nature of emptiness.

I vow soon to reach the shore of awakening.

I vow to overcome all obstacles.

I vow to take the boat of Perfect Understanding.

Namo Avalokiteshvara, I vow to be present in all three bodies.

I vow to realize the fruits of liberation.

I vow to cultivate great compassion.

I vow to understand deeply the Tathagata Store.

I vow to purify my mind.

Namo Avalokiteshvara, please help me get out of the abyss of craving.

Please help me dissolve the worries of my mind.

Please give me skillful means.

Please help me build Sangha.

Please help me transform my anger and hatred.

Please help me uproot my ignorance.

Please help me hold the high torch of right faith.

Please give me the clear eyes of understanding.


Namo Avalokiteshvara, please place in my hand the golden lotus.

Please allow me to see the Dharma Body.

I vow to build brotherhood and sisterhood.

I vow to show gratitude to my spiritual lineage.

I vow to practice loving speech.

I vow to look with loving eyes.

Namo Avalokiteshvara, I vow to practice deep listening

I vow to live mindfully and with clarity.

I vow to realize meditative concentration.

I vow to walk mindfully night and day.

I vow to abide peacefully in the ground of reality.

I vow to cultivate the five kinds of eyes, and the six miraculous powers.

Namo Avalokiteshvara,

Please come with me to the war zones to stop the killing and bombing.

Please walk with me to the places of sickness and suffering, bringing compassionate nectar and medicine.

Please walk with me to the realm of the hungry ghosts, bringing the Dharma food of understanding and love

Please walk with me to the realm of hell in order to cool the heat of afflictions.

Please walk with me to places of conflict in order to remove hatred and anger and help the source of love to flow again.

**Namo the Great Compassionate**

**Avalokiteshvara Bodhisattva.**

(3 times) (ooo)

***

# 34. THE THREE EARTH TOUCHINGS
## (Thích Nhất Hạnh)

Practicing the Three Earth Touchings gives us an opportunity to deeply touch the reality of interbeing across space and time.

To begin this practice, we invite you join your palms in front of your chest in the shape of a lotus bud. If you are with others, one of you may like to take the role of bell master, and invite the bell and read the text for others to practice. If you are alone, you may like to invite the bell, and read the text out loud. (o)

Then, gently lower yourself to the ground so that all four limbs and your forehead are resting comfortably on the floor. While touching the Earth, turn your palms face up, showing your openness to the Three Jewels - the Buddha, Dharma, and Sangha. When we touch the Earth, we breathe in all the strength and stability of the Earth, and breathe out our suffering – our feelings of anger, hatred, fear, inadequacy and grief.

Enjoy your practice. After practicing with

this standard text, we encourage you to write your own, so that you can go even deeper into your practice. (o)


# 1. TOUCHING THE EARTH, I CONNECT WITH ANCESTORS AND DESCENDANTS OF BOTH MY SPIRITUAL AND MY BLOOD FAMILIES.

[invite the bell, touch the earth]

My spiritual ancestors include the Buddha, the bodhisattvas, the noble Sangha of Buddha's disciples, [insert names of others you would like to include], and my own spiritual teachers still alive or already passed away. They are present in me because they have transmitted to me seeds of peace, wisdom, love, and happiness. They have woken up in me my resource of understanding and compassion. (o)

When I look at my spiritual ancestors, I see those who are perfect in the practice of the mindfulness trainings, understanding, and compassion, and those who are still imperfect. I accept them all because I see within myself shortcomings and weaknesses. Aware that my practice of the mindfulness trainings is not always perfect, and that I am not always as understanding and compassionate as I would like to be, I open my heart and accept all my spiritual descendants. Some of my descendants practice the mindfulness trainings, understanding, and compassion in a way which invites confidence and respect, but there are also those who come across many difficulties and are constantly subject to ups and downs in their practice. (o)

In the same way, I accept all my ancestors on my mother's side and my father's side of the family. I accept all their good qualities and their virtuous actions, and I also accept all their weaknesses. I open my heart and accept all my blood descendants with their good qualities, their talents, and also their weaknesses.

My spiritual ancestors, blood ancestors, spiritual descendants, and blood descendants are all part of me. I am them, and they are me. I do not have a separate self. All exist as part of a wonderful stream of life which is constantly moving. (o)

[three breaths, bell, stand up]

## 2. TOUCHING THE EARTH, I CONNECT WITH ALL PEOPLE AND ALL SPECIES THAT ARE ALIVE AT THIS MOMENT IN THIS WORLD WITH ME.

[bell, touch the earth]

I am one with the wonderful pattern of life that radiates out in all directions. I see the close connection between myself and others, how we share happiness and suffering. I am one with those who were born disabled or who have become disabled because of war, accident, or illness. I am one with those who are caught in a situation of war or oppression. I am one with those who find no happiness in family life, who have no roots and no peace of mind, who are hungry for understanding and love, and who are looking for something beautiful, wholesome, and true to embrace and to believe in. I am someone at the point of death who is very afraid and does not know what is going to happen. I am a child who lives in a place where there is miserable poverty and disease, whose legs and arms are like sticks and who has no future. (o)

I am also the manufacturer of bombs that are sold to poor countries. I am the frog swimming in the pond and I am also the snake who needs the body of the frog to nourish its own body. I am the caterpillar or the ant that the bird is looking for to eat, and I am also the bird that is looking for the caterpillar or the ant. I am the forest that is being cut down. I am the rivers and the air that are being polluted, and I am also the person who cuts down the forest and pollutes the rivers and the air. I see myself in all species, and I see all species in me. (o)

I am one with the great beings who have realized the truth of no-birth and no-death and are able to look at the forms of birth and death, happiness and suffering, with calm eyes. I am one with those people who can be found a little bit everywhere-who have sufficient peace of mind, understanding and love, who are able to touch what is wonderful, nourishing, and healing, who also have the capacity to embrace the world with a heart of love and arms of caring action. I am someone who has enough peace, joy, and freedom and is able to offer fearlessness and joy to living beings around themselves. I see that I am not lonely and cut off. The love and the happiness of great beings on this planet help me not to sink in despair. They help me to live my life in a meaningful way, with true peace and happiness. I see them all in me, and I see myself in all of them. (o)

[three breaths, bell, stand up]


## 3. TOUCHING THE EARTH, I LET GO OF MY IDEA THAT I AM THIS BODY AND MY LIFE SPAN IS LIMITED.

[invite the bell, touch the earth]

I see that this body, made up of the four elements, is not really me and I am not limited by this body. I am part of a stream of life of spiritual and blood ancestors that for thousands of years has been flowing into the present and flows on for thousands of years into the future. I am one with my ancestors. I am one with all people and all species, whether they are peaceful and fearless, or suffering and afraid. At this very moment, I am present everywhere on this planet. I am also present in the past and in the future. The disintegration of this body does not touch me, just as when the plum blossom falls it does not mean the end of the plum tree. (o)

I see myself as a wave on the surface of the ocean. My nature is the ocean water. I see myself in all the other waves and see all the other waves in me. The appearance and disappearance of the form of the wave does not affect the ocean. My Dharma body and spiritual life are not subject to birth and death. I see the presence of myself before my body manifested and after my body has disintegrated. Even in this moment, I see how I exist elsewhere than in this body. Seventy or eighty years is not my life span. My life span, like the life span of a leaf or of a Buddha, is limitless. I have gone beyond the idea that I am a body that is separated in space and time from all other forms of life. (ooo)

**Namo Shakyamunaye Buddhaya. (3 times) (ooo)**

***

# 35. KNOWING THE BETTER WAY TO CATCH A SNAKE

## (220.Arittha Sutra, Madhyama Agama, 22.Alagaddupama Sutta, Majjhima Nikaya)

I heard these words one time when the Buddha was staying at the Anathapindika Monastery in the Jeta Grove, near Shravasti. At that time, the Bhikshu Arittha, who before being ordained had been a vulture trainer, had the wrong view that according to the teachings of the Buddha, sense pleasures are not an obstacle to the practice. After hearing this, many bhikshus went to Arittha and asked, "Brother Arittha, do you really believe that the Buddha teaches that sense pleasures are not an obstacle to the practice?"

Arittha replied, "Yes, friends, it is true that I believe the Buddha does not regard sense pleasures as an obstacle to the practice."

The bhikshus scolded him, "Brother Arittha, you misrepresent the Buddha's teachings and even slander him. The Lord has never said that sense pleasures are not an obstacle to the practice. In fact, he uses many examples to teach that sense pleasures are an obstacle to the practice. You should aban- don your wrong view." Although the bhikshus counseled Arittha in this way, he was not moved to change his view. Three times they asked him to abandon his wrong view, and three times he refused, continuing to say that he was right and the others were wrong.

Having advised him like this to no effect, they stood up and left. They went to the Buddha and recounted all that they had seen and heard.

The Buddha summoned Arittha, admonished him, and taught all of the bhik- shus, "Monks, it is important to understand my teachings thoroughly before you teach or put them into practice. If you have not understood the meaning of any teaching I give, please ask me or one of the elder brothers in the Dhar- ma or one of the others who is excellent in the practice about it. There are always some people who do not understand the letter or the spirit of a teach- ing and, in fact, take it the opposite way of what was intended, whether the teachings are offered in the form of verse or prose, predictions, verse summaries, interdependent origination, similes, spontaneous utterances, quotations, stories of previous births, wonderful occurrences, detailed commentaries, or clarifications with definitions. There are always some people who study only to satisfy their curiosity or win arguments, and not for the sake of liberation. With such a motivation, they miss the true spirit of the teaching. They may go through much hardship, endure difficulties that are not of much benefit, and eventually exhaust themselves.

"Bhikshus, a person who studies that way can be compared to a man trying to catch a poisonous snake in the wild. If he reaches out his hand, the snake may bite his hand, leg, or some other part of his body. Trying to catch a snake that way has no advantages and can only create suffering.

"Bhikshus, understanding my teaching in the wrong way is the same. If you do not practice the Dharma correctly, you may come to understand it as the opposite of what was intended. But if you practice intelligently, you will understand both the letter and the spirit of the teachings and will be able to explain them correctly. Do not practice just to show off or argue with others. Practice to attain liberation, and if you do, you will have little pain or exhaustion.

## HOW TO CATCH A POISONOUS SNAKE

"Bhikshus, an intelligent student of the Dharma is like a man who uses a forked stick to catch a snake. When he sees a poisonous snake in the wild, he places the stick right below the head of the snake and grabs the snake's neck with his hand. Even if the snake winds itself around the man's hand, leg, or another part of his body, it will not bite him. This is the better way to catch a snake, and it will not lead to pain or exhaustion.

"Bhikshus, a son or daughter of good family who studies the Dharma needs to apply the utmost skill to understanding the letter and the spirit of the teachings. He or she should not study with the aim of boasting, debating, or arguing, but only to attain liberation. Studying in this way, with intelligence, he or she will have little pain or exhaustion.

"Bhikshus, I have told you many times the importance of knowing when it is time to let go of a raft and not hold onto it unnecessarily. When a mountain stream overflows and becomes a torrent of floodwater carrying

debris, a man or woman who wants to get across might think, 'What is the safest way to cross this floodwater?' Assessing the situation, she may decide to gather branches and grasses, construct a raft, and use it to cross to the other side. But, after arriving on the other side, she thinks, 'I spent a lot of time and energy building this raft. It is a prized possession, and I will carry it with me as I continue my journey.' If she puts it on her shoulders or head and carries it with her on land, bhikshus, do you think that would be intelligent?"

The bhikshus replied, "No, World-Honored One."

The Buddha said, "How could she have acted more wisely? She could have thought, 'This raft helped me get across the water safely. Now I will leave it at the water's edge for someone else to use in the same way.' Wouldn't that be a more intelligent thing to do?"

The bhikshus replied, "Yes, World-Honored One."

The Buddha taught, "I have given this teaching on the raft many times to remind you how necessary it is to let go of all the true teachings, not to mention teachings that are not true."

## SIX BASES FOR VIEWS

"Bhikshus, there are six bases for views. This means that there are six grounds of wrong perception that we need to drop. What are the six?

"First, there is form. Whether belonging to the past, the future, or the present, whether it is our own form or the form of someone else, whether subtle or gross, ugly or beautiful, near or far, such form is not mine, is not me, is not the self. Bhikshus, please look deeply so that you can see the truth concerning form.

"Second, there are feelings. "Third, there are perceptions.

"Fourth, there are mental formations. Whether these phenomena belong to the past, the future, or the present, whether they are our own or someone else's, whether they are subtle or gross, ugly or beautiful, near or far, such phenomena are not mine, are not me, are not the self.

"Fifth, there is consciousness. Whatever we see, hear, perceive, know, mentally grasp, observe, or think about at the present time or any other time is not ours, is not us, is not the self.

"Sixth, there is the world. Some people think, 'The world is the self. The self is the world. The world is me. I will continue to exist without changing even after I die. I am eternal. I will never disappear.' Please meditate so you can see that the world is not mine, is not me, is not the self. Please look deeply so you can see the truth concerning the world."

## FEAR AND ANXIETY

Upon hearing this, one bhikshu stood up, bared his right shoulder, joined his palms respectfully, and asked the Buddha,

"World-Honored One, can fear and anxiety arise from an internal source?"

The Buddha replied, "Yes, fear and anxiety can arise from an internal source. If you think, 'Things that did not exist in the past have come to exist, but now no longer exist,' you will feel sad or become confused and despair- ing. This is how fear and anxiety can arise from an internal source."

The same bhikshu then asked, "World-Honored One, can fear and anxiety from an internal source be prevented from arising?"

The Buddha replied, "Fear and anxiety from an internal source can be prevented from arising. If you do not think, 'Things that did not exist in the past have come to exist, but now no longer exist,' you will not feel sad or become confused and despairing. This is how fear and anxiety from an internal source can be prevented from arising."

"World-Honored One, can fear and anxiety arise from an external source?"

The Buddha taught, "Fear and anxiety can

arise from an external source. You may think, 'This is a self. This is the world. This is myself. I will exist forever.' Then if you meet the Buddha or a disciple of the Buddha who has the understanding and intelligence to teach you how to let go of all views of attachment to the body, the self, and the objects of the self with a view to giving up pride, internal knots (samyojana), and energy leaks, and you think, 'This is the end of the world. I have to give up everything. I am not the world. I am not me. I am not the self. I will not exist forever. When I die, I will be completely annihilated. There is nothing to look forward to, to be joyful about, or to remember,' you will feel sad and become confused and despairing. This is how fear and anxiety can arise from an external source."

## FIVE AGGREGATES AND THE SELF

The Buddha asked, "Bhikshus, do you think the Five Aggregates and the self are permanent, changeless, and not subject to destruction?" "No, reverend teacher."

"Is there anything you can hold onto with attachment that will not cause anxiety, exhaustion, sorrow, suffering, and despair?"

"No, reverend teacher."

"Is there any view of self in which you can take refuge that will not cause anxiety, exhaustion, sorrow, suffering, and despair?"

"No, reverend teacher."

"Bhikshus, you are quite correct. Whenever there is an idea of self, there is also an idea of what belongs to the self. When there is no idea of self, there is no idea of anything that belongs to the self. Self and what belongs to the self are two views that are based on trying to grasp things that cannot be grasped and to establish things that cannot be established." Such wrong perceptions cause us to be bound by internal knots that arise the moment we are caught by ideas that cannot be grasped or established and have no basis in reality. Do you see that these are wrong perceptions? Do you see the consequences of such wrong perceptions in the case of Bhikshu Arittha?"

# THE WAY OF THE TATHAGATA ATTAINED LIBERATION

The Buddha continued, "If, when he considers the six bases for wrong views, a bhikshu does not give rise to the idea of 'I' or 'mine,' he is not caught in the chains of this life. Since he is not caught in the chains of this life, he has no fear. To have no fear is to arrive at nirvana. Such a person is no longer troubled by birth and death; the holy life has been lived; what needs to be done has been done; there will be no further births or deaths; and the truth of things as they are is known. Such a bhikshu has filled in the moat, crossed the moat, destroyed the enemy citadel, unbolted the door, and is able to look directly into the mirror of highest understanding.

"Bhikshus, that is the Way of the Tathagata and those who have attained liberation. Indra, Prajapati, Brahma, and the other gods in their entourage, how- ever hard they look, cannot find any trace or basis for the consciousness of a Tathagata. The Tathagata is a noble fount of freshness and coolness. There is no great heat and no sorrow in this state. When recluses and brahmans hear me say this, they may slander me, saying that I do not speak the truth, that the monk Gautama proposes a theory of nihilism and teaches absolute nonexistence, while in fact living beings do exist. Bhikshus, the Tathagata has never taught the things they say. In truth, the Tathagata teaches only the ending of suffering in order to attain the state of non-fear. If the Tathagata is blamed, criticized, defamed, or beaten, he does not care. He does not become angry, walk away in hatred, or do anything in revenge. If someone blames, criticizes, defames, or beats the Tathagata, how does he react? The Tathagata thinks, 'If someone respects, honors, or makes offerings to a Tathagata, the Tathagata would not on that account feel pleased. He would think only that someone is doing this because the Tathagata has attained the fruits of awakening and transformation.'

Having heard the Buddha speak thus, the bhikshus, with great joy, put the teachings into practice.

**Namo Shakyamunaye Buddhaya.**
(3 times) (ooo)


***


# 36. THE LAND OF GREAT HAPPINESS

(Sukhavati-Vyuha Sutra,
Taisho Revised Tripitaka 366)


This is what I heard the Buddha say one time when he was staying in the Ana-thapindika Monastery in the Jeta Grove. At that time the Buddha had with him a Sangha of 1,250 bhikshus, all arhats and the most well-known among his senior disciples, including Shariputra, Mahamaudgalyayana, Mahakashyapa, Mahakatyayana, Mahakaushthila, Revata, Shuddhipanthaka, Nanda, Ananda, Rahula, Gavampati, Pindolabharadvaja, Kalodayin, Mahakapphina, Vakkula, and Aniruddha. There were also present Bodhisattvas of great stature like Manjushri, Ajita, Gandhahastin, Nityodyukta and many other great Bodhisat- tvas as well as countless heavenly beings including Indra.

At that time the Buddha called Shariputra to him and said: "If you go from here in the western direction and pass through hundreds of thousands of millions of Buddha Worlds you will come to a world called Sukhavati (Great Happiness). In that world there is a Buddha whose name is Amitabha and who is at this very moment teaching the Dharma.

"Shariputra, why is that land called Great Happiness? Because the people who live there do not have to go through any suffering. They are al- ways enjoying many kinds of happiness. And that is why that world is called Great Happiness.

"Shariputra, around Sukhavati there are seven rows of rails, seven rows of spread out netting and seven rows of trees. All are made of the four kinds of precious jewels. That is why the land is called Great Happiness.

"Furthermore Shariputra, in the land of Great Happiness there are many lakes of the seven precious stones, full of the water of the eight virtues. The bed of the lake is made wholly of pure golden sand and on the shores are paths of gold, silver, and crystal. Above these paths are countless pavilions which are built of and decorated with gold, silver, crystal, mother-of-pearl, red agate, and carnelians. The lotus flowers in these lakes are as large as cart-wheels. The blue lotuses give out a halo of blue light, the golden lotuses a halo of golden light, the red lotuses a halo of red light and the white lotuses a halo of white light. The fragrance of the lotuses is subtle, wonderful, sweet, and pure.

"Shariputra, Sukhavati is adorned with such beauties as these.

"Furthermore Shariputra, in this Buddha Land people can always hear the sound of heavenly music. The earth is made of pure gold. During the six periods of the day, flowers rain down multitudes of mandarava from the sky. In the morning the people of this land like to take flower baskets made of cloth and fill them with these wonderful flowers in order to make offerings to the Buddhas who live in countless other Buddha Lands. When it is time for the midday meal, everyone returns to Sukhavati and after eating does walking meditation. Shariputra, that is how extraordinarily beautiful Sukhavati is.

"Furthermore Shariputra, in Sukhavati you can always see different species of birds of many wonderful colors, like white cranes, peacocks, ori- oles, egrets, kavalinkara, and jivanjva birds. These birds sing with harmoni- ous, sweet sounds throughout the six periods of the day. In the song of the birds people can hear teachings on different Dharma doors such as the Five Faculties, the Five Powers, the Seven Factors of Awakening, and the Noble Eightfold Path. When the people of this land hear the teachings in the form of bird songs, their minds are in perfect concentration and they come back to practicing mindfulness of Buddha, Dharma, and Sangha.

"Shariputra, do not think that the birds in Sukhavati have been born as the result of past bad actions. Why? Because the three lower realms of hells, hungry ghosts, and animals do not exist in the land of Amitabha Bud- dha. Shariputra, in this land the names of the lower realms do not even exist, how much less their actuality!

These birds are manifestations of the Buddha Amitabha so that the Dharma can be proclaimed widely in his land.

"Shariputra, in this Buddha Land, whenever a light breeze moves the rows of trees and the jeweled netting, people hear a wonderful sound as if a hundred thousand musical instruments are being played together at the same time. When the people hear this sound, they all naturally return to mindful recollection of the Buddha, the Dharma, and the Sangha. Shariputra, that is how beautiful Sukhavati is.

"Shariputra, why do you think that Buddha is called Amitabha (Limit- less Light)? Because he is infinite light which is able to illuminate all worlds in the Ten Directions and this light and radiance never comes to an end. That is why he is called Amitabha.

"What is more, Shariputra, the life span of Amitabha as well as the life span of everyone who lives in his Buddha Land is limitless. It lasts for innumerable kalpas, that is why he is called Amitabha.

"Shariputra, from the time when Amitabha Buddha realized enlight- enment until now can be reckoned as ten kalpas. Moreover

Shariputra, the number of his hearer disciples who have attained the fruit of arhatship is also limitless. It is not possible to calculate them, so great is their number. The number of bodhisattvas in that land is also limitless.

"Shariputra, the land of Amitabha is made out of such beautiful qualities as these.

"Shariputra, everyone who is born in Sukhavati naturally has the capacity of non-regression. Among the people living there, many will attain Buddhahood in one more lifetime. The number of these bodhisattvas is infinite, and there is no method of calculation to number them. It may only be expressed by the term limitless.

"Shariputra, when living beings everywhere hear Sukhavati spoken about, they should bring forth the great wish to be born in such a land. Why? Be- cause having been born in that land they will be able to live with and be very close to so many noble practitioners.

"Shariputra, one cannot be born in this land with a lack of merit or wholesome roots. Therefore, Shariputra, whenever men or women of good families hear the name of Amitabha Buddha, they should mindfully repeat that name and wholeheartedly practice visualization with a mind that is one- pointed and not dispersed for one, two, three, four, five, six, or seven days. When that person passes from this life, they will see Amitabha Buddha and the Holy Ones of that land right before their eyes. At the time of their passing, their mind will abide in meditative concentration and will not be deluded or dispersed. That is why they can be born in the Land of Great Happiness.

"Shariputra, it is because I have seen the enormous benefit of this land that I want to tell all who are listening now to bring forth the great wish to be born there.

"Shariputra, as I am now commending the inestimably great benefits and virtues of Buddha Amitabha, there are in the east, in the south, in the west, in the north, above and below, Buddhas as numberless as the sands of the Ganges, each one seated in his own Buddha Field, each one with the long tongue of a Buddha which is able to embrace the three chiliocosms, announcing with all sincerity, 'Living beings in all worlds, you should have confidence in this sutra, which all the Buddhas in the entire cosmos whole- heartedly commend and protect by recollection.'

"Shariputra, why do you think this sutra is wholeheartedly commend- ed and protected by the recitation of all Buddhas? The reason is that when sons or daughters of good families hear this sutra or hear the name of the Buddha Amitabha and wholly put it into practice and maintain mindful reci- tation of Buddha Amitabha's name, they will be protected by the recollection of all the Buddhas, and they will attain the highest fruit of awakening from which they will never regress. So you should have faith in what I am saying and what all other Buddhas are also saying.

"Shariputra, if there is anyone who has already brought forth the great aspiration, is aspiring now or will aspire in the future to be born in Amitab- ha's land, at the very moment when that person makes the aspiration, they already attain the fruit of the highest awakening from which they will never regress, and they are dwelling already in the Buddha Field of Amitabha. It is not necessary that they have been born or are being born or will be born there in order to be present within the Buddha Field of Amitabha.

"Shariputra, while I am praising the unimaginably great qualities of the Buddhas, the Buddhas are also praising my unimaginably great qualities saying, 'Buddha Shakyamuni is very rare. In the Saha world which is full of the five impurities - the cloudiness of time, the cloudiness of views, the cloudiness of unwholesome mental states, the cloudiness of the idea of living being and life span - he is able to realize the fruit of the highest awakening and is able to communicate to living beings the Dharma doors, which people will find hard to believe if they have had no preparation.

"Shariputra, understand that to stay in a world which is full of the five kinds of impurity and to be able to attain the fruit of the highest awakening and also to be able to transmit to all beings Dharma doors which people find hard to believe, like this Dharma door of being born in Sukhavati, is some- thing extremely difficult."

When Shariputra as well as all the bhikshus, heavenly beings, bo- dhisattvas, warrior gods, and others heard the Buddha deliver this sutra, they all had faith in it, joyously accepted the teaching and paid respect to the Bud- dha before returning to their dwelling places.

**Namo Shakyamunaye Buddhaya.**
(3 times) (ooo)

***

# 37. THE TEACHINGS TO BE GIVEN TO THE SICK

(51.8. Ekottara Agama, in consultation with
143.Majjhima Nikaya and
26. Madhyama Agama)

Translated by Thích Nhất Hạnh

I heard these words of the Buddha one time when the Lord was staying in the monastery in the Jeta Grove in Anathapindika's park, near Shravasti. At that time the householder Anathapindika was seriously ill. When the Venerable Shariputra was told this, he immediately went to Ananda and said, "Brother Ananda, let us go and visit the layman Anathapindika.

The Venerable Ananda put on his robe, and holding his bowl, went into the town of Shravasti with the Venerable Shariputra to make the almsround. The two of them stopped at every house until they came to the house of the layman Anathapindika, and they went in to visit him. After he had sat down, the Venerable Shariputra asked the layman Anathapindika, "How is your illness? Is it getting better or worse? Is the physical pain easing at all or is it getting greater?" The householder Anathapindika replied, "Venerable monks, it does not seem to be getting better. The pain is not easing. It is getting greater all the time." Shariputra said, "Friend Anathapindika, let us now practice together the recollection of the Buddha, the Dharma, and the Sangha. The recollection goes like this:

"The Buddha has gone to Suchness, is fully and truly awakened, has perfected understanding and action, has arrived at true happiness, understands the nature of the world, is unequaled in understanding, has conquered the afflictions of human beings, is a teacher of gods and humans, and is the Awakened One, the one who liberates the world.

"The Dharma is the teaching of love and understanding that the Tathagata has expounded. It is deep and lovely, worthy of the highest respect, and very precious. It is a teaching that cannot be compared to ordinary teachings. It is a path of practice for the Noble Ones.

"The Sangha is the community of practice, guided by the teachings of the Tathagata. The community is in harmony, and within it all aspects of the practice can be realized. The community is respected and precious. It practices the precepts and realizes concentration, insight, and liberation. The Sangha is the highest field of merit in the world.

"Friend Anathapindika, if you recollect the Buddha, the Dharma, and the Sangha in this way, the beneficial effects are beyond measure. Recollecting in this way, you can put an end to the obstacles of wrong deeds and the afflictions. You can harvest a fruit that is as fresh and sweet as the nectar of deathlessness. Anyone practicing an upright way of life who knows how to recollect the Three Jewels will have no chance of falling into the three lower realms but will be reborn as a human or a god.

"Friend Anathapindika, now is the time to practice the meditation on the Six Sense Bases:

These eyes are not me. I am not caught in these eyes.

These ears are not me. I am not caught in these ears.

This nose is not me. I am not caught in this nose.

This tongue is not me. I am not caught in this tongue.

This body is not me. I am not caught in this body.

This mind is not me. I am not caught in this mind.

"Now continue your meditation with the Six Sense Objects:

These forms are not me. I am not caught in these forms.

These sounds are not me. I am not caught in these sounds.

These smells are not me. I am not caught in these smells.

These tastes are not me. I am not caught in these tastes.

These contacts with the body are not me. I am not caught in these contacts with the body.

These thoughts are not me. I am not caught in these thoughts.

"Now continue your meditation on the Six Sense Consciousnesses:

Sight is not me. I am not caught in sight.

Hearing is not me. I am not caught in hearing.

Consciousness based on the nose is not me. I am not caught in the consciousness based on the nose.

Consciousness based on the tongue is not me. I am not caught in consciousness based on the tongue.

Consciousness based on the body is not me. I am not caught in consciousness based on the body.

Consciousness based on the mind is not me. I am not caught in consciousness based on the mind.

"Now continue your meditation on the Six Elements:

The earth element is not me. I am not caught in the earth element.

The water element is not me. I am not caught in the water element.

The fire element is not me. I am not caught in the fire element.

The air element is not me. I am not caught in the air element.

The space element is not me. I am not caught in the space element.

The consciousness element is not me. I am not caught in the consciousness element.

"Now continue your meditation on the Five Aggregates:

Form is not me. I am not limited by the form aggregate.

Feelings are not me. I am not limited by the feeling aggregate.

Perceptions are not me. I am not limited by the perception aggregate.

Mental formations are not me. I am not limited by the mental formation aggregate.

Consciousness is not me. I am not limited by the consciousness aggregate.

"Now continue your meditation on the Three Times:

The past is not me. I am not limited by the past.

The present is not me. I am not limited by the present.

The future is not me. I am not limited by the future.

"Friend Anathapindika, everything arises and ceases due to causes and conditions. In reality, the nature of everything is not born and does not die, does not come and does not go. When eyes arise, they arise, but they do not come from anywhere. When eyes cease to be, they cease to be, but they do not go anywhere. Eyes are neither nonexistent before they arise, nor are they existent after they arise. Everything that is comes to be because of a combination of causes and conditions. When the causes and conditions are sufficient, eyes are present. When the causes and conditions are not sufficient, eyes are absent. The same is true of ears, nose, tongue, body, and mind; form, sound, smell, taste, touch, and thought; sight, hearing, smelling, tasting, somatosensory and mind consciousness; the Six Elements, the Five Aggregates, and the Three Times.

"In the Five Aggregates, there is nothing that we can call 'I,' a 'person,' or a 'lifespan.' Ignorance is the inability to see this truth. Because there is ignorance, there are wrong perceptions of formations. Because there are wrong perceptions of formations, there is wrong consciousness. Because there is wrong consciousness, there is the distinction between the perceiver and the perceived. Because there is the distinction between the perceiver and the perceived, there is the distinction between the six organs and the six objects of sense. Because there is the distinction between the six organs and the six objects of sense, there is contact. Because there is contact, there is feeling. Because there is feeling, there is craving. Because there is craving, there is grasping. Because there is grasping, there is being and then birth, death, and the inexpressible mass of suffering and grief.

"Friend Anathapindika, you have meditated that everything that arises is due to causes and conditions and does not have a separate self. That is called 'the meditation on emptiness.' It is the highest and the most profound meditation."

When he had practiced to this point, the layman Anathapindika began to cry and tears flowed down his cheeks. Venerable Ananda asked him, "Friend, why are you crying? Has your meditation not been successful? Do you have some regret?" The layman Anathapindika replied, "Venerable Ananda, I do not regret anything. The meditation has been most successful. I am crying because I am so deeply moved. I have been fortunate to have been able to serve the Buddha and his community for many years, yet I have never heard a teaching so wonderful and precious as the teaching transmitted by the Venerable Shariputra today."

Then the Venerable Ananda said to the layman Anathapindika, "Do you not know, friend, that the Buddha often gives this teaching to bhikshus and bhikshunis?" The layman Anathapindika replied, "Venerable Ananda, please tell the Buddha that there are also laypeople with the capacity to listen, understand, and put into practice these deep and wonderful teachings."

After listening to and practicing with the two venerable monks, Anathapindika felt free and at ease, and gave rise to the highest mind. The Venerables Shariputra and Ananda bade him farewell and went back to the monastery, and Anathapindika passed away and was born in the thirty-third heaven.

**Namo Shakyamunaye Buddhaya.**
(3 times) (ooo)

***

# 38. HAPPINESS IN THE PRESENT MOMENT
(Thích Nhất Hạnh)

The past has already gone,
and the future has not yet come.

Let us not drown ourselves in regret for what has passed

or in expectations and worry for the future.

The Buddha has said that we can be peaceful, happy, and free

in this present moment.

Let us hear the Buddha's words

and let go of our sadness and anxiety.

Let us come back to ourselves

and establish ourselves in what is present right now.

Let us learn to recognize he conditions for happiness that are present within us and around us.


Can we hear the birds singing and the wind in the pines?

Can we see the green mountains, the white clouds, the golden moon?

The Pure Land is available

in the present moment.

Every day we can enjoy ourselves

in the Buddha Land.

Every mindful breath and step takes us to the Pure Land, revealing all the wonders

of the Dharma body.

I am determined to let go of hurrying, competing,

being busy and disgruntled.

I shall not run after fame, power, riches, and sex

because I know

that this does not lead to true happiness.

All it will bring me is

misery and misfortune.


I shall learn to know what is sufficient,

to live simply,

so that I have time to live deeply every moment of my daily life,

giving my body and mind a chance to heal, and to have the time to look after and protect those I have vowed to love.


I shall practice for my mind to grow in love and compassion, so that I have the ability to help beings anywhere

who are drowning in craving.

I ask the Buddhas everywhere to protect and guide me,

to support me on my path,

so that I can live in peace, joy, and freedom every day, fulfilling the deepest aspiration as your disciple

whom you trust and love. (ooo)

**Namo Amitabha Buddhaya.** (3 times) (ooo)

***

## 39. WE ARE TRULY PRESENT
Thích Nhất Hạnh

**With heart established in mindfulness, we are truly present for sitting and walking meditation, and for reciting the sutras.**

**May this practice center with its Four fold Sangha be supported by three Jewels and Holy Beings,**

well-protected from the eight misfortunes and the three paths of suffering.

May parents, teachers, friends, and all beings within the three Realms be filled with the most divine grace, and may it be found that in the world there is no place at war.

May the winds be favorable, the rains seasonable, and the people's hearts at peace. May the practice of the noble community, diligent and steady, ascend the Ten Bodhisattva Stages with ease and energy. May the Sangha body live peacefully, fresh and full of joy, a refuge for all, offering happiness and insight. (o)

The wisdom of the Awakened Mind shines out like the full moon. (o)

The body of the Awakened One is pure and clear as crystal. (o)

In the world, the Awakened One relieves bitterness and suffering. (o)

In every place, the Awakened Mind reveals love and compassion.

**Namo Shakyamunaye Buddhaya**

(3 times) (ooo)

# 40. THE HAPPINESS
## (2.4.Maṅgala Sutta, Sutta Nipāta)
## Translated by Thích Nhất Hạnh

I heard these words of the Buddha one time when the Lord was living in the vicinity of Savatthi at the Anathapindika Monastery in the Jeta Grove. Late at night, a deva appeared whose light and beauty made the whole Jeta Grove shine radiantly. After paying respects to the Buddha, the deva asked him a question in the form of a verse:

"Many gods and men are eager to know

what are the greatest blessings

which bring about a peaceful and happy life.

Please, Tathagata, will you teach us?"


(This is the Buddha's answer):

"Not to be associated with the foolish ones,

to live in the company of wise people,

honoring those who are worth honoring -

this is the greatest happiness.

"To live in a good environment,
to have planted good seeds,
nd to realize that you are on the right path
-this is the greatest happiness.

"To have a chance to learn and grow,
to be skillful in your profession or craft,
practicing the precepts and loving speech
-this is the greatest happiness.

"To be able to serve and support your
parents,
to cherish your own family,
to have a vocation that brings you joy -
this is the greatest happiness.
"To live honestly, generous in giving,
to offer support to relatives and friends,
living a life of blameless conduct -
this is the greatest happiness.

"To avoid unwholesome actions,

not caught by alcoholism or drugs,

and to be diligent in doing good things -

this is the greatest happiness.


"To be humble and polite in manner,

to be grateful and content with a simple life,

not missing the occasion to learn the Dharma -

this is the greatest happiness.


"To persevere and be open to change,

to have regular contact with monks and nuns,

and to fully participate in Dharma discussions -

this is the greatest happiness.


"To live diligently and attentively,

to perceive the Noble Truths,

and to realize Nirvana -

this is the greatest happiness.

"To live in the world
with your heart undisturbed by the world,
with all sorrows ended, dwelling in peace -
this is the greatest happiness.

"For he or she who accomplishes this,
unvanquished wherever she goes,
always he is safe and happy -
happiness lives within oneself."
Namo Shakyamunaye Buddhaya.
(3 times) (ooo)

***

## 41. THE YOUTH AND HAPPINESS

(Samiddhi Sutta, Samyukta Agama 1078
Corresponds to Samyutta Nikaya
1.20. Also Taisho 99)

I heard these words of the Buddha one time when the Lord was staying at the Bamboo Forest Monastery near the town of Rajagriha. At that time there was a bhikshu who, in the very early morning, came to the banks of the river, took off his upper robe and left it on the bank, and went down to the river to bathe. After bathing, he came out of the river, waited until his body was dry, and then put on his upper robe. At that time a goddess appeared, whose body, surrounded by light, lit up the entire bank of the river. The goddess said to the bhikshu, "Venerable, you've recently become a monk. Your hair is still black; you are very young. At this time in your life, shouldn't you be perfumed with oils, adorned with gems and fragrant flowers, enjoying the five kinds of sensual desire? Why have you abandoned your loved ones and turned your back on the worldly life, living alone? You've shaved your hair and beard, donned the monk's robe, and placed your faith in monastic prac- tice. Why have you abandoned the pleasures of this moment to seek pleasures in a distant future?"

The bhikshu replied, "I have not abandoned the present moment in order to seek pleasures in a distant future. I have abandoned pleasures that are untimely for the deepest happiness of this moment."

The goddess asked, "What do you mean?"

And the bhikshu replied, "The World-Honored One has taught: in the joy associated with sensual desire there is little sweetness and much bitter- ness, tiny benefits, and a great potential to lead to disaster. Now, as I dwell in the Dharma that is available here and now, I've given up the burning fire of afflictions. The Dharma is available here and now. It is outside of time, and it always invites us to come and see it. It is to be realized and experienced by each of us for ourselves. That is what is meant by abandoning untimely pleasures in order to arrive at the deepest happiness of the present moment." The goddess asked the bhikshu again, "Why does the World-Honored.

One say that in the untimely pleasure of sensual desire there is little sweet- ness and much bitterness, its benefit is tiny but its potential to lead to disaster is great? Why does he say that if we dwell in the Dharma that is available here and now we are able to give up the flames of the afflictions that burn us? Why does he say that this Dharma belongs to the present moment, is outside of time, always invites us to come and see it, is available here and now, and is realized and experienced by each of us for ourselves?"

The bhikshu replied, "I have only been ordained for two years. I do not have the skill to explain to you the true teachings and the wonderful pre- cepts that the World-Honored One has proclaimed. The World-Honored One is presently nearby, in the Bamboo Forest. Why don't you go to him and ask your questions directly? The Tathagata will offer you the Right Dharma, and you will be able to receive and practice his guidance as you see fit."

The goddess replied, "Venerable bhikshu, at this moment the Tathaga- ta is surrounded by powerful and influential gods and goddesses. It would be difficult for me to have the chance to approach him and ask about the Dharma. If you would be willing to ask the Tathagata these questions on my behalf, I will accompany you."

The bhikshu replied, "I will help you."

The goddess said, "Venerable, then I will follow you."

The bhikshu went to the place where the Buddha was staying, bowed his head and prostrated before the Buddha, then withdrew a little and sat down to one side. He repeated the conversation he had just had with the god- dess, and then said, "World-Honored One, if this goddess had not spoken sincerely, she would not have come here with me." At that moment, there was a sound from afar, "Venerable monk, I am here. I am here."

The World-Honored One immediately offered this gatha: "Beings produce wrong perceptions

concerning objects of desire.

That is why they are caught in desire.

Because they do not know what desire really is,

they proceed on the path to Death."

The Buddha then asked the goddess, "Do you understand this gatha? If not,

please say so."

The goddess addressed the Buddha, "I have not understood, World-

Honored One. I have not understood, Well-

Gone One."

So the Buddha recited another gatha for the goddess: "When you know the true nature of desire,

the desiring mind will not be born.

When there is no desire, and no perception based on it,

at that time, no one is able to tempt you."


Then Buddha asked the goddess, "Have you understood this gatha? If

not, please say so."

The goddess addressed the Buddha: "I have not understood, World-

Honored One. I have not understood, Well-Gone One."

So the Buddha recited another gatha for the goddess: "If you think you are greater, less than, or equal,

you cause dissension.

When those three complexes have ended, nothing can agitate your mind."


Then Buddha asked the goddess, "Have

you understood this gatha? If not, please say so."

The goddess addressed the Buddha, "I have not understood, World-

Honored One. I have not understood, Well-Gone One."

So the Buddha recited another gatha for the goddess: "Ending desire, overcoming the three complexes,

our mind is stilled, we have nothing to long for. We lay aside all affliction and sorrow,

in this life and in lives to come."


Then Buddha asked the goddess, "Have you understood this gatha? If

not, please say so."

The goddess addressed the Buddha, "I have understood, World-Hon-

ored One. I have understood, Well-Gone One."

The Buddha had finished the teaching. The goddess was delighted at what she had heard. Practicing in accord with these teachings, she disap- peared. Not a trace of her was to be seen anywhere.

## Namo Shakyamunaye Buddhaya.
(3 times) (ooo)

***

# 42. THE DEEP KINDNESS OF PARENTS AND THE DIFFICULTY OF REPAYING IT

Translated by: Upasika Terri Nicholson

Reviewed by: Bhikshuni Heng Tao

Edited by: Bhikshuni Heng Ch'ih and Upasika Susuan Rounds

Certified by: Venerable Abbot Hua and Bhikshuni Heng Tao

Thus I have heard, at one time, the Buddha dwelt at Shravasti, in the Jeta Grove, in the Garden of the Benefactor of Orphans and the Solitary, together with a gathering of great Bhikshus, twelve hundred fifty in all, and with all of the Bodhisattvas, thirty-eight thousand in all.

At that time, the World Honored One led the great assembly on a walk toward the south. Suddenly they came upon a pile of bones beside the road. The World Honored One turned to face them, placed his five limbs on the ground, and bowed respectfully.

Ananda put his palms together and asked the World Honored One, 'The Tathagatha is the Great Teacher of the Triple Realm and the compassionate father of beings of the four kinds of births. He has the respect and reverence of the entire assembly. What is the reason that he now bows to a pile of dried bones?"

The Buddha told Ananda, "Although all of you are my foremost disciples and have been members of the Sangha for a long time, you still have not achieved far-reaching understanding. This pile of bones could have belonged to my ancestors from former lives. They could have been my parents in many past lives. That is the reason I now bow to them." The Buddha continued speaking to Ananda. "These bones we are looking at can be divided into two groups. One group is composed of the bones of men, which are heavy and white in color. The other group is composed of the bones of women, which are light and black in color."

Ananda said to the Buddha, "World Honored One, when men are alive in the world they adorn their bodies with robes, belts, shoes, hats and other fine attire, so that they clearly assume a male appearance. When women are alive, they put on cosmetics, perfumes, powders, and elegant fragrances to adorn their bodies, so that they clearly assume a female appearance. Yet, once men and women die, all that is left are their bones. How does one tell them apart? Please teach us how you are able to distinguish them."

The Buddha answered Ananda, "If when men are in the world, they enter temples, listen to explanations of Sutras and Vinaya texts, make obeisance to the Triple Jewel, and recite the Buddha's names, then when they die their bones will be heavy and white in color. Most women in the world have little wisdom and are saturated with emotion. They give birth to and raise children, feeling that this is their duty. Each child relies on its mother's milk for life and nourishment, and that milk is a transformation of the mother's blood. Each child drinks one thousand two hundred gallons of its mother's milk. Because of this drain on the mother's body whereby the child takes milk for its nourishment, the mother becomes worn and haggard and so her bones turn black in color and are light in weight." When Ananda heard these words, he felt a pain in his heart as if he had been stabbed and wept silently. He said to the World Honored One, "How can one repay one's mother's kindness and virtue?"

The Buddha told Ananda, "Listen well, and I will explain it for you in detail. The fetus grows in its mother's womb for ten lunar months. What bitterness she goes through while it dwells there! In the first month of pregnancy, the life of the fetus is as precarious as a dewdrop on grass: how likely that it will not last from morning to evening but will evaporate by mid-day!

"During the second lunar month, the embryo congeals like curds. In the third month it is like coagulated blood. During the fourth month of pregnancy the fetus begins to assume a slightly human form.

During the fifth month in the womb, the child's five limbs-two legs, two arms, and a head--start to take shape. In the sixth lunar month of pregnancy, the child begins to develop the essences of the six sense faculties: the eyes, ears, nose, tongue, body and mind. During the seventh month, the three hundred sixty bones and joints are formed, and the eighty-four thousand hair pores are also complete. In the eight lunar month of the pregnancy the intellect and the nine apertures are formed. By the ninth month the fetus has learned to assimilate the different nutrients of the foods it eats. For example, it can assimilate the essence of peaches, pears, certain plant roots and the five kinds of grains.

"Inside the mother's body, the solid internal organs, used for storing, hang downward, while the hollow internal organs, used for processing, spiral upward. These can be likened to three mountains which arise from the face of the earth. We can call these mountains Mount Sumeru, Karma Mountain, and Blood Mountain. These analogous mountains come together and form a single range in a pattern of upward peaks and downward valleys. So, too, the coagulation of the mother's blood from her internal organs forms a single substance, which becomes the child's food.

During the tenth month of pregnancy, the body of the fetus is completed and ready to be born. If the child is extremely filial, it will emerge with palms joined together in respect and the birth will be peaceful and auspicious. The mother will remain uninjured by the birth and will not suffer pain. However, if the child is extremely rebellious in nature, to the extent that it is capable of commiting the five rebellious acts, then it will injure its mother's womb, rip apart its mother's heart and liver, or get entangled in its mother's bones. The birth will feel like the slices of a thousand knives or like ten thousand sharp swords stabbing her heart. Those are the agonies involved in the birth of a defiant and rebellious child.

To explain more clearly, there are ten types of kindness bestowed by the mother on the child:

The first is the kindness of providing protection and care while the child is in the womb.

The second is the kindness of bearing suffering during the birth.

The third is the kindness of forgetting all the pain once the child has been born.

The fourth is the kindness of eating the bitter herself and saving the sweet for the child.

The fifth is the kindness of moving the child to a dry place and lying in the wet herself.

The sixth is the kindness of suckling the child at her breast and nourishing and bringing up the child.

The seventh is the kindness of washing away the unclean.

The eighth is the kindness of always thinking of the child when it has travelled far.

The ninth is the kindness of deep care and devotion.

The tenth is the kindness of ultimate pity and sympathy.

## 1. THE KINDNESS OF PROVIDING PROTECTION AND CARE WHILE THE CHILD IS IN THE WOMB

The causes and conditions from accumulated kalpas grows heavy,

Until in this life the child ends up in its mother's womb.

As the months pass, the five vital organs develop;

Within seven weeks the six sense organs start to grow.

The mother's body becomes as heavy as a mountain;

The stillness and movements of the fetus are like a kalpic wind disaster.

The mother's fine clothes no longer hang properly,
And so her mirror gathers dust.

## 2. THE KINDNESS OF BEARING SUFFERING DURING BIRTH

The pregnancy lasts for ten lunar months

And culminates in difficult labor at the approach of the birth.

Meanwhile, each morning the mother is

seriously ill

And during every day is drowsy and sluggish.

Her fear and agitation are difficult to describe;

Grieving and tears fill her breast.

She painfully tells her family

That she is only afraid that death will overtake her.

## 3. THE KINDNESS OF FORGEITING ALL THE PAIN ONCE THE CHILD HAS BEEN BORN

On the day the compassionate mothers bears the child,

Her five organs all open wide,

Leaving her totally exhausted in body and mind.

The blood flows as from a slaughtered lamb;

Yet, upon hearing that the child is healthy,

She is overcome with redoubling joy,

But after the joy, the grief returns,

And the agony wrenches her very insides.

## 4. THE KINDNESS OF EATING THE BITTER HERSELF AND SAVING THE SWEET FOR THE CHILD

The kindness of both parents is profound and deep,

Their care and devotion never cease.

Never resting, the mother saves the sweet for the child,

And without complaint she swallows the bitter herself.

Her love is weighty and her emotion difficult to bear;

Her kindness is deep and so is her compassion.

Only wanting the child to get its fill,

The compassionate mother doesn't speak of her own hunger.

## 5. THE KINDNESS OF MOVING THE CHILD TO A DRY PLACE AND LYING IN THE WET HERSELF

The mother is willing to be wet So that the child can be dry.

With her two breasts she satisfies its

hunger and thirst;

Covering it with her sleeve, she protects it from the wind and cold.

In kindness, her head rarely rests on the pillow,

And yet she does this happily,

So long as the child is comfortable,

The kind mother seeks no solace for herself.

## 6. THE KINDNESS OF SUCKUNG THE CHILD AT HER BREAST AND NOURISHING AND BRINGING UP THE CHILD

The kind mother is like the great earth.

The stern father is like the encompassing heaven

One covers from above' the other supports from below.

The kindness of parents is such that

They know no hatred or anger toward their offspring,

And are not displeased, even if the child is born crippled.

After the mother carries the child in her

womb and gives birth to it,

The parents care for and protect it together until the end of their days.

## 7. KINDNESS OF WASHING AWAY THE UNCLEAN

Originally she had a pretty face and a beautiful body,

Her spirit was strong and vibrant.

Her eyebrows were like fresh green willows,

And her complexion would have put a red rose to shame.

But her kindness is so deep she will forego a beautiful face.

Although washing away the filth injures her constituion,

The kind mother acts solely for the sake of her sons and daughters

And willingly allows her beauty to fade.

## 8. THE KINDNESS OF ALWAYS THINKING OF THE CHILD WHEN IT HAS TRAVELLED FAR

The death of loved ones is difficult to endure.

But separation is also painful.

When the child travels afar,

The mother worries in her village.

From morning until night, her heart is with her child,

And a thousand tears fall from her eyes.

Like the monkey weeping silently in love for her child,

Bit-by-bit her heart is broken.

## 9. THE KINDNESS OF DEEP CARE AND DEVOTION

How heavy is the parents' kindness and emotional concern!

Their kindness is deep and difficult to repay.

Willingly they undergo suffering on their child's behalf.

If the child toils, the parents are uncomfortable.

If they hear that he has travelled afar,

They worry that at night he will have to lie

in the cold.

Even a moment's pain suffered by their sons or daughters

Will cause the parents sustained distress.

## 10. THE KINDNESS OF ULTIMATE PITY AND SYMPATHY

The kindness of parents is profound and important.

Their tender concern never ceases.

From the moment they awake each day, their thoughts are with their children.

Whether the children are near or far away, the parents think of them often.

Even if a mother lives for a hundred years,

She will constantly worry about her eighty-year-old child!

Do you wish to know when such kindness and love ends?

It doesn't even begin to dissipate until her life is over.

The Buddha told Ananda, "When I contemplate living beings, I see that although they are born as human beings, nonetheless, they are stupid and dull in their thoughts and actions. They don't consider their parents' great kindness and virtue. They are disrespectful and turn their backs on kindness and what is right. They lack humaneness and are neither filial nor compliant.

For ten months while the mother is with child, she feels discomfort each time she rises, as if she were lifting a heavy burden. Like a chronic invalid, she is unable to keep her food and drink down. When the ten months have passed and the time comes for the birth, she undergoes all kinds of pain and suffering so that the child can be born. She is afraid of her own mortality, like a pig or lamb waiting to be slaughtered. Then the blood flows all over the ground. These are the sufferings she undergoes.

Once the child is born, she saves what is sweet for him and swallows what is bitter herself. She carries the child and nourishes it, washing away its filth. There is no toil or difficulty that she does not willingly undertake for the sake of her child. She endures both cold and heat and never even mentions what she has gone through. She gives the dry place to her child and sleeps in the dump herself. For three years she nourishes the baby with milk, which is transformed from the blood of her own body.

Parents continually instruct and guide their children in the ways of propriety and morality as the youngsters mature into adults. They arrange marriages for them and provide them with property and wealth or deviseways to get it for them. They take this responsibility and trouble upon themselves with tremendous zeal and toil, never speaking about their care and kindness.

When a son or daughter becomes ill, parents are worried and afraid to the point that they may even grow ill themselves. They remain by the child's side providing constant care, and only when the child gets well are the parents happy once again. In this way, they care for and raise their children with the sustained hope that their off-spring will soon grow to be mature adults.

How sad that all too often the children are unfilial in return! In speaking with relatives whom they should honor, the childre~n display no compliance. When they ought to be polite, they have no manners. They glare at those whom they should venerate, and insult their uncles and aunts. They scold their siblings and destroy any family feeling that might have existed among them. Children like that have no respect or sense of propriety.

Children may be well taught, but if they are unfilial, they will not heed the instructions or obey the rules. Rarely will they rely upon the guidance of their parents. They are contrary and rebellious when interacting with their brothers. They come and go from home without ever reporting to their parents. Their speech and actions are very arrogant and they act on impulse without consulting others. Such children ignore the admonishments and punishments set down by their parents and pay no regard to their uncles' warnings. Yet, at the same time, they are immature and always need to be looked after and protected by their elders.

As such children grow up, they become more and more obstinate and uncontrollable. They are entirely ungrateful and totally contrary. They are defiant and hateful, rejecting both family and friends. They befriend evil people and under their influence soon adopt the same kinds of bad habits. They come to take what is false to be true.

Such children may be enticed by others to leave their families and run away to live in other towns, thus denouncing their parents and rejecting their native town. They may become salesmen or crvil servants who languish in comfort and luxury. They may marry in haste and that new bond provides yet another obstruction which prevents them from returning home for long periods of time.

Or, in going to live in other towns, these children may be incautious and find themselves plotted against or accused of doing evil. They may be unfairly locked up in prison. Or they may meet with illness and become enmeshed in disasters and hardships, subject to the terrible pain of poverty, starvation, and emaciation. Yet no one there will care for them. Being scorned and disliked by others, they will be abandoned on the street. In such circumstances, their lives may come to an end. No one bothers to try to save them. Their bodies swell up, rot, decay, and are exposed to the sun and blown away by the wind. The white bones entirely disintegrate and scatter as these children come to their final rest in the dirt of some other town. These children will never again have a happy reunion with their relatives and kin. Nor will they ever know how their ageing parents mourn for and worry about them. The parents may grow blind from weeping or become sick from extreme grief and despair. Constantly dwelling on the memory of their children, they may pass away, but even when they become ghosts, their souls still cling to this attachment and are unable to let it go.

Others of these unfilial children may not aspire to learning, but instead become interested in strange and bizarre doctrines. Such children may be villainous, coarse, and stubborn, delighting in practices that are utterly devoid of benefit. They may become involved in fights and thefts, setting themselves at odds with the town by drinking and gambling. As if their own debauchery were not enough, they drag their brothers into it as well, to the further distress of their parents.

If such children do live at home, they leave early in the morning and do not return until late at night. Never do they ask about the welfare of their parents or make sure that they don't suffer from heat or cold. They do not inquire after their parents' well being in the morning or the evening, nor even on the first and fifteenth of the lunar month. In fact, it never occurs to these unfilial children to ever ask whether their parents have slept comfortably or rested peacefully. Such children are simply not concerned in the least about their parents' well being. When the parents of such children grow old and their appearance becomes more and more withered and emaciated, they are made to feel ashamed to be seen in public and are subjected to abuse and oppression.

Such unfilial children may end up with a father who is a widower or a mother who is a widow. The solitary parents are left alone in empty houses, feeling like guests in their own homes. They may endure cold and hunger, but no one takes heed of their plight. They may weep incessantly from morning to night, sighing and lamenting. It's only right that children should provide for ageing parents with food and drink of delicious flavours, but irresponsible children are sure to overlook their duties. If they ever do attempt to help their parents out in any way, they feel embarrassed and are afraid people will laugh at them. Yet, such offspring may lavish wealth and food on their own wives and children, disregarding the toil and weariness involved in doing so. Other unfilial offspring may be so intimidated by their wives that they go along with all of their wishes. But when appealed to by their parents and elders, they ignore them and are totally unfazed by their pleas.

It may be the case that daughters were quite filial to their parents before their own marriages, but that they become progressively rebellious after they marry. This situation may be so extreme that if their parents show even the slightest signs of displeasure, the daughters become hateful and vengeful toward them. Yet they bear their husband's scolding and beatings with sweet tempers, even though their spouses are outsiders with other surnames and family ties. The emotional bonds between such couples are deeply entangled, and yet those daughters hold their parents at a distance. They may follow their husbands and move to other towns, leaving their parents behind entirely. They do not long for them and simply cut off all communication with them. When the parents continue to hear no word from their daughters, they feel incessant anxiety. They become so fraught with sorrow that it is as if they were suspended upside down. Their every thought is of seeing their children, just as one who is. thirsty longs for something to drink. Their kind thoughts for their offspring never cease.

The virtue of one's parents' kindness is boundless and limitless. If one has made the mistake of being unfilial, how difficult it is to repay that kindness!"

At that time, upon hearing the Buddha speak about the depth of one's parents' kindness, everyone in the Great Assembly threw themselves on the ground and began beating their breasts and striking themselves until all their hairpores flowed with blood. Some fell unconscious to the ground, while others stamped their feet in grief. It was a long time before they could control themselves. With loud voices they lamented, "Such suffering! What suffering! How painful! How painful! We are all offenders. We are criminals who have never awakened, like those who travel in a dark night. We have just now understood our offenses and our very insides are torn to bits. We only hope that the World Honored One will pity us and save us. Please tell us how we can repay the deep kindness of our parents!"

At that time the Tathagata used eight kinds of profoundly deep and pure sounds to speak to the assembly. "All of you should know this. I will now explain for you the various aspects of this matter.

"If there were a person who carries his father on his left shoulder and his mother on his right shoulder until his bones were ground to powder by their weight as they bore through to the marrow, and if that person were to circumambulate Mount Sumem for a hundred thousand kalpas until the blood that flowed out from his feet covered his ankles, that person would still not have repayed the deep kindness of his parents.

"If there were a person who, during the period of a kalpa fraught with famine and starvation, sliced the flesh off his own body to feed his parents and did this as many times as there are dust motes as he passed through hundreds of thousands of kalpas, that person still would not have repayed the deep kindness of his parents.

"If there were a person who, for the sake of his parents, took a sharp knife and cut out his eyes and made an offering of them to the Tathagatas, and continued to do that for hundreds of thousands of kalpas, that person still would not have repayed the deep kindness of his parents.

"If there were a person who, for the sake of his father and mother, used a sharp knife to cut out his heart and liver so that the blood flowed and covered the ground and if he continued in this way to do this for hundreds of thousands of kalpas, never once complaining about the pain, that person still would not have repayed the deep kindness of his parents.

"If there were a person who, for the sake of his parents, took a hundred thousand swords and stabbed his body with them all at once so that they enteredone side and came out the other, and if he continued in this way to do this for hundreds of thousands of kalpas, that person still would not have repayed the deep kindness of his parents.

"If there were a person who, for the sake of his parents, beat his bones down to the marrow and continued in this way to do this for hundreds of thousands of kalpas, that person still would not have repayed the deep kindness of his parents. "If there were a person who, for the sake of his parents, swallowed molten iron pellets and continued in this way to do this for hundreds of thousands of kalpas, that person still would not have repayed the deep kindness of his parents."

At that time, upon hearing the Buddha speak about the kindness and virtue of parents, everyone in the Great Assembly wept silent tears and felt searing pain in their hearts. They reflected deeply, simultaneously brought forth shame and said to the Buddha, " World Honored One, how can we repay the deep kindness of our parents?"

The Buddha replied, "Disciples of the Buddha, if you wish to repay your parents' kindness, write out this Sutra on their behalf. Recite this Sutra on their behalf. Repent of transgressions and offenses on their behalf. For the sake of your parents, make offerings to the Triple Jewel. For the sake of your parents, hold the precept of pure eating. For the sake of your parents, practice giving and cultivate blessings. If you are able to do these things, you are being a filial child. If you do not do these things, you are a person destined for the hells."

The Buddha told Ananda, "If a person is not filial, when his life ends and his body decays, he will fall into the Spaceless, Avici Hell. This great hell is eighty thousand yojanas in circumference and is surrounded on all four sides by iron walls.

Above, it is covered over by nets, and the ground is also made of iron. A mass of fire bums fiercely, while thunder roars and bright bolts of lightning set things afire. Molten brass and iron fluids are poured over the offenders' bodies. Brass dogs and iron snakes constantly spew out fire and smoke which burns the offenders and broils their flesh and fat to a pulp.

"Oh, such suffering! Difficult to take, difficult to bear! There are poles, hooks, spears, and lances, iron halberds and iron chains, iron hammers, and iron awls. Wheels of iron knives rain down from the air. The offender is chopped, hacked, or stabbed, and undergoes these cruel punishments for kalpas without respite.

Then they enter the remaining hells, where their heads are capped with fiery basins, while iron wheels roll over their bodies, passing both horizontally and vertically until their guts are ripped open and their bones and flesh are squashed to a pulp. Within a single day, they experience myriad births and myriad deaths. Such sufferings are a result of committing the five rebellious acts and of being unfilial when one was alive."

At that time, upon hearing the Buddha speak about the virtue of parents' kindness, everyone in the Great Assembly wept sorrowfully and addressed the Tathagata, "On this day, how can we repay the deep kindness of our parents?"

The Buddha said, "Disciples of the Buddha, if you wish to repay their kindness, then for the sake of your parents print this Sutra. This is truly repaying their kindness. If one can print one copy, then one will get to see one Buddha. If one can print ten copies, then one will get to see ten Buddhas. If one can print one hundred copies, then one will get to see one hundred Buddhas. If one can print one thousand copies, then one will get to see one thousand Buddhas. If one can print ten thousand copies, then one will get to see ten thousand Buddhas. This is the power derived when good people print Sutras. All Buddhas will forever protect such people with their kindness and can immediately cause the parents of such people to be reborn in the heavens, to enjoy all kinds of happiness, and to leave behind the sufferings of the hells."

At that time, Ananda and the rest of the Great Assembly--the asuras, garudas, kinnaras, mahoragas, people, non-people, and others, as well as the gods, dragons, yakshas, gandarvas, wheel-turning sage kings, and all the lesser kings--felt all the hairs on their bodies stand on end when they heard what the Buddha had said. They wept grievously and were unable to stop themselves. Each one of them made a vow saying, "All of us, from now until the exhaustion of the bounds of the future, would rather that our bodies be pulverized into small particles of dust for a hundred thousand kalpas, than to ever go against the Thus Come One's sagely teachings. We would rather that our tongues be plucked out, so that they would extend for a full yojana, and that for a hundred thousand kalpas an iron plough would run over them; we would rather have a hundred-thousand bladed wheel roll freely over our bodies, than ever go against the Tathagata's sagely teachings. We would rather that our bodies be ensnared in an iron net for a hundred thousand kalpas, than ever go against the Tathagata's sagely teachings. We would rather that for a hundred thousand kalpas our bodies would be chopped, hacked, mutilated, and chiselled into ten million pieces so that our skin, flesh, joints, and bones would be completely disintegrated, than ever go against the Tathagata's sagely teachings."

At that time, Ananda, with a dignity and a sense of peace, rose from his seat and asked the Buddha, "World Honored One, what name shall this Sutra have when we accord with it and uphold it?"

The Buddha told Ananda, "This Sutra is called THE SUTRA ABOUT THE DEEP KINDNESS OF PARENTS AND THE DIFFICULTY OF REPAYING IT. Use this name when you accord with it and uphold it."

At that time, the Great Assembly, the gods, humans, asuras, and the others, hearing what the Buddha has said, were completely delighted. They believed it, received it, and offered up their conduct in accord with it, and then bowed and withdrew.

**Namo Shakyamunaye Buddhaya.**
(3 times) (ooo)

***

# 43. KALAMA SUTRA
# -THE INSTRUCTION TO THE KALAMAS

(Anguttara Nikaya 3.56)

Translated from the Pali by Soma Thera

## THE KALAMAS OF KESAPUTTA GO TO SEE THE BUDDHA

1. I heard thus. Once the Blessed One, while wandering in the Kosala country with a large community of Bhikkhus, entered a town of the Kalama people called Kesaputta. The Kalamas who were inhabitants of Kesaputta: "Reverend Gautama, the monk, the son of the Sakyans, has, while wandering in the Kosala country, entered Kesaputta. The good repute of the Reverend Gautama has been spread in this way: Indeed, the Blessed One is thus consummate, fully enlightened, endowed with knowledge

and practice, sublime, knower of the worlds, peerless, guide of tamable men, teacher of divine and human beings, which he by himself has through direct knowledge understood clearly. He set forth the Dhamma, good in the beginning, good in the middle, good in the end, possessed of meaning and the letter, and complete in everything; and he proclaims the holy life that is perfectly pure. Seeing such consummate ones is good indeed."

2. Then the Kalamas who were inhabitants of Kesaputta went to where the Blessed One was. On arriving there some paid homage to him and sat down on one side; some exchanged greetings with him and after the ending of cordial memorable talk, sat down on one side; some saluted him raising their joined palms and sat down on one side; some announced their name and family and sat down on one side; some without speaking, sat down on one side.

THE KALAMAS OF KESAPUTTA ASK FOR GUIDANCE FROM THE BUDDHA

3. The Kalamas who were inhabitants

of Kesaputta sitting on one side said to the Blessed One: "There are some monks and Brahmins, venerable sir, who visit Kesaputta. They expound and explain only their own doctrines; the doctrines of others they despise, revile, and pull to pieces. Some other monks and Brahmins too, venerable sir, come to Kesaputta. They also expound and explain only their own doctrines; the doctrines of others they despise, revile, and pull to pieces. Venerable sir, there is doubt; there is uncertainty in us concerning them. Which of these reverend monks and Brahmins spoke the truth and which falsehood?"

## THE CRITERION FOR REJECTION

4. "It is proper for you, Kalamas, to doubt, to be uncertain; uncertainty has arisen in you about what is doubtful. Come, Kalamas. Do not go upon what has been acquired by repeated hearing; nor upon tradition; nor upon rumor; nor upon what is in a scripture; nor upon surmise; nor upon an axiom; nor upon specious reasoning; nor upon a bias towards a

notion that has been pondered over; nor upon another's seeming ability; nor upon the consideration, 'The monk is our teacher.' Kalamas, when you yourselves know: 'These things are bad; these things are blamable; these things are censured by the wise; undertaken and observed, these things lead to harm and ill,' abandon them.

## GREED, HATE, AND DELUSION

5. "What do you think, Kalamas? Does greed appear in a man for his benefit or harm?" -- "For his harm, venerable sir." -- "Kalamas, being given to greed, and being overwhelmed and vanquished mentally by greed, this man takes life, steals, commits adultery, and tells lies; he prompts another too, to do likewise. Will that be long for his harm and ill?" -- "Yes, venerable sir."

6. "What do you think, Kalamas? Does hate appear in a man for his benefit or harm?" -- "For his harm, venerable sir." -- "Kalamas, being given to hate, and being overwhelmed and vanquished mentally by hate, this man takes life,

steals, commits adultery, and tells lies; he prompts another too, to do likewise. Will that be long for his harm and ill?" -- "Yes, venerable sir."

7. "What do you think, Kalamas? Does delusion appear in a man for his benefit or harm?" -- "For his harm, venerable sir." -- "Kalamas, being given to delusion, and being overwhelmed and vanquished mentally by delusion, this man takes life, steals, commits adultery, and tells lies; he prompts another too, to do likewise. Will that be long for his harm and ill?" -- "Yes, venerable sir."

8. "What do you think, Kalamas? Are these things good or bad?" -- "Bad, venerable sir" -- "Blamable or not blamable?" -- "Blamable, venerable sir." -- "Censured or praised by the wise?" -- "Censured, venerable sir." -- "Undertaken and observed, do these things lead to harm and ill, or not? Or how does it strike you?" -- "Undertaken and observed, these things lead to harm and ill. Thus it strikes us here."

9. "Therefore, did we say, Kalamas, what was said thus, 'Come Kalamas. Do not

go upon what has been acquired by repeated hearing; nor upon tradition; nor upon rumor; nor upon what is in a scripture; nor upon surmise; nor upon an axiom; nor upon specious reasoning; nor upon a bias towards a notion that has been pondered over; nor upon another's seeming ability; nor upon the consideration, "The monk is our teacher." Kalamas, when you yourselves know: "These things are bad; these things are blamable; these things are censured by the wise; undertaken and observed, these things lead to harm and ill," abandon them.'

## THE CRITERION FOR ACCEPTANCE

10. "Come, Kalamas. Do not go upon what has been acquired by repeated hearing; nor upon tradition; nor upon rumor; nor upon what is in a scripture; nor upon surmise; nor upon an axiom; nor upon specious reasoning; nor upon a bias towards a notion that has been pondered over; nor upon another's seeming ability; nor upon the consideration, 'The monk is our

teacher.' Kalamas, when you yourselves know: 'These things are good; these things are not blamable; these things are praised by the wise; undertaken and observed, these things lead to benefit and happiness,' enter on and abide in them.

## ABSENCE OF GREED, HATE, AND DELUSION

11. "What do you think, Kalamas? Does absence of greed appear in a man for his benefit or harm?" -- "For his benefit, venerable sir." -- "Kalamas, being not given to greed, and being not overwhelmed and not vanquished mentally by greed, this man does not take life, does not steal, does not commit adultery, and does not tell lies; he prompts another too, to do likewise. Will that be long for his benefit and happiness?" -- "Yes, venerable sir."

12. "What do you think, Kalamas? Does absence of hate appear in a man for his benefit or harm?" -- "For his benefit, venerable sir." -- "Kalamas, being not given to hate, and being

not overwhelmed and not vanquished mentally by hate, this man does not take life, does not steal, does not commit adultery, and does not tell lies; he prompts another too, to do likewise. Will that be long for his benefit and happiness?" -- "Yes, venerable sir."

13. "What do you think, Kalamas? Does absence of delusion appear in a man for his benefit or harm?" -- "For his benefit, venerable sir." -- "Kalamas, being not given to delusion, and being not overwhelmed and not vanquished mentally by delusion, this man does not take life, does not steal, does not commit adultery, and does not tell lies; he prompts another too, to do likewise. Will that be long for his benefit and happiness?" -- "Yes, venerable sir."

14. "What do you think, Kalamas? Are these things good or bad?" -- "Good, venerable sir." -- "Blamable or not blamable?" -- "Not blamable, venerable sir." -- "Censured or praised by the wise?" -- "Praised, venerable sir." -- "Undertaken and observed, do these things lead to benefit and happiness,

or not? Or how does it strike you?" -- "Undertaken and observed, these things lead to benefit and happiness. Thus it strikes us here."

15. "Therefore, did we say, Kalamas, what was said thus, 'Come Kalamas. Do not go upon what has been acquired by repeated hearing; nor upon tradition; nor upon rumor; nor upon what is in a scripture; nor upon surmise; nor upon an axiom; nor upon specious reasoning; nor upon a bias towards a notion that has been pondered over; nor upon another's seeming ability; nor upon the consideration, "The monk is our teacher." Kalamas, when you yourselves know: "These things are good; these things are not blamable; these things are praised by the wise; undertaken and observed, these things lead to benefit and happiness," enter on and abide in them.'

## THE FOUR EXALTED DWELLINGS

16. "The disciple of the Noble Ones, Kalamas, who in this way is devoid of coveting, devoid of ill will, un-deluded,

clearly comprehending and mindful, dwells, having pervaded, with the thought of amity, one quarter; likewise the second; likewise the third; likewise the fourth; so above, below, and across; he dwells, having pervaded because of the existence in it of all living beings, everywhere, the entire world, with the great, exalted, boundless thought of amity that is free of hate or malice.

"He lives, having pervaded, with the thought of compassion, one quarter; likewise the second; likewise the third; likewise the fourth; so above, below, and across; he dwells, having pervaded because of the existence in it of all living beings, everywhere, the entire world, with the great, exalted, boundless thought of compassion that is free of hate or malice.

"He lives, having pervaded, with the thought of gladness, one quarter; likewise the second; likewise the third; likewise the fourth; so above, below, and across; he dwells, having pervaded because of the existence in it of all living beings, everywhere, the entire world, with the great, exalted, boundless thought of gladness that is free of hate or malice.

"He lives, having pervaded, with the thought of equanimity, one quarter; likewise the second; likewise the third; likewise the fourth; so above, below, and across; he dwells, having pervaded because of the existence in it of all living beings, everywhere, the entire world, with the great, exalted, boundless thought of equanimity that is free of hate or malice.

## THE FOUR SOLACES

17. "The disciple of the Noble Ones, Kalamas, who has such a hate-free mind, such a malice-free mind, such an undefiled mind, and such a purified mind, is one by whom four solaces are found here and now.

"'Suppose there is a hereafter and there is a fruit, result, of deeds done well or ill. Then it is possible that at the dissolution of the body after death, I shall arise in the heavenly world, which is possessed of the state of bliss.' This is the first solace found by him.

"'Suppose there is no hereafter and there is no fruit, no result, of deeds done well or ill. Yet in this world, here and now, free from hatred, free from malice, safe and sound, and happy, I keep myself.' This is the second solace found by him.

"'Suppose evil (results) befall an evil-doer. I, however, think of doing evil to no one. Then, how can ill (results) affect me who do no evil deed?' This is the third solace found by him.

"'Suppose evil (results) do not befall an evil-doer. Then I see myself purified in any case.' This is the fourth solace found by him.

"The disciple of the Noble Ones, Kalamas, who has such a hate-free mind, such a malice-free mind, such an undefiled mind, and such a purified mind, is one by whom, here and now, these four solaces are found."

"So it is, Blessed One. So it is, Sublime one. The disciple of the Noble Ones, venerable sir, who has such a hate-free mind, such a malice-free mind, such an undefiled mind, and such a purified mind, is one by whom, here and now, four solaces are found.

"'Suppose there is a hereafter and there is a fruit, result, of deeds done well or ill. Then it is possible that at the dissolution of the body after death, I shall arise in the heavenly world, which is possessed of the state of bliss.' This is the first solace found by him.

"'Suppose there is no hereafter and there is no fruit, no result, of deeds done well or ill. Yet in this world, here and now, free from hatred, free from malice, safe and sound, and happy, I keep myself.' This is the second solace found by him.

"'Suppose evil (results) befall an evil-doer. I, however, think of doing evil to no one. Then, how can ill (results) affect me who do no evil deed?' This is the third solace found by him.

"'Suppose evil (results) do not befall an evil-doer. Then I see myself purified in any case.' This is the fourth solace found by him.

"The disciple of the Noble Ones, venerable sir, who has such a hate-free mind, such a malice-free mind, such an undefiled mind, and such a purified mind, is one by whom, here and now, these four solaces are found.

"Marvelous, venerable sir! Marvelous, venerable sir! As if, venerable sir, a person were to turn face upwards what is upside down, or to uncover the concealed, or to point the way to one who is lost or to carry a lamp in the darkness, thinking, 'Those who have eyes will see visible objects,' so has the Dhamma been set forth in many ways by the Blessed One. We, venerable sir, go to the Blessed One for refuge, to the Dhamma for refuge, and to the Community of Bhikkhus for refuge. Venerable sir, may the Blessed One regard us as lay followers who have gone for refuge for life, from today."

**Namo Shakyamunaye Buddhaya.**
(3 times) (ooo)

# 44. MASTERING ANGER
## (Thích Nhất Hạnh)

I bow my head and touch the Earth

before the highest charioteer who trains humankind.

Stretch out your arms of compassion;

bring us to the shore of peace and solidity.

For so long, confusion has inhabited us

so that we have not had the chance to learn, and we have often acted foolishly,

allowed seeds of anger and violence

to be watered in our deep consciousness.


Whenever seeds of irritation or fury arise and operate in my mind,

They always cause wounds and resentment

in myself and in so many others.

Listening to Avalokita's teaching,

I begin right now with a deep aspiration:
Whenever anger arises,

I shall come back to myself,

taking refuge in my mindful breathing and

steps so as to look after and embrace,

to protect and recognize

the painful mental formations in me.

I shall remember to look deeply to see
the true nature and source of hatred and
anger.

Heeding the Buddha's teachings,

I shall know how to guard my mind.

When anger arises in me

I shall not do or say anything

until I have mastered it.

I shall look deeply to see

the real nature of my pain.

The seed of ignorance

is the cause of my suffering, and the
reason why the seed of

anger in me has grown so strong.

The person who makes me angry

has so much suffering himself, herself.

Such a person has had no chance

to learn how to protect, to come home to himself or herself to take care and to transform

the deep-seated habit energies within.

Contemplating in this way,

I will be able to bring about understanding and acceptance, and help the other person to practice and to transform

the suffering within him or her.

The Blessed One has said,

When we are capable of conquering our anger,

we bring a double victory to ourself and to the other person.

I want to practice with all my heart

in order to respond to the Great Grace.

May the Three Jewels give me energy and blessing so that we can reach promptly

the shore of peace and happiness.

Namo Shakyamunaye Buddhaya.
(3 times) (ooo)

# 45. THE TEN WHOLESOME WAYS OF ACTION

Translated to English by
Saddhaloka Bhikkhu

## 1. GIVING UP TAKING LIFE

Oh Dragon King, if one gives up taking life hen one will accomplish ten ways of being free from vexations. What are the ten?

i. One give universally to all beings without fear

ii. One always has a heart of great compassion towards all beings

iii. All habitual tendencies of hate in oneself will be cut off forever

iv. One's body is always free from illness

v. One's life is long

vi. One is constantly protected by non-human beings

vii. One is always without bad dreams, one sleeps and wakes happily

viii. The entanglement of enmity is eradicated and one is free from all hatred

ix. One is free from the dread of evil

destinies

x. When one's life comes to an end one will be born as a deva.

These are the ten. If one is one who is able to turn-towards the Highest Perfect Illumination, one will later at the time one becomes Buddha attain to the ability peculiar to the Buddha, to live as long as one wishes.

## 2. GIVING UP STEALING

Again, oh Dragon King, if one gives up stealing then one will attain to ten kinds of dharmas which can protect one's confidence. what are the ten?

i. One's wealth will increase and accumulate and cannot be scattered or destroyed by Kings, robbers, floods, fires, and careless sons.

ii. One is thought of with fondness by many people.

iii. People do not take advantage of one.

iv. Everywhere one is praised

v. One is above the worry, that one oneself could be injured.

vi. One's good name spreads

vii. One is without fear in public.

viii. One is endowed with wealth, long life, strength, peace, happiness, and skill in speech, without deficiencies

ix. One always thinks of giving

x. At the end of one's life, one will be born as a deva

These are the ten. If one is one who is able to turn towards the Highest Perfect Illumination, one will later at the time one becomes Buddha, attain to the realization of the purified great illumination wisdom.

## 3. GIVING UP WRONG CONDUCT

Again the Dragon King, if one gives up wrong conduct one will attain to four kinds of dharmas which are praised by the wise. What are the four?

i. All one's faculties are tuned and adjusted.

ii. One is free from turmoil and excitement.

iii. One is praised and extolled by the world

iv. One's wife cannot be encroached upon by anybody

These are the four. If one is one who is able to turn towards the Highest Perfect Illumination one will later at the time one becomes Buddha, attain the mastersign of the Buddha, of a concealed organ.

## 4. GIVING UP LYING

Again, oh Dragon King, if one gives up lying then one will attain to the eight dharmas which are praised by the devas. What are the eight?

i. One's mouth is always pure and has the fragrance of a blue lotus flower.

ii. One is trusted and obeyed by all the world.

iii. What one says is true and one is loved by men and devas.

iv. One always comforts beings with loving words.

v. One attains to excellent bliss of mind and one's actions, speech, and thoughts are pure.

vi. One's speech is faultless and one's mind is always joyful.

vii. One's words are respected and are

followed by men and devas.

viii. One's wisdom is extraordinary and cannot be subdued These are the eight. If one is one who is able to turn towards the Highest Perfect Illumination, one will later at the time one becomes Buddha, attain to the true speech of the Tathagata.

## 5. GIVING UP SLANDERING ONE

Again, oh Dragon King, if one gives up slandering one will then attain to five kinds of incorruptible dharmas.

What are the five?

i. One attains to an incorruptible body because no harm can be done to one.

ii. One gets an incorruptible family because no one can destroy it.

iii. One attains to incorruptible confidence because

this is in line with one's own actions.

iv. One attains to an incorruptible spiritual life because what one cultivates is firmly grounded.

v. One gets incorruptible spiritual friends because one does not mislead or delude anybody.

These are the five. If one is one who is able to turn-towards the Highest Perfect Illumination, one will later  at the time one becomes Buddha, gets a holy retinue which cannot be corrupted by any Mara or heretic.

## 6. GIVING UP HARSH LANGUAGE

Again, oh Dragon King, if one gives up harsh language  then one will attain to the accomplishment of eight kinds of pure actions. What are the eight?

i. One's speech is meaningful and reasonable

ii. All that one says is profitable.

iii. One's words are bound to be truthful.

iv. One's language is beautiful and marvelous.

v. One's words are accepts (by others).

vi. One's words are trusted.

vii. One's words cannot be ridiculed.

viii. All one's words are being loved and enjoyed (by others)

These are the eight. If one is one who is able to turn towards the Highest Perfect Illumination, be endowed with the perfect characteristic of the Brahma voice of the Tathagata.

## 7. GIVING UP FRIVOLOUS SPEECH

Again, oh Dragon King, if one gives up frivolous speech then one will attain to the accomplishment of the three certainties. What are the three?

i. One is certain to be loved by the wise

ii. One is certain to be able to answer questions

with wisdom and according to reality

iii. One is certain to have the most excellent dignity and virtue among men and devas and one is without falsehood.

These are the three. If one is one who is able to turn towards the Highest Perfect Illumination, one will later at the time one becomes Buddha, attain to the Tathagata's (ability) to predict everything, none (of the predictions) are ever in vain.

## 8. GIVING UP LUST

Again, oh Dragon King, if one gives up lust, then one will attain to the accomplishment of the five kinds of freedom. What are the five?

i. Freedom of bodily, verbal, and mental actions because one's six faculties are perfect

ii. Freedom as regards property because all enemies and robbers cannot rob one.

iii. Freedom with regard to merit because whatever one wishes one will be provided with.

iv. Freedom of being in the position of a King, because precious, rare and marvelous things  will be reverently offered to one.

v. The things one will get will surpass in excellency by a hundred times that what one is  looking for, because in times by-gone one was  neither stingy nor envious

These are the five. If one is one who is able to turn towards the Highest Perfect Illumination, one will later at the time becomes Buddha, be especially revered in all three realms all (the beings of the three realms) will all respectfully make offering to one.

## 9. GIVING UP HATRED

Again, oh Dragon King, if one gives up hatred then one will attain to eight kinds of dharmas of joy of mind. What the eight?

i. One's mind is free from (the want) to injure and to

annoy (others)

ii. One's mind is free from hatred

iii. One's mind is free from (the desire) to dispute and to argue

iv. One's mind is gentle and upright

v. One has attained to the mind of loving kindness of a saint

vi. One is of a mind that always acts beneficially giving peace to beings

vii. One's bodily appearance is dignified and one is respectfully by all

viii. Because one is kind and forbearing, one will be born soon in the Brahma World.

These are the eight. If one is one who is able to turn towards to the Highest Perfect

Illumination, one will later at the times one becomes Buddha, attain to the mind of the Buddha that is free from obstacles. People will not become tired of looking at him.

## 10. GIVING UP WRONG VIEWS

Again, Oh Dragon King, if one gives up wrong views, one will attain to the accomplishment of ten meritorious dharmas. What are the ten?

i. One attains to genuinely good bliss of mind and one gets genuinely good companions

ii. One has deep confidence in (the law of) cause and effect and one would rather lose one's life than do evil.

iii. One takes refuge in the Buddha only and not in devas or others.

iv. One is of a straight mind and right views, and leaves behind the net of doubts about good and evil  fortune.

v. One will not be born again in an evil course of existence but will always be born as a man or deva

vi. Immeasurable blessings and wisdom

will increase sublimely from turn to turn

vii. One will forever leave the wrong path and tread the holy path.

viii. The view of a personality will not arise (in one) and one gives up all evil actions.

ix. One will abide in unobstructed understanding.

x. One will not fall into any difficult conditions.

These are the ten. If one is one who is able to turn towards the Highest Perfect Illumination, one will later at the time one becomes Buddha, realize quickly all Buddha-dharmas and accomplish the mastery of the higher spiritual powers.

**Namo Shakyamunaye Buddhaya.**
(3 times) (ooo)

***

# 46. TURNING TO THE TATHAGATA
## (Thích Nhất Hạnh)

I touch the Earth deeply, turning to the Tathagata,

the lighthouse that shines over the ocean of dust and suffering.

Lord of Compassion, embrace us with your love,

for today we are determined to return to our true home. (o)

We, your spiritual children, still owe so much gratitude to our parents, teachers, friends, and all other beings. Looking over the Three Realms and across the Four Quarters, we see all species drowning in an ocean of misfortune.

It wakes us with a start.

Although we have turned in the right direction, the shore of awakening still lies very far away. Fortunately, we see the hands of the Compassionate One bringing relief to every corner of the world. (o)

With one-pointed mind, we return, taking

refuge.

We aspire to be the spiritual children of the Tathagata. We unify our body and mind before the Buddha's throne, releasing all attachment and negativity.

With great respect, we now aspire to receive the wonderful teachings.

We shall always practice diligently and carefully, our mindfulness trainings and concentration nourished to maturity,

for the fruit of understanding to be ripened in the future. We ask the Bodhisattvas to protect us day and night.

May the Buddha, Dharma, and Sangha show us their compassion. (o)

We know that the fruits of our past actions are still heavy, that the merit from our virtues is still frail,

that we are often full of wrong perceptions, that our capacity to understand is poor,

that the impurities of our mind still arise very easily,

that our practices of listening and contemplation are not firm.

In this moment we entrust ourselves to the Lotus Throne,

and, with our five limbs resting gently on the Earth, we now pray.

Infinite loving kindness, please expand and envelop us so that we too may open our hearts. (o)

We, your spiritual children for countless past lives, have chased after worldly things,

unable to recognize the clear, pure basis of our True Mind.

Our actions of body, speech, and mind have been unwholesome. We have drowned in ignorant cravings, jealousy, hatred, and anger.

But now the sound of the great bell has caused us to awaken with a heart that is determined to renew our body and our mind. Please help us completely remove the red dust of all wrongdoings, mistakes, and faults. (o)


We, your spiritual children in this moment,

make the vow to leave all our habit energies

behind,

and for the whole of our life to go for refuge to the Sangha.

Awakened One, please place your hand over us in protection,

so that loving kindness and compassion will guide and assist us.

We promise that when we practice meditation, when we take part in Dharma discussion, when we stand, walk, lie, or sit, when we cook, wash, work, or play, when we recite the names of the Buddhas and Bodhisattvas, when we offer incense or when we touch the Earth, every step will bring peace and joy to the world, every smile will be resplendent with freedom.

We will live mindfully in each and every moment to demonstrate the way of liberation from suffering. We vow to touch the Pure Land with every step.

We promise in every contact to be in touch with the ultimate dimension, taking steps on the soil of reality, breathing the air of true emptiness, lighting up wisdom to make resplendent the wonderful True Mind, drawing aside the dark curtain of ignorance, with our body and mind peaceful and happy,

free and at leisure until the moment when we leave this life, our heart with no regrets, our body without pain, our thoughts unclouded by ignorance,

our mindfulness clear and bright, and our six senses calm as when entering meditative concentration. (o)


If necessary to be reborn, we will always do so as the spiritual children of the Tathagata.

We will continue in the work of helping other beings, bringing them all over to the shore of awakening. Realizing the Three Bodies and the Four Wisdoms, using the Five Eyes and the Six Miracles, manifesting thousands of appropriate forms, being present at the same time in all the three worlds, coming in and going out in freedom and with ease, we will not abandon anyone, helping all beings to transform, bringing all to the shore of no regression. (o)

Space is without limit. There are infinite

living beings, and the same is true with afflictions and results of past actions. We pray that our aspirations will also become infinite.

We bow to the Awakened One as we make this vow.

We will maintain virtue, sharing the merit with countless others in order to fully repay the gratitude that we owe and to teach the practice everywhere within the Three Realms.

May we, alongside all species of living beings, fully realize the Great Awakened Understanding. (ooo)

**Namo Shakyamunaye Buddhaya.**
(3 times) (ooo)


***


# 47. THE FORTY-TWO SECTION DISCOURSE

(Translated by the Buddhist Text Translation Society)


When the World Honored One had attained the Way, he thought, "To leave desire behind and to gain calmness and tranquillity is supreme." He abided in deep meditative concentration and subdued every demon and externalist.

In the Deer Park he turned the Dharma-wheel of the Four Noble Truths and took across Ajnata-kaundinya and the other four disciples, who all realized the fruition of the Way.

Then the Bhikshus expressed their doubts and asked the Buddha how to resolve them. The World Honored One taught and exhorted them, until one by one they awakened and gained enlightenment. After that, they each put their palms together, respectfully gave their assent, and followed the Buddha's instructions.

## Section 1

# LEAVING HOME AND BECOMING AN ARHAT

The Buddha said, "People who take leave of their families and go forth from the householder's life, who know their mind and penetrate to its origin, and who understand the unconditioned Dharma are calle47.d *Shramanas.* They constantly observe the 250 precepts, and they value purity in all that they do. By practicing the four true paths, they can become *Arhats.*"

This is the first section of the *Sutra in Forty-two Sections.* It says that a Shramana can become an Arhat.

## Section 2
## ELIMINATING DESIRE
## AND ENDING SEEKING

The Buddha said, "Those who have left the home-life and become Shramanas cut off desire, renounce love, and recognize the source of their minds. They penetrate the Buddha's profound principles and awaken to the unconditioned Dharma. Internally they have nothing to attain, and externally they seek nothing. They are not mentally bound to the Way, nor are they tied to karma. They are free of thought and action; they neither cultivate nor attain certification; they do not pass through the various stages, and yet they are highly revered. This is the meaning of the Way."

## Section 3

# SEVERING LOVE
# AND RENOUNCING GREED

The Buddha said, "Shaving their hair and beards, they become Shramanas who accept the Dharmas of the Way. They renounce worldly wealth and riches. In receiving alms, they accept only what's enough. They take only one meal a day at noon, pass the night beneath trees, and are careful not to seek more than that. Craving and desire are what cause people to be stupid and dull."

## Section 4

# CLARIFYING GOOD AND EVIL

The Buddha said, "Living beings may perform Ten Good Deeds or Ten Evil Deeds. What are the ten? Three are done with the body, four are done with the mouth, and three are done with the mind. The three done with the body are killing, stealing, and lust. The four done with the mouth are duplicity, harsh speech, lies, and frivolous speech. The three done with the mind are jealousy, hatred, and stupidity. Thus these ten are not in accord with the Way of Sages and are called the Ten Evil Deeds. To put a stop to these evils is to perform the Ten Good Deeds."

## Section 5

# REDUCING THE SEVERITY OF OFFENSES

The Buddha said, "If a person has many offenses and does not repent of them, but cuts off all thought of repentance, the offenses will engulf him, just as water returning to the sea will gradually become deeper and wider. If a person has offenses and, realizing they are wrong, reforms and does good, the offenses will dissolve by themselves, just as a sick person who begins to perspire will gradually be cured."

## Section 6

# TOLERATING EVIL-DOERS AND AVOIDING HATRED

The Buddha said, "When an evil person hears about your goodness and intentionally comes to cause trouble, you should restrain yourself and not become angry or blame him. Then the one who has come to do evil will do evil to himself."


## Section 7

# EVIL RETURNS TO THE DOER

The Buddha said, "There was a person who, upon hearing that I observe the Way and practice great humane kindness, intentionally came to berate me. I was silent and did not reply. When he finished abusing me, I asked, If you are courteous to people and they do not accept your courtesy, the courtesy returns to you, does it not?'

"It does,' he replied. I said, Now you are scolding me, but I do not receive it, so the misfortune returns to you and must remain with you. It is as inevitable as an echo that follows a sound, or as a shadow that follows a form. In the end you cannot avoid it. Therefore, be careful not to do evil."

## Section 8

# ABUSING OTHERS DEFILES ONESELF

The Buddha said, "An evil person who harms a sage is like one who raises his head and spits at heaven. Instead of reaching heaven, the spittle falls back on him. It is the same with someone who throws dust against the wind. Instead of going somewhere else, the dust returns to defile his own body. The sage cannot be harmed. Misdeeds will inevitably destroy the doer."

## Section 9

# BY RETURNING TO THE SOURCE, YOU FIND THE WAY

The Buddha said, "Deep learning and a love of the Way make the Way difficult to attain. When you guard your mind and revere the Way, the Way is truly great!"

## Section 10

## JOYFUL CHARITY BRINGS BLESSINGS

The Buddha said, "When you see someone who is practicing giving, aid him joyfully, and you will obtain vast and great blessings."

A Shramana asked, "Is there an end to those blessings?"

The Buddha said, "Consider the flame of a single torch. Though hundreds and thousands of people come to light their own torches from it so that they can cook their food and ward off darkness, the first torch remains the same. Blessings, too, are like this."

## Section 11

## THE INCREASE IN MERIT GAINED BY BESTOWING FOOD

The Buddha said, "Giving food to a hundred bad people is not as good as giving food to a single good person.

Giving food to a thousand good people is not as good as giving food to one person who holds the Five Precepts. Giving food to ten thousand people who hold the Five Precepts is not as good as giving food to a single Srotaapanna. Giving food to a million Srotaapannas is not as good as giving food to a single Sakridagamin. Giving food to ten million Sakridagamins is not as good as giving food to a single Anagamin. Giving food to a hundred million Anagamins is not as good as giving food to a single Arhat. Giving food to one billion Arhats is not as good as giving food to a single Pratyekabuddha. Giving food to ten billion Pratyekabuddhas is not as good as giving food to a Buddha of the three periods of time. Giving food to a hundred billion Buddhas of the three periods of time is not as good as giving food to a single person who is without thoughts, without dwelling, without cultivation, and without accomplishment."

# Section 12

# A LIST OF DIFFICULTIES AND AN EXHORTATION TO CULTIVATE

The Buddha said, "People encounter twenty different kinds of difficulties: It is difficult to give when one is poor. It is difficult to study the Way when one has wealth and status. It is difficult to abandon life and face the certainty of death. It is difficult to encounter the Buddhist sutras. It is difficult to be born at the time of a Buddha. It is difficult to be patient with lust and desire. It is difficult to see fine things and not seek them. It is difficult to be insulted and not become angry. It is difficult to have power and not abuse it. It is difficult to come in contact with things and have no thought of them. It is difficult to be vastly learned and well-read. It is difficult to get rid of pride. It is difficult not to slight those who have not yet studied. It is difficult to practice equanimity of mind. It is difficult not to gossip. It is difficult to meet a Good and Wise Advisor. It is difficult to see one's own nature and study the Way. It is difficult to teach and save people according to their potentials. It is difficult to see a state and not be moved by it. It is difficult to have a good understanding of skill-in-means."

## Section 13

# QUESTIONS ABOUT THE WAY AND PAST LIVES

A Shramana asked the Buddha, "By what causes and conditions can I know my past lives and understand the ultimate Way?" The Buddha said, "By purifying your mind and preserving your resolve, you can understand the ultimate Way. Just as when you polish a mirror, the dust vanishes and brightness remains, so too, if you cut off desire and do not seek, you then can know past lives."

## Section 14

# ASKING ABOUT GOODNESS AND GREATNESS

A Shramana asked the Buddha, "What is goodness? What is the foremost greatness?" The Buddha said, "To practice the Way and uphold the truth is goodness. To unite your will with the Way is greatness."

## Section 15

# ASKING ABOUT STRENGTH AND BRILLIANCE

A Shramana asked the Buddha, "What is the greatest strength? What is the utmost brilliance?"

The Buddha said, "Patience under insult is the greatest strength, because people who are patient do not harbor hatred, and they gradually grow more peaceful and strong. Patient people, since they are not evil, will surely gain the respect of others.

"When the mind's defilements are gone completely, so that it is pure and untainted, that is the utmost brilliance. When there is nothing, from before the formation of the heavens and the earth until now, in any of the ten directions that you do not see, know, or hear; when you have attained omniscience, that may be called brilliance."

## Section 16

# CASTING ASIDE LOVE
# AND ATTAINING THE WAY

The Buddha said, "People who cherish love and desire do not see the Way. Just as when you stir clear water with your hand, those who stand beside it cannot see their reflections, so, too, people who are entangled in love and desire have turbidity in their minds, and therefore they cannot see the Way. You Shramanas should cast aside love and desire. When the stains of love and desire disappear, you will be able to see the Way."

## Section 17

# WHEN LIGHT ARRIVES,
# DARKNESS DEPARTS

The Buddha said, "Those who see the Way are like someone holding a torch who enters a dark room, dispelling the darkness so that only light remains. When you study the Way and see the truth, ignorance vanishes and light remains forever."

## Section 18

# THOUGHTS AND SO FORTH
# ARE BASICALLY EMPTY

The Buddha said, "My Dharma is the mindfulness that is both mindfulness and non-mindfulness. It is the practice that is both practice and non-practice. It is words that are words and non-words, and cultivation that is cultivation and non-cultivation. Those who understand are near to it; those who are confused are far away, indeed. It is not accessible by the path of language. It is not hindered by physical objects. If you are off by a hairsbreadth, you will lose it in an instant."

## Section 19

# CONTEMPLATING BOTH
# THE FALSE AND THE TRUE

The Buddha said, "Contemplate heaven and earth, and be mindful of their impermanence. Contemplate the world, and be mindful of its impermanence. Contem-plate the efficacious, enlightened nature: it is the Bodhi nature. With this awareness, one quickly attains the Way."

## Section 20

# REALIZE THAT THE SELF IS TRULY EMPTY

The Buddha said, "You should be mindful of the four elements within the body. Though each has a name, none of them is the self. Since they are not the self, they are like an illusion."

## Section 21

# FAME DESTROYS LIFE'S ROOTS

The Buddha said, "There are people who follow emotion and desire and seek to be famous. By the time their reputation is established, they are already dead. Those who are greedy for worldly fame and do not study the Way simply waste their effort and wear themselves out. By way of analogy, although burning incense gives off fragrance, when it has burned down, the remaining embers bring the danger of a fire that can burn one up."

## Section 22

# WEALTH AND SEX CAUSE SUFFERING

The Buddha said, "People are unable to renounce wealth and sex. They are just like a child who cannot resist honey on the blade of a knife. Even though the amount is not even enough for a single meal's serving, he will lick it and risk cutting his tongue in the process."

## Section 23

# A FAMILY IS WORSE THAN A PRISON

The Buddha said, "People are bound to their families and homes to such an extent that these are worse than a prison. Eventually one is released from prison, but people never think of leaving their families. Don't they fear the control that emotion, love, and sex have over them? Although they are in a tiger's jaws, their hearts are blissfully oblivious. Because they throw themselves into a swamp and drown, they are known as ordinary people. Pass through the gateway! Get out of the defilement and become an Arhat!"

## Section 24

# SEXUAL DESIRE OBSTRUCTS THE WAY

The Buddha said, "Of all longings and desires, there is none as strong as sex. Sexual desire has no equal. Fortunately, it is one of a kind. If there were something else like it, no one in the entire world would be able to cultivate the Way."

## Section 25

# THE FIRE OF DESIRE BURNS

The Buddha said, "A person with love and desire is like one who carries a torch while walking against the wind: he is certain to burn his hand."

## Section 26

# DEMONS FROM THE HEAVENS TRY TO TEMPT THE BUDDHA

The heaven spirit offered beautiful maidens to the Buddha, hoping to destroy his resolve. The Buddha said, "What have you skin-bags full of filth come here for? Go away, I've got no use for you."

Then the heaven spirit became very respectful and asked about the meaning of the Way. The Buddha explained it for him, and he immediately attained the fruition of Srotaapanna.

## Section 27

# ONE ATTAINS THE WAY AFTER LETTING GO OF ATTACHMENTS

The Buddha said, "A person who follows the Way is like a floating piece of wood that courses along with the current. If it does not touch either shore; if people do not pluck it out; if ghosts and spirits do not intercept it; if it is not trapped in whirlpools; and if it does not rot, I guarantee that the piece of wood will reach the sea. If students of the Way are not deluded by emotion and desire, and if they are not caught up in the many crooked views, but are vigorous in their cultivation of the unconditioned, I guarantee that they will certainly attain the Way."

## Section 28

# DON'T INDULGE THE WILD MIND

The Buddha said, "Be careful not to believe your own mind; your mind is not to be believed. Be careful not to get involved with sex; involvement with sex leads to disaster. After you have attained Arhatship, you can believe your own mind."

## Section 29

# PROPER CONTEMPLATION COUNTERACTS SEXUAL DESIRE

The Buddha said, "Be careful not to look at women, and do not talk with them. If you must speak with them, be properly mindful and think, am a Shramana living in a turbid world. I should be like the lotus flower, which is not stained by the mud.' Think of elderly women as your mothers, of those who are older than you as your elder sisters, of those who are younger as your younger sisters, and of very young girls as your daughters. Bring forth thoughts to rescue them, and put an end to bad thoughts."

## Section 30

# STAY FAR AWAY FROM THE FIRE OF DESIRE

The Buddha said, "People who cultivate the Way are like dry grass: it is essential to keep it away from an oncoming fire. People who cultivate the Way look upon desire as something they must stay far away from."

## Section 31

# WHEN THE MIND IS STILL, DESIRE IS DISPELLED

The Buddha said, "There was once someone who was plagued by ceaseless sexual desire and wished to castrate himself. The Buddha said to him, 'To cut off your sexual organ would not be as good as to cut off your mind. Your mind is like a supervisor: if the supervisor stops, his employees will also quit. If the deviant mind is not stopped, what good does it do to cut off the organ?'"

The Buddha spoke a verse for him:

Desire is born from your intentions.

Intentions are born from thoughts.

When both aspects of the mind are still,

There is neither form nor activity.

The Buddha said, "This verse was spoken by the Buddha Kashyapa."

## Section 32

## EMPTYING OUT THE SELF QUELLS FEAR

The Buddha said, "People worry because of love and desire. That worry then leads to fear. If you transcend love, what worries will there be? What will be left to fear?"

## Section 33

## WISDOM AND CLARITY DEFEAT THE DEMONS

The Buddha said, "People who cultivate the Way are like a soldier who goes into battle alone against ten thousand enemies. He dons his armor and goes out the gate. He may prove to be a coward; he may get halfway to the battlefield and retreat; he may be killed in combat; or he may return victorious.

"Shramanas who study the Way must make their minds resolute and be vigorous, courageous, and valiant. Not fearing what lies ahead, they should defeat the hordes of demons and obtain the fruition of the Way."

## Section 34

# BY STAYING IN THE MIDDLE, ONE ATTAINS THE WAY

One evening a Shramana was reciting the *Sutra of the Teaching Bequeathed by the Buddha Kashyapa*. The sound of his voice was mournful as he reflected remorsefully on his wish to retreat in cultivation. The Buddha asked him, "In the past when you were a householder, what did you do?"

He replied, "I was fond of playing the lute."

The Buddha said, "What happened when the strings were slack?"

He replied, "They didn't sound."

"What happened when they were too tight?"

He replied, "The sounds were cut short."

"What happened when they were tuned

just right between slack and tight?"

He replied, "The sounds car-ried."

The Buddha said, "It is the same with a Shrama-na who studies the Way.

If his mind is harmonious, he can attain the Way. If he is impetuous about the Way, his impetuousness will tire out his body; and if his body is tired, his mind will become afflicted. If his mind becomes afflicted, then he will retreat from his practice.

If he retreats from his practice, his offenses will certainly increase. You need only be pure, peaceful, and happy, and you will not lose the Way."

## Section 35

# WHEN ONE IS PURIFIED OF DEFILE-MENTS, THE BRILLIANCE REMAINS

The Buddha said, "People smelt metal by burning the dross out of it in order to make high quality implements. It is the same with people who study the Way: first they must get rid of the defilements in their minds; then their practice becomes pure."

## Section 36

# THE SEQUENCE THAT LEADS TO SUCCESS

The Buddha said, "It is difficult for one to leave the evil destinies and become a human being.

"Even if one does become a human being, it is still difficult to become a man rather than a woman.

"Even if one does become a man, it is still difficult to have the six sense organs complete and perfect.

"Even if the six sense organs are complete and perfect, it is still difficult for one to be born in a central country.

"Even if one is born in a central country, it is still difficult to be born at a time when there is a Buddha in the world.

"Even if one is born at a time when there is a Buddha in the world, it is still difficult to encounter the Way.

"Even if one does encounter the Way, it is still difficult to bring forth faith.

"Even if one brings forth faith, it is still difficult to resolve one's mind on Bodhi.

"Even if one does resolve one's mind on Bodhi, it is still difficult to be beyond cultivation and attainment."

## Section 37

## STAYING MINDFUL OF MORAL PRECEPTS BRINGS US CLOSE TO THE WAY

The Buddha said, "My disciples may be several thousand miles away from me, but if they remember my moral precepts, they will certainly attain the fruition of the Way. "If those who are by my side do not follow my moral precepts, they may see me constantly, but in the end they will not attain the Way."

## Section 38

## BIRTH LEADS TO DEATH

The Buddha asked a Shramana, "How long is the human life span?" He replied, "A few days." The Buddha said, "You have not yet understood the Way."

He asked another Shramana, "How long is the human life span?" The reply was, "The space of a meal." The Buddha said, "You have not yet understood the Way."

He asked another Shramana, "How long is the human life span?" He replied, "The length of a single breath." The Buddha said, "Excellent. You have understood the Way."

## Section 39

## THE BUDDHA'S INSTRUCTIONS ARE NOT BIASED

The Buddha said, "Students of the Buddha's Way should believe in and accord with everything that the Buddha teaches. When you eat honey, it is sweet on the surface and sweet in the center; it is the same with my sutras."

## Section 40

## THE WAY IS PRACTICED IN THE MIND

The Buddha said, "A Shramana who practices the Way should not be like an ox turning a millstone. Such a one walks the Way with his body, but his mind is not on the Way. If the mind is concentrated on the Way, what further need is there to practice?"

## Section 41

# A STRAIGHT MIND GETS RID OF DESIRE

The Buddha said, "One who practices the Way is like an ox pulling a heavy load through deep mud. The ox is so extremely exhausted that it dares not glance to the left or right. Only when it gets out of the mud can it rest. The Shramana should regard emotion and desire as being worse than deep mud; and with an undeviating mind, he should be mindful of the Way. Then he can avoid suffering."

## Section 42

# UNDERSTANDING THAT THE WORLD IS ILLUSORY

The Buddha said, "I look upon royalty and high positions as upon the dust that floats through a crack. I look upon treasures of gold and jade as upon broken tiles. I look upon fine silk clothing as upon cheap cotton. I look upon a great thousand-world universe as upon a small nut kernel. I look upon the waters of the Anavatapta Lake as upon oil used to anoint the feet."

**Namo Shakyamunaye Buddhaya.**
(3 times) (ooo)

***

# 48. THE KARMA DISCOURSE

Transcribed in English by Jason Chau

This Sutra has changed the lives of many who have read it, for it explains the direct results of causes. It is also called the Golden Precepts by Lord Buddha and is reproduced here in its entirety:

"Once upon a gathering attended by 1,250 followers, the venerable Ananda, after circling thrice with folded hands around the Buddha and bowing with respect asked: "In the present dark age where the majority of our people are indulgent in unrighteousness, disrespectful to the Lord's teaching, undutiful to their parents, immoral, miserable and sordid, among them some are deaf, some blind, some mute, some idiotic, some handicapped in other aspects, and most people inured to killing, how could we understand the cryptic and fundamental principle or causes that have brought about this reality and what consequences each individual is to suffer eventually for his deeds. My Lord, would you kindly explain these to us?'.

The World-honoured One then answered, "Listen carefully, I will now expound the Law of Karma. Because of Karmic effects inherited from previous lives, some people are poor, some rich, some happy and some miserable. These are four rules inseparable in obtaining happiness and prosperity for your next life. They are: to be dutiful to parents; to be respectful to Buddhas, to Buddha's teaching, and to Buddhist monks; to abstain from killing and setting free sentient beings; and to abstain from eating meat and be charitable." Then the Buddha proceeded on the Karmic Sutra:

"Destiny is aggregate karmic effects from the past. To believe in and practice this Sutra will bring you eternal prosperity and happiness.

**Learn the Law of Karma expounded as follows:**

'To be able to hold office in the Government is a reward for your building Buddha's statues in previous lives. For building Buddha's statues is likened to molding yourself, and to protect the Tathagata is protecting yourself. To be a public officer cannot be taken for granted, for without practicing Buddhism it will not befall you. Having helped in the construction of bridges and roads in your past life is conducive to your present enjoyment of various transportation facilities which prevent you from getting foot-worn.

To donate clothing to monks will ensure you to be well provided with clothing in future or in your next life.

To be free from want in food is the result of your providing food to the poor in your previous life.

To be miserly and unwilling to help the needy gives rise to future starvation and clothlessness.

To have ample housing is a reward for

donating food to monastries in your past life.

To build temples and public shelters will give you future prosperity and happiness.

To be pretty and handsome is the reward for your respecting and offering flowers to Buddha's altar in the past.

To abstain from eating meat and to pray constantly to Buddha wil assure you to be born a very intelligent child in your next incarnation.

To have a good wife and son is reward for your disseminating Buddha's teaching in your past life.

Furnishing Buddhist temples with hangings and tapestries will enable you to have a good marriage in your next rebirth.

To have good parents is a reward for your respecting and helping those who were lonely and desolate in your past life.

Being a bird hunter in your previous life has resulted in your being an orphan now.

To have plenty of children is attributable to your setting free birds in your previous life.

To have destroyed flowers habitually in your previous life has caused you to be heirless now.

Your longevity is due to your setting free sentient beings in your past life.

Being short-lived is the result of your committing too many killings in your previous life.

To steal the wife of another man will cause you to have no spouse in your next reincarnation.

To be a widow now is due to your disrespecting your husband in your previous life.

Being ungrateful in your previous life has caused you to be a serf at present.

To covet another man's wife will cause you to have no spouse in your next reincarnation.

To distort truths habitually will cause you to suffer blindness in your next life.

To have wry mouth is due to your intentionally blowing out candles before Buddha's altar in your past life.

To vituperate (abuse) your parents will

cause you to be reborn a deaf mute in your next incarnation.

Being a hunchback is punishment for jeering at the Buddha's followers in your previous life.

To have committed evil with your hands in your past life is the cause for you having disabled hands now.

Your being lame is imputable to your being a robber in your previous life.

To be reborn a horse or an ox is the result of your denying your debts in your previous life.

To be reborn a pig or a dog is the punishment for your deceiving and hurting others in your previous life.

Offering flesh to monks in your past life has given rise to your constant illness now.

To be healthy is a reward for your offering drugs and medications to save the sick and wounded in your past life.

Relentlessly perpetrating evil in your previous life is the cause for your present imprisonment.

Plugging snake-pit and mouse holds habitually will cause you to starve to death in your next incarnation.

To intentionally poison a river or water-source will cause you to die of poison in your next life.

Being forlorn and friendless is the punishment for being unfaithful and deceitful to others in your past life.

Disrespecting the Buddha's teaching will bring you constant starvation in your next rebirth.

To spew blood is the punishment for eating meat while praying to Buddha.

To have attended Buddhist instruction with levity in your previous life is the cause for your present deafness.

To be afflicted with ulcers is the punishment for offering flesh before the Buddha's altar in your past life.

To have bad bodily odour is the punishment for selling incense with dishonesty in your previous life.

To hunt animals with rope and net will predestine your death by hanging in your next incarnation.

Being unduly envious and jealous in your past life is the cause for being so lonely or being refect of spouse at present.

To be struck by lightning or burn by fire will be the punishment for dishonest trade dealings.

Being wounded by beasts or snakes tells you that those creatures were your enemies in your previous life.

Whatever you do will come back to you, so accept whatever justice and retribution that befalls you.

Be not mistaken that karma is fallicious. You will live to bear its consequences, either in this lifetime or in your future life.

Should you doubt the virtue of practising Buddhism, could you not see the happiness of Buddha's followers?

Past karma determine your present destiny. Present karmas are to mold your next life.

Whoever slanders this Sutra will not be reborn again a human being.

Whoever accepts this Sutra will witness the truth.

Whoever writes this Sutra will prosper in successful lives.

Whoever carries this Sutra will be free from mishaps.

Whoever preaches this Sutra will become a very intelligent person in successive lives.

Whoever recites this Sutra will be well-respected by people in his next incarnation.

Whoever distributes this Sutra free to all will become a leader to humanity in his next life.

If karma did not produce effect, what prompted Wu-Lin, a dutiful son, to rescue his mother under grave danger?

Whoever is faithful to this Sutra will not fail to witness the eternal paradise.

The Law of Karma works forever, and the fruit of good deed will come in due course."

Having spoken the above Sutra to Ananda and the followers, the World-honoured One added "There are innumerable examples of Karmic Law, but I have only mentioned in generalisation."

Then Ananda said, "Until the end of the present Dark Age, most human beings would have through successive lives accumulated countless misdeeds because of their ignorance of the karmic consequences, but thanks to our Lord and the Sutra he has so kindly given to us, whoever writes and reads, prints and distributes this Sutra, upon praying to the Buddha, will be blessed with eternal happiness and be admitted to see Amitabha Buddha, Avalokiteshvara Bodhisattva and all the other Buddhas in the heavenly paradise."

After Ananda spoke, all Buddha's disciples and followers felt ecstatic and enlightened and, after bowing respectfully and vowing to abide by his Sutra, took their journey home.

**Namo Shakyamunaye Buddhaya.**
(3 times) (ooo)

***

# 49. THE INNUMERABLE MEANINGS
## (The Threefoldlotus Sutra)

Thus have i heard. Once the Buddha was staying at the City of Royal Palaces on Mount Grdhrakuta with a great assemblage of great bhlkshus, in all twelve thousand. The Buddha taught that,

The trainer of gods and men, elephants and horses,
His moral breeze and virtuous fragrance
Deeply permeate all.

Serene is his wisdom, calm his emotion,
And stable his prudence.

His thought is settled, his consciousness is extinct,
And thus his mind is quiet.

Long since, he removed false thoughts
And conquered all the laws of existence.

His body is neither existing nor nonexisting;

Without cause or condition,

Without self or others;

Neither square nor round,

Neither short nor long;

Without appearance or disappearance,
Without birth or death;
Neither created nor emanating,
Neither made nor produced;
Neither sitting nor lying,
Neither walking nor stopping;
Neither moving nor rolling,
Neither calm nor quiet;
Without advance or retreat,
Without safety or danger;
Without right or wrong,
Without merit or demerit;
Neither that nor this,
Neither going nor coming;
Neither blue nor yellow,
Neither red nor white;
Neither crimson nor purple,
Without a variety of color.
Born of commandments, meditation,
Wisdom, emancipation, and knowledge;
Merit of contemplation, the six divine faculties,

And the practice of the way;

Sprung of benevolence and compassion,

The ten powers, and fearlessness;

He has come in response

To good karmas of living beings.

He reveals his body,

Ten feet six inches in height,

Glittering with purple gold,

Well proportioned, brilliant,

And highly bright.

The mark of hair curls as the moon,

In the nape of the neck there is a light as of the sun.

The curling hair is deep blue,

On the head there is a protuberance.

The pure eyes, like a stainless mirror,

Blink up and down.

The eyebrows trail in dark blue,

The mouth and cheeks are well formed.

The lips and tongue appear pleasantly red,

Like a scarlet flower.

The white teeth, forty in number,

Appear as snowy agate.
Broad the forehead, high-bridged the nose,
And majestic the face.
The chest, with a swastika mark,
Is like a lion's breast.
The hands and feet ate flexible,
With the mark of a thousand spokes.
The sides and palms are well rounded,
And show in fine lines.
The arms are elongated,
And the fingers are straight and slender.
The skin is delicate and smooth,
And the hair curls to the right.
The ankles and knees are well defined,
And the male organ is hidden
Like that of a horse.
The fine muscles, the collarbone,
And the thigh bones are slim
Like those of a deer.
The chest and back are shining,
Pure and without blemish,

Untainted by any muddy water,

Unspotted by any speck of dust.

There are thirty-two such signs,

The eighty kinds of excellence are visible,

And truly, there is nothing

Of form or nonform.

All visible forms are transcended;

His body is formless and yet has form.

This is also true

Of the form of the body of all living beings.
5*

Living beings adore him joyfully,

Devote their minds to him,

And pay their respects wholeheartedly.

By cutting off arrogance and egotism,

He has accomplished such a wonderful body.

Now we, the assemblage of eighty thousand,

Making obeisance all together,

Submit ourselves to the saint of nonattachment,

The trainer of elephants and horses,

Detached from the state of thinking,

Mind, thought, and perception.

We make obeisance,

And submit ourselves to the Law-body,

To all commands, meditation, wisdom,

Emancipation, and knowledge.

We make obeisance,

And submit ourselves to the wonderful character.

We make obeisance,

And submit ourselves to the unthinkable.

The sacred voice sounds eight ways, 6*

As the thunder sounds.

It is sweet, pure, and greatly profound.

He preaches the Four Noble Truths,

The Six Paramitas, and the Twelve Causes,

According to the working of the minds of living beings.

One never hears without opening one's mind

And breaking the bonds of the infinite chain of life and death.

One never hears without reaching, srotaapanna,

Sakrdagamin, anagamin, and arhat;

Reaching the state of pratyekabuddha,

Of nonfault and noncondition;

Reaching the state of bodhisattva

Of nonlife and nondeath;

Of obtaining the infinite dharani

And-the unhindered power of discourse,

With which one recites profound and wonderful verses,

Plays and bathes in the pure pond of the Law,

Or displays supernatural motion

By jumping and flying up,

Or freely goes in or out of water and fire.

The aspect of the Tathagata's Law-wheel is like this.

It is pure, boundless, and unthinkable.

Making obeisance all together,

We Submit ourselves to him

When he rolls the Law-wheel.

We make obeisance,

And submit ourselves to the sacred voice.

We make obeisance,

And submit Ourselves to the Causes, Truths, and Paramitas.

For infinite past kalpas,

The World-honored One has practiced

All manner of virtues with effort

To bring benefits to us human beings,

Heavenly beings, and dragon kings,

Universally to all living beings.

He abandoned all things hard to abandon,

His treasures, wife, and child,

His country and his palace.

Unsparing of his person as of his possessions,

He gave all, his head, eyes, and brain,

To people as alms.

Keeping the buddhas' precepts of purity,

He never did any harm,

Even at the cost of his life.

He never became angry,

Even though beaten with sword and staff,

Or though cursed and abused.

He never became tired,

In spite of long exertion.

He kept his mind at peace day and night,

And was always in meditation.

Learning all the law-ways,

With his deep wisdom

He has seen into the capacity of living beings.

As a result, obtaining free power,

He has become the Law-king,

Who is free in the Law.

Making obeisance again all together,

We submit ourselves to the one,

Who has completed all hard things.

Namo Amitabha Buddhaya. (3 times) (ooo)

***

# 50. MEDITATING FOUR IMMEASURABLES OF LOVING-KINDNESS.

(Compassion, Sympathetic Joy and Equanimity. 13. Digha Nikaya)

(Translated by Bhikkhu Sujato)

## 1. LOVING-KINDNESS (METTA)

Here, monks, a disciple dwells pervading one direction with his heart filled with loving-kindness, likewise the second, the third, and the fourth direction; so above, below and around; he dwells pervading the entire world everywhere and equally with his heart filled with loving-kindness, abundant, grown great, measureless, free from enmity and free from distress.

## 2. COMPASSION (KARUNA)

Here, monks, a disciple dwells pervading one direction with his heart filled with compassion, likewise the second, the third and the fourth direction; so above, below and around; he dwells pervading the entire world everywhere and equally with his heart filled with compassion, abundant, grown great, measureless, free from enmity and free from distress.

## 3. SYMPATHETIC JOY (MUDITA)

Here, monks, a disciple dwells pervading one direction with his heart filled with sympathetic joy, likewise the second, the third and the fourth direction; so above, below and around; he dwells pervading the entire world everywhere and equally with his heart filled with sympathetic joy, abundant, grown great, measureless, free from enmity and free from distress.

## 4. EQUANIMITY (UPEKKHA)

Here, monks, a disciple dwells pervading one direction with his heart filled with equanimity, likewise the second, the third and the fourth direction; so above, below and around; he dwells pervading the entire world everywhere and equally with his heart filled with equanimity, abundant, grown great, measureless, free from enmity and free from distress.

## CONTEMPLATIONS ON THE FOUR SUBLIME STATES

### 1. LOVE (METTA)

*Love*, without desire to possess, knowing well that in the ultimate sense there is no possession and no possessor: this is the highest *love*.

*Love*, without speaking and thinking of "I," knowing well that this so-called "I" is a mere delusion.

*Love*, without selecting and excluding, knowing well that to do so means to create love's own contrasts: dislike, aversion and hatred.

*Love*, embracing all beings: small and great, far and near, be it on earth, in the water or in the air.

*Love*, embracing impartially all sentient beings, and not only those who are useful, pleasing or amusing to us.

*Love*, embracing all beings, be they noble-minded or low-minded, good or evil. The noble and the good are embraced because *Love* is flowing to them spontaneously. The low-minded and evil-minded are included because they are those who are most in need of *Love*. In many of them the seed of goodness may have died merely because warmth was lacking for its growth, because it perished from cold in a loveless world.

*Love*, embracing all beings, knowing well that we all are fellow wayfarers through this round of existence -- that we all are overcome by the same law of suffering.

*Love*, but not the sensuous fire that burns, scorches and tortures, that inflicts more wounds than it cures -- flaring up now, at the next moment being extinguished, leaving behind more coldness and loneliness than was felt before.

Rather, *Love* that lies like a soft but firm hand on the ailing beings, ever unchanged in its sympathy, without wavering, unconcerned with any response it meets. *Love* that is comforting coolness to those who burn with the fire of suffering and passion; that is life-giving warmth to those abandoned in the cold desert of loneliness, to those who are shivering in the frost of a loveless world; to those whose hearts have become as if empty and dry by the repeated calls for help, by deepest despair.

*Love*, that is a sublime nobility of heart and intellect which knows, understands and is ready to help.

*Love*, that *is* strength and *gives* strength: this is the highest *Love*.

*Love*, which by the Enlightened One was named "the liberation of the heart," "the most sublime beauty": this is the highest *Love*.

And what is the highest manifestation of *Love*?

To show to the world the path leading to the end of suffering, the path pointed out, trodden, and realized to perfection by Him, the Exalted One, the Buddha.

## 2. COMPASSION (KARUNA)

The world suffers. But most men have their eyes and ears closed. They do not see the unbroken stream of tears flowing through life; they do not hear the cry of distress continually pervading the world. Their own little grief or joy bars their sight, deafens their ears. Bound by selfishness, their hearts turn stiff and narrow. Being stiff and narrow, how should they be able to strive for any higher goal, to realize that only release from selfish craving will effect their own freedom from suffering?

It is *compassion* that removes the heavy bar, opens the door to freedom, makes the narrow heart as wide as the world. *Compassion* takes away from the heart the inert weight, the paralyzing heaviness; it gives wings to those who cling to the lowlands of self.

Through *compassion* the fact of suffering remains vividly present to our mind, even at times when we personally are free from it. It gives us the rich experience of suffering, thus strengthening us to meet it prepared, when it does befall us.

*Compassion* reconciles us to our own destiny by showing us the life of others, often much harder than ours.

Behold the endless caravan of beings, men and beasts, burdened with sorrow and pain! The burden of every one of them, we also have carried in bygone times during the unfathomable sequence of repeated births. Behold this, and open your heart to *compassion*!

And this misery may well be our own destiny again! He who is without *compassion* now, will one day cry for it. If sympathy with others is lacking, it will have to be acquired through one's own long and painful experience. This is the great law of life. Knowing this, keep guard over yourself!

Beings, sunk in ignorance, lost in delusion, hasten from one state of suffering to another, not knowing the real cause, not knowing the escape from it. This insight into the general law of suffering is the real foundation of our *compassion*, not any isolated fact of suffering.

Hence our *compassion* will also include those who at the moment may be happy, but act with an evil and deluded mind. In their present deeds we shall foresee their future state of distress, and *compassion* will arise.

The *compassion* of the wise man does not render him a victim of suffering. His thoughts, words and deeds are full of pity. But his heart does not waver; unchanged it remains, serene and calm. How else should he be able to help?

May such *compassion* arise in our hearts!

*Compassion* that is sublime nobility of heart and intellect which knows, understands and is ready to help.

*Compassion* that *is* strength and *gives* strength: this is highest *compassion*.

And what is the highest manifestation of *compassion*?

To show to the world the path leading to the end of suffering, the path pointed out, trodden and realized to perfection by Him, the Exalted One, the Buddha.


## 3. SYMPATHETIC JOY (MUDITA)

Not only to compassion, but also to *joy with others* open your heart!

Small, indeed, is the share of happiness and joy allotted to beings! Whenever a little happiness comes to them, then you may rejoice that at least one ray of joy has pierced through the darkness of their lives, and dispelled the gray and gloomy mist that enwraps their hearts.

Your life will gain in joy by sharing the happiness of others as if it were yours. Did you never observe how in moments of happiness men's features change and become bright with joy? Did you never notice how joy rouses men to noble aspirations and deeds, exceeding their normal capacity? Did not such experience fill your own heart with joyful bliss? It is in your power to increase such experience of *symapthetic joy*, by producing happiness in others, by bringing them joy and solace.

Let us teach real joy to men! Many have unlearned it. Life, though full of woe, holds also sources of happiness and joy, unknown to most. Let us teach people to seek and to find real joy within themselves and to rejoice with the joy of others! Let us teach them to unfold their joy to ever sublimer heights!

Noble and sublime joy is not foreign to the Teaching of the Enlightened One. Wrongly the Buddha's Teaching is sometimes considered to be a doctrine diffusing melancholy. Far from it: the Dhamma leads step by step to an ever purer and loftier happiness.

Noble and sublime joy is a helper on the path to the extinction of suffering. Not he who is depressed by grief, but one possessed of joy finds that serene calmness leading to a contemplative state of mind. And only a mind serene and collected is able to gain the liberating wisdom.

The more sublime and noble the joy of others is, the more justified will be our own *symapthetic joy*. A cause for our *joy with others* is their noble life securing them happiness here and in lives hereafter. A still nobler cause for our *joy with others* is their faith in the Dhamma, their understanding of the Dhamma, their following the Dhamma. Let us give them the *help* of the Dhamma! Let us strive to become more and more able ourselves to render such help!

*Symapthetic joy* means a sublime nobility of heart and intellect which knows, understands and is ready to help.

*Symapthetic joy* that *is* strength and *gives* strength: this is the highest joy.

And what is the highest manifestation of *symapthetic joy*?

To show to the world the path leading to the end of suffering, the path pointed out, trodden, and realized to perfection by Him, the Exalted One, the Buddha.

# 4. EQUANIMITY (UPEKKHA)

*Equanimity* is a perfect, unshakable balance of mind, rooted in insight.

Looking at the world around us, and looking into our own heart, we see clearly how difficult it is to attain and maintain balance of mind.

Looking into life we notice how it continually moves between contrasts: rise and fall, success and failure, loss and gain, honor and blame. We feel how our heart responds to all this with happiness and sorrow, delight and despair, disappointment and satisfaction, hope and fear. These waves of emotion carry us up and fling us down; and no sooner do we find rest, than we are in the power of a new wave again. How can we expect to get a footing on the crest of the waves? How can we erect the building of our lives in the midst of this ever restless ocean of existence, if not on the Island of Equanimity.

A world where that little share of happiness allotted to beings is mostly secured after many disappointments, failures and defeats;

a world where only the courage to start anew, again and again, promises success;

a world where scanty joy grows amidst sickness, separation and death;

a world where beings who were a short while ago connected with us by *symapthetic joy*, are at the next moment in want of our *compassion* - such a world needs *equanimity*.

But the kind of equanimity required has to be based on vigilant presence of mind, not on indifferent dullness. It has to be the result of hard, deliberate training, not the casual outcome of a passing mood. But equanimity would not deserve its name if it had to be produced by exertion again and again. In such a case it would surely be weakened and finally defeated by the vicissitudes of life. True equanimity, however, should be able to meet all these severe tests and to regenerate its strength from sources within. It will possess this power of resistance and self-renewal only if it is rooted in insight.

Equanimity is the crown and culmination of the four sublime states. But this should not be understood to mean that equanimity is the negation of love, compassion and sympathetic joy, or that it leaves them behind as inferior. Far from that, equanimity includes and pervades them fully, just as they fully pervade perfect equanimity.

**Namo Shakyamunaye Buddhaya.**
(3 times) (ooo)

***

# 51. THE LARGER SUKHAVATIVYUHA

(The Sutra on the Buddha of Eternal Life)

Translated by The Sutra Translation Committee of United Canada

**Om.**

**Adoration to the Three Treasures!**

**Om.**

**Adoration to all the glorious Buddhas and Bodhisattvas!**

**Adoration to all Buddhas, Bodhisattvas, Aryas, Sravakas, and Pratyekabuddhas, past, present, and to come, who dwell in the unlimited and endless world systems**

of the ten quarters!

Adoration to Amitabha!

Adoration to him whose soul is endowed with incomprehensible virtues!

Adoration to Amitabha, to the Jina, to thee, O Sage!

I go to Sukhavati through thy compassion also;

To Sukhavati, with its groves, resplendent with gold,

The delightful, adorned with the sons of Sugata,--

I go to it, which is full of many jewels and treasures;

And the refuge of thee, the famous and wise.

Thus it was heard by me. At one time the Bhagavat dwelt in Rajagriha, on the mountain Gridhrakuta, with a large assembly of Bhikkhus, with thirty-two thousands of Bhikkhus, all arhats, Bodhisattva Ajita, with gods, men, spirits, mighty birds, and fairies.

Then at that time, the Bhagavat recited these verses:

1. 'As there are Buddha countries equal to the sand of the river Ganges in the eastern quarter, whence all the Bodhisattvas come to worship the Buddha, the lord Amitayu;

2. 'And they having taken many bunches of flowers of different colors, sweetly-scented and delightful, shower them down on the best leader of men, on Amitayu, worshipped by gods and men;

3. 'In the same manner there are as many Buddha countries in the southern, western, and northern quarters, whence they come with the Bodhisattvas to worship the Buddha, the lord Amitayus.

4. 'And they having taken many handfulls of scents of different colors, sweetly scented and delightful, shower them down on the best leader of men, on Amitayus, worshipped by gods and men.

5. 'These many Bodhisattvas having worshipped and revered the feet of Amitaprabha, and having walked round him respectfully, speak thus: "Oh, the country of Buddha shines wonderfully!"

6. 'And they cover him again with handfulls of flowers, with thoughts jubilant, with incomparable joy, and proclaim their wish before that lord: "May our country also be such as this."

7. 'And what was thrown there as handfuls of flowers arose in the form of an umbrella extending over a hundred yojanas, and the beautiful country shines and is well adorned, and flowers cover the whole body of Buddha.

8. 'These Bodhisattvas having thus honored him, how do they act? Delighted they pronounce this speech: "Gains by those people are well gained, by whom the name of the best man has been heard.

9. "By us also all the gain has been well gained, because we have come to this Buddha country. See this dream-like country, how beautiful it is, which was made by the teacher during a hundred thousand kalpas.

10. "Look, the Buddha possessed of a mass of the best virtues shines, surrounded by Bodhisattvas. Endless is his splendor, and endless the light,

and endless the life, and endless the assembly."

11.   'And the lord Amitayus makes a smile of thirty-six nayutas of kotis of rays, which rays having issued from the circle of his mouth light up the thousand kotis of Buddha countries.

12.   'And all these rays having returned there again settle on the head of the lord; gods and men perceive the delight, because they have seen there this light of him.

13.   'There rises the Buddha-son, glorious, he indeed the mighty Avalokitesvara, and says: "What is the reason there, O Bhagavat, what is the cause, that thou smilest, O lord of the world ?

14.   "Explain this, for thou knowest the sense, and art full of kind compassion, the deliverer of many living beings. All beings will be filled with joyful thoughts, when they have thus heard this excellent and delightful speech.

15.   "And the Bodhisattvas who have come from many worlds to Sukhavati in order to see the Buddha, having heard

it and having perceived the great joy, will quickly inspect this country.

16. "And beings, come to this noble country, (quickly) obtain miraculous power, divine eye and divine ear, they remember their former births, and know the highest wisdom."

17. 'Then Buddha Amitayus preaches: "This prayer was mine formerly, so that beings having in any way whatever heard my name should for ever go to my country.

18. "And this my excellent prayer has been fulfilled, and beings having quickly come here from many worlds into my presence, never return from here, not even for one birth."

19. 'If a Bodhisattva wishes here that his country should be such as this, and that he also should deliver many beings, through his name, through his preaching, and through his sight.

20. 'Let him quickly and with speed go to the world Sukhavati, and having gone near Amitaprabha, let him worship a thousand kotis of Buddhas.

21.  'Having worshipped many kotis of Buddhas, and having gone to many countries by means of their miraculous power, and having performed adoration in the presence of the Sugatas, they will go to Sukhavati with devotion.

At that time this universe, the three millions of worlds, trembled in six ways. And various miracles were seen. On earth everything was perfect, and human and divine instruments were played, and the shout of joy was heard as far as the world of the Akanishthas.

Thus spoke the Bhagavat enraptured, and the noble-minded Bodhisattva Ajita, and the blessed Ananda, the whole Assembly, and the world, with gods, men, spirits, mighty birds, and fairies, applauded the speech of the Bhagavat. The praise of the beauty of the excellences of Sukhavati, the country of the blessed Amitabha, the Tathagata, the entry of the Bodhisattva on the stage of never returning, the story of Amitabha, the Mahayanasutra of the Description of Sukhavati is finished.

Namo Amitabha Buddhaya. (3 times) (ooo)

# 52. BEGINNING ANEW

## (Thích Nhất Hạnh)

With great respect, we turn towards the conqueror of afflictions, offering heartfelt words of repentance.

We have lived in forgetfulness for a long time.

As we have not had the opportunity to encounter the Dharma,

our habit-energies have led us into suffering.

We have made many mistakes out of unskillfulness.

We have been blinded by our wrong perceptions

for a very long time.

Our heart's garden is sown with attachment, hatred, and pride. In us are seeds of killing, stealing, sexual misconduct, and lies. Our everyday deeds and words do damage.

All these wrong actions are obstacles to our peace and joy. Let us begin anew. (o)

We see that we have been thoughtless,

straying from the path of mindfulness.

We have stored up afflictions and ignorance,

which have brought about so much aversion and sorrow.

There are times we have been weary of life

because we are so full of anxiety. Because we do not understand others, we are angry and resentful. (o)


First we try to reason with each other, then we blame. Every day the suffering increases, making the rift greater.

There are days when we are unwilling to speak to each other,

unwilling to look each other in the face.

And we create internal formations, which last for a long time. Now we turn to the Three Jewels.

Sincerely recognizing our errors, we bow our heads. (o)


We know so well that in our consciousness

are buried all the wholesome seeds -

seeds of love and understanding and seeds of peace and joy.

But because we do not know how to water them,

the wholesome seeds do not sprout fresh and green.

We continue to allow sorrow to overwhelm us until there is no light in our lives.

When we chase after a distant happiness, life becomes but a shadow of the reality. Our mind is occupied by the past,

or worrying about this or that in the future.

We cannot let go of our anger,

and we consider of no value the precious gifts of life which are already in our hands,

thereby trampling on real happiness.

As month follows month, we are sunk in sorrow. So now in the precious presence of the Buddha, fragrant with sandalwood incense, we recognize our errors and begin anew. (o)


With all our heart we go for refuge,

turning to the Buddhas in the Ten Directions

and all the Bodhisattvas, noble disciples, and self-achieved Buddhas.

Very sincerely we recognize our errors

and the mistakes of our wrong judgments.

Please bring the balm of clear water

to pour on the roots of our afflictions. Please bring the raft of the true teachings to carry us over the ocean of sorrows.

We vow to live an awakened life, to practice smiling and conscious breathing, and to study the teachings, authentically transmitted. Diligently, we shall live in mindfulness. (o)


We come back to live in the wonderful present, to plant our heart's garden with good seeds,

and to make strong foundations of understanding and love. We vow to train ourselves in mindfulness and concentration, practicing to look and understand deeply

to be able to see the nature of all that is,

and so to be free of the bonds of birth and death.

We learn to speak lovingly, to be affectionate,

to care for others whether it is early morn or late afternoon, to bring the roots of joy to many places,

helping people to abandon sorrow, to respond with deep gratitude

to the kindness of parents, teachers, and friends. With deep faith we light up the incense of our heart. We ask the Lord of Compassion to be our protector on the wonderful path of practice.

We vow to practice diligently, cultivating the fruits of this path. (o)

**Namo Shakyamunaye Buddhaya.**
(3 times) (ooo)

***

# 53. TAKING REFUGE IN ONESELF

(Samyukta Agama 639,
Taisho Revised Tripitaka 99)

I heard these words of the Buddha one time when the Lord was staying in the Mango Grove in the cool shade of the mango trees along the bank of a river in the land of Magadha. The elders Shariputra and Maudgalyayana had recently passed away. It was the full-moon day of the Uposatha Ceremony and the precepts were recited.

The Buddha spread out his sitting mat and sat facing the community. After looking out at those gathered, he said, "As I look at our community, I see a large space left by the Venerables Shariputra and Maudgalyayana. In our Sangha, these venerables were the monks who were the most eloquent in giving Dharma talks, encouraging and instructing all the other monks, nuns, and laypeople.

"O monks, people seek two kinds of riches - material riches and the riches of the Dharma. In their search for material riches, they can go to world- ly people. In their search for the riches of the Dharma, they could always go to the Venerables Shariputra and Maudgalyayana. The Tathagata is someone who is not searching for anything, whether it is material or the Dharma.

"O monks, do not be sad or anxious because Shariputra and Maudga- lyayana have passed into nirvana. On large trees, filled with leaves, sumptu- ous fruits, and flowers, the largest branches always die or are broken first. On jeweled mountains, don't the highest peaks always erode before the smaller ones? In the Sangha of the Tathagata, the Venerables Shariputra and Maud- galyayana were the greatest students. So it is natural that these venerables would enter nirvana first. Do not give rise to feelings of sorrow or anguish.

"All phenomena that are born, exist, and are subject to the influence of other phenomena, in other words, all phenomena that are composite, must abide by the law of impermanence and eventually cease to exist. They cannot exist eternally, without someday being destroyed. Everything we cherish and hold dear today, we will have to let go of and be separated from in the future. In not too long a time, I will also pass away. Therefore, I urge you to practice being an island unto yourself, knowing how to take refuge in yourself, and not taking refuge in anyone or anything else.

"Practice taking refuge in the island of the Dharma. Know how to take refuge in the Dharma, and do not take refuge in any other island or per- son. Meditate on the body in the body, nourishing Right Understanding and mindfulness to master and transform your cravings and anxieties. Observe the elements outside the body in the elements outside the body, nourishing Right Understanding and mindfulness to master and transform your cravings and anxieties. That is the way to take refuge in the island of self, to return to yourself in order to take refuge in the Dharma, and not to take refuge in any other island or thing."

When the bhikshus heard the Buddha offer this teaching, they were all very happy to put it into practice.

Namo Shakyamunaye Buddhaya.
(3 times) (ooo)

# 54. JOYFULLY SHARING THE MERIT
## Thích Nhất Hạnh

Blessed Ones who dwell in the world, grant to us compassion.

In this and countless lives before, from beginningless time,

our mistakes have caused much suffering to ourselves and others.

We have done wrong, encouraged others to do wrong,

and given our consent to acts of killing, stealing, deceiving,

sexual misconduct, and other harmful actions

among the Ten Unwholesome Deeds.

Whether our faults are known to others or whether they are hidden, they have brought us to the realms of hell, hungry ghosts, and animals, causing us to be born in places filled with pain and suffering.

We have not yet had the chance to realize our full potential. Today we are determined, with one-pointed concentration, to repent the obstacles of our past unwholesome

**actions**. (o)

**Blessed Ones, be our witness and look upon us with compassion.**

**We surrender before you and make this aspiration:**

**If at all within this very life and countless lives before,**

**we have given, even if only a handful of food or simple garment; if we have ever spoken kindly, even if only a few words;**

**if we have ever looked with eyes of compassion, even if only for a moment;**

**if we have ever comforted or consoled, even if only once or twice;**

**if we have ever listened carefully to wonderful teachings,**

**even if only to one talk;**

**if we have ever offered a meal to monks and nuns, even if only once;**

**if we have ever saved a life, even if only that of an ant or a worm;**

**if we have ever recited a sutra, even if only one or two lines;**

if we have ever been a monk or a nun, even if only for one life; if we have ever supported others on the path of practice, even if only two or three people;

if we have ever observed the mindfulness trainings, even if imperfectly;

all of this merit has slowly formed wholesome seeds within us. Today we gather them together like a fragrant flower garland and, with great respect, we offer it to all Awakened Ones -

a contribution to the fruit of the highest path. (o)

Opening our hearts wide to the Perfect Highest Awakening,

we are resolved to attain Great Understanding.

We will realize compassion and embody deep love. We will practice diligently, transforming our suffering and the suffering of all other species.

Please transfer the merits of body, speech, and mind

to the happiness of people and all other beings.

Apart from bodhicitta and apart from the thirst

for great understanding and the embodiment of love,

there is no other desire within us.

All Buddhas in the Three Times and the Ten Directions

have offered their merit as we are doing today. Repenting all our faults, we joyfully contribute to the immeasurable ocean of merit and the towering peaks of the Highest Understanding.

The Buddhas and the Ancestral Teachers

are the light which shows us the way.

In this solemn moment, with all my life's force,

I come back to myself and bow deeply with respect. (ooo)

**Namo Shakyamunaye Buddhaya.**
(3 times) (ooo)

***

# III. CONCLUSION

## 1. THE INSIGHT THAT BRINGS US TO THE OTHER SHORE

The Heart of Prajnaparamita
(Perfect Wisdom)

Avalokiteshvara while practicing deeply with the Insight that Brings Us to the Other Shore, suddenly discovered that all of the five Skandhas are equally empty, and with this realization he overcame all Ill-being (suffering). (o)

Listen Sariputra, this Body itself is Emptiness and Emptiness itself is this Body.

This Body is not other than Emptiness and Emptiness is not other than this Body.

The same is true of Feelings, Perceptions, Mental Formations, and Consciousness. (o)

Listen Sariputra, all phenomena bear the mark of Emptiness; their true nature is the nature of neither Birth nor Death, neither Being nor Non-being, neither

Defilement nor Purity, neither Increasing nor Decreasing. (o)

That is why in Emptiness, Body, Feelings, Perceptions, Mental Formations and Consciousness are not separate self-entities. The Eighteen Realms of Phenomena which are the six Sense Organs, six Sense Objects, and six Consciousnesses are also not separate self-entities. (o)

The Twelve Links of Interdependent Arising and their Extinction are also not separate self-entities. Ill-being, the Causes of Ill-being, the End of Ill-being, the Path, insight and attainment, are also not separate self-entities. Whoever can see this no longer needs anything to attain. (o)

Bodhisattvas who practice the Insight that Brings Us to the Other Shore see no more obstacles in their mind, and because there are no more obstacles in their mind, they can overcome all fear, destroy all wrong perceptions and realize Perfect Nirvana. All Buddhas in the past, present and future by practicing the Insight that Brings Us to the Other Shore, are all capable of attaining Authentic and Perfect Enlightenment. (o)

Therefore, Sariputra, it should be known that the Insight that Brings Us to the Other Shore is a Great Mantra, the most illuminating mantra, the highest mantra, a mantra beyond compare, the True Wisdom that has the power to put an end to all kinds of suffering. (o)

Therefore, let us proclaim a mantra. To praise the Insight that Brings Us to the Other Shore. *Gone, gone, gone beyond, gone to the other shore, awake, rejoice!* (3 times) (o)

Namo the Great Compassionate Avalokiteshvara Bodhisattva.
(3 times) (ooo)

# 2. INVOKING THE BODHISATTVAS' NAMES

## 2.1. AVALOKITESHVARA

We invoke your name, Avalokiteshvara. We aspire to learn your way of listening in order to help relieve the suffering in the world. You know how to listen in order to understand. We invoke your name in order to practice listening with all our attention and openheartedness. We will sit and listen without any prejudice. We will sit and listen without judging or reacting.

We will sit and listen in order to understand. We will sit and listen so attentively that we will be able to hear what the other person is saying and also what is being left unsaid. We know that just by listening deeply we already alleviate a great deal of pain and suffering in the other person. (o)

## 2.2. MANJUSHRI

We invoke your name, Manjushri. We aspire to learn your way, which is to be still and to look deeply into the heart of things and into the hearts of people. We will look with all our attention and openheartedness. We will look with unprejudiced eyes. We will look without judging or reacting. We will look deeply so that we will be able to see and understand the roots of suffering and the impermanent and selfless nature of all that is. We will practice your way of using the sword of understanding to cut through the bonds of suffering, thus freeing ourselves and other species. (o)

## 2.3. SAMANTABHADRA

We invoke your name, Samantabhadra. We aspire to practice your vow to act with the eyes and heart of compassion, to bring joy to one person in the morning and to ease the pain of one person in the afternoon. We know that the happiness of others is our own happiness, and we aspire to practice joy on the path of service. We know that every word, every look, every action, and every smile can bring happiness to others. We know that if we practice wholeheartedly, we ourselves may become an inexhaustible source of peace and joy for our loved ones and for all species. (o)

## 2.4. KSHITIGARBHA

We invoke your name, Kshitigarbha. We aspire to learn your way of being present where there is darkness, suffering, oppression, and despair, so we can bring light, hope, relief, and liberation to those places. We are determined not to forget about or abandon those in desperate situations. We will do our best to establish contact with those who cannot find a way out of their suffering, those whose cries for help, justice, equality, and human rights are not being heard. We know that hell can be found in many places on Earth. We will do our best not to contribute to creating more hells on Earth, and we will help transform the hells that already exist. We will practice in order to realize the qualities of perseverance and stability, so that, like the Earth, we can always be supportive and faithful to those in need. (o)

## 2.5. SADAPARIBHUTA

We invoke your name Sadaparibhuta. We aspire to learn your way of looking deeply with the eyes of nondiscrimination in order to see the virtuous qualities of others. Whenever you meet anyone, you bow respectfully and say in appreciation: I respect you deeply. You are a future Buddha. We vow to look deeply into ourselves to recognize the positive qualities that are there, to accept and to love ourselves. We vow only to water positive seeds in ourselves and in those around us. Then our thoughts, words, and deeds will give rise to self-confidence and acceptance in ourselves, our children, grandchildren, and all those we know. We vow to look deeply with the eyes of nondiscrimination to see that your joy and success is also our joy and success. We vow to behave and to speak with humility and respect. We vow to practice loving speech to help people who underestimate themselves see that they are wonders of the universe. We know that only when we are able to transcend the barriers of a separate self, shall we be able to transform the superiority, inferiority, and equality complexes and realize true happiness and freedom. (o)

**Namo the Great Bodhisattva Mahasattvas.** (3 times) (ooo)

# 3. READ THE NAMES OF BUDDHAS & BODHISATTVAS

The river of attachment is ten thousand miles long.

The waves on the ocean of confusion stretch so far.

If you wish to go beyond the realms of samsara,

Recollect the Buddha with one pointed mind. (o)


The Pure Land is available in our True Mind.

Amitabha manifests from the true nature of things,

Shining light on the three worlds and the ten directions,

Always abiding in the present moment.

May I go back to Amitabha Buddha,

The founder of the Pure Land,

The source of limitless lifespan.

May I with one heart visualize

And recollect this holy name.


Namo Shakyamuni Buddha, the Fully Awakened One. (3 times) (o)

Namo Amitabhaya Buddhaya, the Buddha of Infinite Light. (3 times) (o)

**Namo Manjushri, the Bodhisattva of Great Understanding.** (3 times) (o)

**Namo Samantabhadra, the Bodhisattva of Great Action.** (3 times) (o)

**Namo Avalokiteshvara, the Bodhisattva of Great Compassion.** (3 times) (o)

**Namo Kshitigarbhaya Bodhisattvaya, the Bodhisattva of Great Aspiration.**
(3 times) (o)

# 4. TAKING REFUGE IN AMITABHA BUDDHA

**Taking refuge in the Amitabha Buddha**

**In the wondrous ultimate dimension,**

**I devote my heart to returning to myself**

**And holding to the source of mindfulness.**

**I have vowed to go for refuge to the Amitabha Buddha.** (o)


**I bow my head and ask the Buddha**

**To receive us in his embrace.**

**As the Pure Land manifests,**

**Please bring your torch of light**

To shine onto my thoughts.

Please bring the boat of long lifespan

To carry my body through life

So I live with peace and joy,

So my aspiration can be fully realized.

Buddha, please always protect me. (o)

Not letting my mind grow slack,

So that I end wrong perceptions

And the affliction fall away.

In the present moment

Buddha can be found in this world.

Taking every step with solidity and freedom

We walk in the Pure Land.

When we live the present moment mindfully,

The Pure Land is already a reality.

So whatever form we take in the future,

We can be assured of peace and joy. (o)

If we are able to recollect the Amitabha

With undispersed, one-pointed mind,

The nine lotus grades will appear.

May we enjoy life for ourselves and others

And know in advance our time of death.

At death may our mind not flinch,

Our body not be sick and in pain,

Our thoughts not waiver. (o)

May the Amitabha and his holy assembly

Holding up the golden lotuses

Be present without delay.

Together may we set out in freedom

May we see the Buddha in the opening lotus.

May the Pure Land be our home.

I bow my head to ask Buddha to be my witness

To my never slackening practice. (o)

**Namo Amitabha Buddha** (3 times) (ooo)

## 5. MAY THE DAY & NIGHT BE WELL

May the day be well and the night be well.

May the midday hour bring happiness too.

In every minute and every second, may the day and night be well.

By the blessing of the Triple Gem, may all things be protected and safe.

May all beings born in each of the four ways live in a land of purity.

May all in the Three Realms be born upon Lotus Thrones.

May countless wandering souls realize the three virtuous positions of the Bodhisattva Path.

May all living beings, with grace and ease, fulfill the Bodhisattva Stages.

The countenance of the World-Honored One, like the full moon or like the orb of the sun, shines with the light of clarity.

A halo of wisdom spreads in every direction, enveloping all with love and compassion, joy and equanimity.

**Namo Shakyamunaye Buddhaya.**

(3 times) (ooo)

## 6. GATHA ON IMPERMANENCE

The day is now ended. Our lives are shorter.

Let us look carefully. What have we done?

Noble Sangha, with all our heart,

let us be diligent, engaging in the practice.

Let us live deeply, free from our afflictions, aware of impermanence so that life does not drift away without meaning. (ooo)

## 7. PRAYER

Namo the Buddhas, Bodhisattvas

and the Dharma Protective Deities prove,

Today, we (the leader...) and the sangha have gathered at... (the place...) to recite..., invoke the Buddhas' and Bodhisattvas' names, make offerings, as well as transfer the merits to the Buddhists... (the full name, the Dharma name, age...) together with the householders and all Sangha members present here are always healthy, happy and diligent in practice. May all year round be auspicious and joy. May our bodhicitta firm; our wills are steady; and we will gain self-awareness as well as the perfective enlightenment. (o)

Again, we give back this merit to pray for the deceased... (the full name, the Dharma name, longevity...) with our ancestors and parents in the past, the heroic warriors sacrificed for the country, the deceased died in rivers, accidents and other reasons. There are twelve kinds of souls with names or unnamed. May all of them overcome the suffering ocean of the bad karma and be peaceful at the Pure land and practice with Buddhas and Bodhisattvas.

Finally, may all sentient beings soon complete the Way of Love and Understanding.

Namo Amitabha Buddhaya. (ooo)

## 8. SALUTATION THOUSANDS BUDDHAS IN THREE TIMES

There are many the great causes

The ten directions, three lives and realms

I keep my body and mind pure

Pay homage at all without being left behind. (o)

We pay respects sincerely to the four graces of the three realms:

Namo the Buddhas of the kalpa thousands in the past. (o) (1 prostration)

Namo the Buddhas of the kalpa thousands in the present. (o) (1 prostration)

Namo the Buddhas of the kalpa thousands in the future. (o) (1 prostration)

## 9. TAKING REFUGE
## AT THREE JEWELS

-I take refuge in the *Buddha*,

the one who shows me the way in this life.

I take refuge in the *Dharma*,

the way of understanding and of love.

I take refuge in the *Sangha*,

the community that lives in harmony and awareness. (o) (1 prostration)

-Dwelling in the refuge of *Buddha*,

I clearly see the path of light and beauty in the world.

Dwelling in the refuge of *Dharma*,

I learn to open many doors on the path of transformation.

Dwelling in the refuge of *Sangha*,

shining light that supports me, keeping my practice free of obstruction. (o) (1 prostration)

-Taking refuge in the *Buddha* in myself,

I aspire to help all people recognize their own awakened nature,

realizing the Mind of Love.

Taking refuge in the *Dharma* in myself,

I aspire to help all people fully master the ways of practice

and walk together on the path of liberation.

Taking refuge in the *Sangha* in myself,

I aspire to help all people build Fourfold Communities,

to embrace all beings and support their transformation. (ooo) (1 prostration)

## 10. SHARING THE MERIT & VERSE FOR CLOSING

Reciting the sutras, practicing the way of awareness gives rise to benefits without limit.

We vow to share the fruits with all beings.

We vow to offer tribute to parents, teachers, friends, and numerous beings who give guidance and support along the path. (o)


May we be born now in the Pure Land

within the heart of a lotus flower.

In the moment when the lotus blooms,

we touch the reality of no-birth and no-dying.

May Buddhas and Bodhisattvas be our companions

on the wonderful path of practice. (o)


May we end all afflictions

so that understanding can arise,

the obstacles of unwholesome acts be dissolved, and the fruit of awakening be fully realized. (o)

**Namo Amitabha Buddhaya. (ooo)**

# 11. THE DIVINE GATHA

Gods, nagas, asuras and yakshas

Come here, with all your heart listen to the Dharma.

Protect the Buddha-dharma so that it may endure

And all may act in the spirit of the Buddha's teaching.

When you have come to hear the Dharma,

Whether you are under the earth or in the sky,

Look at all beings with the eyes of love.

Day and night abide in the right practice.

May the world always be safe and secure,

Impregnated by the merit of wisdom and love.

May all the obstacles of wrong doing be dissolved.

May we live behind afflictions

and know always how to touch peace and joy.

May the Sangha with determination observe the precepts,

Be diligent in the practice of meditative concentration.

May the flower of awakened understanding bloom beautifully And everywhere may all species have happiness.

**Namo the Dharma Protective Bodhisattva Mahasattva.** (3 times) (ooo)

***

# BẢO ANH LẠC BOOKSHELF
## Dr. Bhikṣuṇī TN Giới Hương composed

## A. THE VIETNAMESE BOOKS

1. *Bồ-tát và Tánh Không Trong Kinh Tạng Pali và Đại Thừa* (Boddhisattva and Sunyata in the Early and Developed Buddhist Traditions).

2. *Ban Mai Xứ Ấn* (The Dawn in India), (3 tập).

3. *Vườn Nai – Chiếc Nôi* (Phật Giáo Deer Park–The Cradle of Buddhism).

4. *Quy Y Tam Bảo và Năm Giới* (Take Refuge in Three Gems and Keep the Five Precepts).

5. *Vòng Luân Hồi* (The Cycle of Life).

6. *Hoa Tuyết Milwaukee* (Snowflake in Milwaukee).

7. *Luân Hồi trong Lăng Kính Lăng Nghiêm* (The Rebirth in *Śūrangama* Sūtra).

8. *Nghi Thức Hộ Niệm, Cầu Siêu* (The Ritual for the Deceased).

9. *Quan Âm Quảng Trần* (The Commentary of Avalokiteśvara Bodhisattva).

10. *Nữ Tu và Tù Nhân Hoa Kỳ* (A Nun and American Inmates).

11. *Nếp Sống Tỉnh Thức của Đức Đạt Lai Lạt Ma Thứ XIV* (The Awakened Mind of the 14th Dalai Lama).

12. *A-Hàm: Mưa pháp chuyển hóa phiền não* (*Agama – A Dharma Rain transforms the Defilement*), 2 tập.

13. *Góp Từng Hạt Nắng Perris* (Collection of Sunlight in

Perris).

14. *Pháp Ngữ của Kinh Kim Cang* (The Key Words of Vajracchedikā-Prajñāpāramitā-Sūtra).

15. *Tập Thơ Nhạc Nắng Lăng Nghiêm* (Songs and Poems of Śūraṅgama Sunlight).

16. *Nét Bút Bên Song Cửa* (Reflections at the Temple Window).

17. *Máy Nghe MP3 Hương Sen* (Hương Sen Digital Mp3 Radio Speaker): Các Bài Giảng, Sách, Bài viết và Thơ Nhạc của Thích Nữ Giới Hương (383/201 bài).

18. *DVD Giới Thiệu về Chùa Hương Sen*, USA (Introduction on Huong Sen Temple).

19. *Ni Giới Việt Nam Hoằng Pháp tại Hoa Kỳ* (Sharing the Dharma - Vietnamese Buddhist Nuns in the United States).

20. *Tuyển Tập 40 Năm Tu Học & Hoằng Pháp của Ni sư Giới Hương* (Forty Years in the Dharma: A Life of Study and Service—Venerable Bhikkhuni Giới Hương), Thích Nữ Viên Quang, TN Viên Nhuận, TN Viên Tiến, and TN Viên Khuông.

21. *Tập Thơ Nhạc Lối Về Sen Nở* (*Songs and Poems of Lotus Blooming on the Way*).

22. *Nghi Thức Công Phu Khuya – Thần Chú Thủ Lăng Nghiêm* (Śūraṅgama Mantra).

23. *Nghi Thức Cầu An – Kinh Phổ Môn* (The Universal Door Sūtra).

24. *Nghi Thức Cầu An – Kinh Dược Sư* (The Medicine Buddha Sūtra).

25. *Nghi Thức Sám Hối Hồng Danh* (The Sūtra of Confession at many Buddha Titles).

26. *Nghi Thức Công Phu Chiều – Mông Sơn Thí Thực* (The Ritual Donating Food to Hungry Ghosts).

27. *Khóa Tịnh Độ – Kinh A Di Đà* (The Amitabha Buddha Sūtra).

28. *Nghi Thức Cúng Linh và Cầu Siêu* (The Rite for Deceased and Funeral Home).

29. *Nghi Lễ Hàng Ngày - 50 Kinh Tụng và các Lễ Vía trong Năm* (The Daily Chanting Rituals and Annual Ceremonies).

30. *Hương Đạo Trong Đời 2022* (Tuyển tập 60 Bài Thi trong Cuộc Thi Viết Văn Ứng Dụng Phật Pháp 2022 - A Collection of Writings on the Practicing of Buddhism in Daily Life in the Writing Contest 2022).

31. *Hương Pháp 2022* (Tuyển Tập Các Bài Thi Trúng Giải Cuộc Thi Viết Văn Ứng Dụng Phật Pháp 2022 - A Collection of the Winning Writings on the Practicing of Buddhism in Daily Life in the Writing Contest 2022).

32. *Giới Hương - Thơm Ngược Gió Ngàn*, Nguyên Hà.

33. *Pháp Ngữ Kinh Hoa Nghiêm* (2 tập). Thích Nữ Giới Hương.

34. *Tinh Hoa Kinh Hoa Nghiêm*. Thích Nữ Giới Hương. NXB Hương Sen.

35. *Phật Giáo và Đại Dịch Coronavirus Covid-19*. Thích Nữ Giới Hương.

36. *Phật Giáo – Tầm Nhìn Lịch Sử Và Thực Hành*. Hiệu đính: Thích Hạnh Chánh và Thích Nữ Giới Hương.

# B. THE ENGLISH BOOKS

1. Boddhisattva and Sunyata in the Early and Developed Buddhist Traditions.

2. *Rebirth Views in the Śuraṅgama Sūtra.*

3. *Commentary of Avalokiteśvara Bodhisattva.*

4. *The Key Words in Vajracchedikā Sūtra.*

5. *Sārnātha-The Cradle of Buddhism in the Archeological View.*

6. *Take Refuge in the Three Gems and Keep the Five Precepts.*

7. *Cycle of Life.*

8. *Forty Years in the Dharma: A Life of Study and Service—Venerable Bhikkhuni Giới Hương.*

9. *Sharing the Dharma -Vietnamese Buddhist Nuns in the United States.*

10. *A Vietnamese Buddhist Nun and American Inmates.*

11. *Daily Monastic Chanting.*

12. *Weekly Buddhist Discourse Chanting.*

13. *Practice Meditation and Pure Land.*

14. *The Ceremony for Peace.*

15. *The Lunch Offering Ritual.*

16. *The Ritual Offering Food to Hungry Ghosts.*

17. *The Pureland Course of Amitabha Sutra.*

18. *The Medicine Buddha Sutra.*

19. *The New Year Ceremony.*

20. *The Great Parinirvana Ceremony.*

21. *The Buddha's Birthday Ceremony.*

22. *The Ullambana Festival (Parents' Day).*

23. *The Marriage Ceremony.*

24. *The Blessing Ceremony for The Deceased.*

25. *The Ceremony Praising Ancestral Masters.*

26. *The Enlightened Buddha Ceremony.*

27. *The Uposatha Ceremony (Reciting Precepts).*

28. *Buddhism: A Historical and Practical Vision.* Edited by Ven. Dr. Thich Hanh Chanh and Ven. Dr. Bhikṣuṇī TN Gioi Huong.

29. *Contribution of Buddhism For World Peace & Social Harmony.* Edited by Ven. Dr. Buddha Priya Mahathero and Ven. Dr. Bhikṣuṇī TN Gioi Huong.

30. *Global Spread of Buddhism with Special Reference to Sri Lanka.* Buddhist Studies Seminar in Kandy University. Edited by Dr. Ven. Kahawatte Siri Sumedha Thero and Dr. Bhikṣuṇī TN Gioi Huong.

31. *Buddhism In Sri Lanka During The Period of 19th to 21st Centuries.* Buddhist Studies Seminar in Colombo. Edited by Prof. Ven. Medagama Nandawansa and Dr. Bhikṣuṇī TN Gioi Huong.

## C. THE BILINGUAL BOOKS
## (VIETNAMESE-ENGLISH)

1. *Bản Tin Hương Sen: Xuân, Phật Đản, Vu Lan* (Hương Sen Newsletter: Spring, Buddha Birthday and Vu Lan, annual/ Mỗi Năm).

2. *Danh Ngôn Nuôi Dưỡng Nhân Cách - Good Sentences*

*Nurture a Good Manner.*

3. *Văn Hóa Đặc Sắc của Nước Nhật Bản-Exploring the Unique Culture of Japan.*

4. *Sống An Lạc dù Đời không Đẹp như Mơ - Live Peacefully though Life is not Beautiful as a Dream.*

5. *Hãy Nói Lời Yêu Thương-Words of Love and Understanding.*

6. *Văn Hóa Cổ Kim qua Hành Hương Chiêm Bái -The Ancient- Present Culture in Pilgrim.*

7. *Nghệ Thuật Biết Sống - Art of Living.*

## D. THE TRANSLATED BOOKS

1. *Xá Lợi Của Đức Phật* (Relics of the Buddha), Tham Weng Yew.

2. *Sen Nở Nơi Chốn Tử Tù* (Lotus in Prison), many authors.

3. *Chùa Việt Nam Hải Ngoại* (Overseas Vietnamese Buddhist Temples).

4. *Việt Nam Danh Lam Cổ Tự* (The Famous Ancient Buddhist Temples in Vietnam).

5. *Hương Sen, Thơ và Nhạc* – (Lotus Fragrance, Poem and Music).

6. *Phật Giáo-Một Bậc Đạo Sư, Nhiều Truyền Thống* (Buddhism: One Teacher – Many Traditions), Đức Đạt Lai Lạt Ma 14th & Ni Sư Thubten Chodren.

7. *Cách Chuẩn Bị Chết và Giúp Người Sắp Chết-Quan Điểm Phật Giáo* (Preparing for Death and Helping the Dying – A Buddhist Perspective).

# BUDDHIST MUSIC ALBUMS
## from POEMS of THÍCH NỮ GIỚI HƯƠNG

1. *Đào Xuân Lộng Ý Kinh* (The Buddha's Teachings Reflected in Cherry Flowers).

2. *Niềm Tin Tam Bảo* (Trust in the Three Gems).

3. *Trăng Tròn Nghìn Năm Đón Chờ Ai* (Who Is the Full Moon Waiting for for Over a Thousand Years?).

4. *Ánh Trăng Phật Pháp* (Moonlight of Dharma-Buddha).

5. *Bình Minh Tỉnh Thức* (Awakened Mind at the Dawn) (*Piano Variations for Meditation*).

6. *Tiếng Hát Già Lam* (Song from Temple).

7. *Cảnh Đẹp Chùa Xưa* (The Magnificent, Ancient Buddhist Temple).

8. Karaoke *Hoa Ưu Đàm Đã Nở* (An Udumbara Flower Is Blooming).

9. *Hương Sen Ca* (Hương Sen's Songs).

10. *Về Chùa Vui Tu* (Happily Go to Temple for Spiritual Practices).

11. *Gọi Nắng Xuân Về* (Call the Spring Sunlight).

12. *Đệ Tử Phật* (The Buddha's Disciples).

*Please consult the **Bảo Anh Lạc Bookshelf** at this website:*

*http://huongsentemple.com/index.php/en/about-us/b-o-anh-l-c-bookshelf*

**WEEKLY BUDDHIST DISCOURSE CHANTING VOL.1**

Author: Bao Anh Lac Bookshelf 55 - Huong Sen Buddhist Temple


HONG DUC PUBLISHING

Tel.: 024.39260024 - Fax : 024.39260031

Email: nhanxuatbanhongduc65@gmail.com


Responsible for publishing

Manager: **Bui Viet Bac**


Responsible for the content

Editor in Chief: **Ly Ba Toan**


Editor: **Phan Thi Ngoc Minh**

Presenter: **Vu Dinh Trong**

Editing the copy: **Vu Dinh Trong**


Printing quantity: 1,000 copies, Size: 14.5 x 20.5 cm

Printed at: Tram Anh Printing,

159/57 Bach Dang, Ward 2, Tan Binh District, HCM City.

Registration number: 3206-2023/CXBIPH/16-92/HĐ

ISBN: 978-604-476-991-2

Publishing decision: 330/QD-NXBHD dated September 29, 2023

Finished printing and deposit in the third quarter of 2023